INTERNATIONAL BUSINESS ENVIRONMENT

READINGS IN BUSINESS ENVIRONMENT SERIES

INTERNATIONAL BUSINESS ENVIRONMENT

Edited by
S. D. SHARMA
PETER REBELLO

ANMOL PUBLICATIONS PVT. LTD.
NEW DELHI-110 002 (INDIA)

ANMOL PUBLICATIONS PVT. LTD.
4374/4B, Ansari Road, Daryaganj
New Delhi-110 002

International Business Environment

First Edition 1998

ISBN 81-7488-898-5

PRINTED IN INDIA

Published by J. L. Kumar for Anmol Publications Pvt. Ltd., New Delhi-110 002 and Printed at Mehra Offset Press, Delhi.

Contents

Preface

The last three decades of the present century have witnessed a sea-change in the nature and contents of the business environment—primarily because more and more national governments, particularly in the Third World, have sought to devise ways and means of coping with the highly competitive nature and new challenges thrown up by several factors: the advent of globalisation, irreversible consumerism, a more insightful awareness of the benefits and long-term gains of economic liberalisation and, above all, the availability of diverse and cost-effective technologies. Economic configurations have been redrawn with the cataclysmic world events: the collapse of the Soviet Union and the emergence of the free market economies; the opening up of China as a major player in the global market place; the staggering fact of the Japanese surplus which has caused much apprehension and rethinking among the developed nations of the west; and the emergence of the new unified economic force on the western horizon, namely, the European Economic Community. On a more regional scale yet equally significant is the reorganisation and resurgence of the Asian nations, from positions of dependence and economic dithering to assertion of self and the search for a rightful place in the global economic system. India too has done well with its far-reaching policies and programmes of economic liberalisation, enabling the entrepreneur to do better business and the industrialist to be part of the world economic order. In brief, the Indian businessmen's dream of a license-free regime and easy availability of capital along with other incentives has come true. The business environment for domestic as well as international business has become near-perfect.

The current series of readings in business environment forms an integral part of the dynamics of modern management and is intended for the student as well as the management professional. The materials are drawn from a wide range of sources, both Indian and foreign, with a view to provide an appropriate window on to the intricate yet enthralling management landscape. Of special interest is the division into four carefully thought out compilations under specific heads, namely, dimensions of regulation and control across various relevant economies; the business firm and the new global challenges; Asian and European experiences; and technological dimensions of business environment. Indian students and management professionals will find particularly useful the papers on the dynamics of the Indian company in a comparative analysis of other leading world economic and business regimes, and also the insights into economic liberalisation and economic reform launched over six years ago to place India firmly in the pilot seat towards progress and prosperity. The case studies of high-profile and high-profit industries—airlines and garment exports—will be of special interest. It is believed that the volumes will be a significant contribution to current literature in the area.

Editors

1

Business and Society: Two Asian Studies

1. JAPAN

Introduction

The social responsibilities of business administrators have recently been studied from various points of view. There are main reasons for this activity. The ownership of shares has been widely spread among large numbers of people, making it almost impossible for the administration of any business to depend solely on individual owners. On the other hand, the increasing complexity of large-scale business administration has created a need for 'professional' management. This has resulted in the separation of ownership and management and the development of a conspicuous tendency for business to be controlled by management. Moreover, the economic power now exercised by the big enterprise, both absolutely and relatively, has grown so vastly that its resulting social effect can never be taken lightly. In the economic world of today a small number of large firms has an overwhelmingly powerful position and wields a monopolistic influence which tends to nullify the salutary effects of free competition so highly commended by classical economists. The result is that some big enterprises and groups pursue their policies and objectives unchecked by the processes of a competitive market. Their unilateral decisions on price, production, investment and employment affect the interests and welfare of the people and the area concerned, as well as the life of the nation as a whole. The social significance of vast economic power exercised by large companies and the responsibility borne—or mission undertaken—by their administrators are indeed worthy of serious study. In brief, the problem is to determine what attitude or method the administrators of large private firms (now free from both the one-sided subjugation to owners or shareholders and the impersonal control of a free market) should adopt in the fulfilment of their social mission as responsible, independent managers.

The Separation of Ownership and Management

The conditions just outlined have reached an advanced stage in Japan A survey of the dispersal of the shares of big companies was made in 1958. There were 4,050,000 shareholders of 120 large corporations, an average of 33,000 shareholders per corporation. Of the 120 corporations, 101 had more than 10,000 shareholders, twenty-five had more than 50,000 and four had more than 100,000. When the shareholders of the same 120 corporations were classified according to ten major types, it was found that individuals possessed 1.5 per cent of the total share value, banks and insurance, trust and investment companies 18.6 per cent and other agents 1.1 per cent. The total of these figures amounts to only 21.2 per cent. The percentage of individual shareholders in strikingly small.[1]

According to another survey, the percentages of share ownership of 346 big corporations listed on the Tokyo Securities Market in 1961 were as follows: 33.0 per cent by financial agents, 2.8 per cent by investment companies, 17.4 per cent by business companies, 45.2 per cent by individuals and 1.6 per cent by foreigners and others. The proportion held by individuals was less than half the total. By contrast, a high proportion was held by legal persons, including financial agents. Moreover, the share of individuals seems to have fallen since the war: the pre-war percentage of financial agents was 11.2 per cent and that of individuals 53.0 per cent. The weight of shareholding by legal persons, including financial agents, was also small after the war.[2] These results show that the conditions for the separation of ownership and management, as a consequence of the dispersal of ownership, are now firmly established in Japan.

In seeking the decisive factor which set the scene for these changes in the Japanese economy, there is no need to look further than the policy of democratisation enforced during the American occupation after the war. The breaking up of the financial combines, and the dismissal of all the business leaders who had been closely connected with the wealthy governing class and its dependants, put an end to a world of self-righteous paternalism and allowed a number of well trained or experienced business administrators to come to the fore. Hand in hand with these changes, a programme for the unionisation of industrial workers was launched. In order to cope with a labour movement which resorted to collected bargaining, business administrators were compelled to cultivate a new social attitude which required them totally to abandon the concept of employer/employee relationships that had been prevalent in pre-war Japan. In this way, the importance which the business administrator had acquired as an owner rapidly diminished in the post-war years. Study of the control of industry after 1950 shows the percentage of corporation shares held by executives and other senior members of corporations to be as low as 2 or 3 per cent of all shares. Thus, the possibility of controlling an enterprise on the basis of ownership has, for all practical purposes, been reduced to nil.[3] In a word, the administrators of large companies have held their own since the war by dint of proven administrative talent and of the social esteem they have thereby earned and not by any right or prestige of ownership.

The Concentration of Economic Power

If the Americans went somewhat too far in the enforcement of economic democratisation, the policy of the dispersal of economic power was nevertheless quite successful. In the process, however, of economic recovery through the rapid absorption of new technology, a new concentration of economic power in a few big enterprises has occurred. A number of studies has pointed to the danger that this recovery may entail something akin to the restoration of the pre-war financial combines.

In 1966, companies with more than 1,000 employees represented only 3 per cent of all companies in Japan (excluding those with fewer than three employees), but accounted for 19.2 per cent of the total number of employees of all firms employing more than three people, and for 34.2 per cent of total added value. If the concentration of general economic power is examined on the basis of the corporation unit, it is found that, in 1962, of a total of some 1,50,000 companies, 422 large firms (0.3 per cent) had a capital of more than 1,000 million yen (some £1.15m.). These accounted for 26.0 per cent of all employees, 61.5 per cent of all tangible fixed capital and 51.8 per cent of total net corporation profit, whereas the small and medium-size firms with a capital of less than 100 m. yen (about £115,000) (98.8 per cent of all companies) accounted for 61.3 per cent of employees, 24.2 per cent of tangible fixed capital and 34.6 per cent of net corporation profit. Of 154 principal industries examined for their degree of concentration in production, in thirteen of them the five largest corporations together accounted for the whole of the industry's production; in ten for 90-100 per cent; and in two for 70-90 per cent. In other words, in twenty-five industries the five biggest corporations account for 70 per cent or more of production. If we take the ten biggest corporations, we find that they account for 100 per cent of production in twenty-two industries and for 75 per cent in eighty—that is, in the majority of the various industries.[4]

These facts not only show that a small number of big corporations in various industries is dominant in production, but also point to the powerful sway they hold over the industrial world through financial influence, the mutual holding of shares and the interchange of executives and staff members. All these factors give the big firms (*zaibatsu*) an important role in the moulding of the economy and the lives of large numbers of people. Opinion both at home and abroad regards this situation as something which can no longer be taken for granted. Indeed, the power and influence of an oligopolistic industrial structure is now severely criticised.

When the Japanese economy, having stabilised itself, began to expand about fifteen years ago, leading industrialists started to think more profoundly about their mission and often themselves declared the importance of their social responsibilities. The Keizai-Doyukai (Japan Committee for Economic Development),[5] one of the most progressive organisations of businessmen, took up this question at its national convention in 1955. At its convention in 1956, a declaration was made on 'The Social Responsibility of Business Administrators: Awareness and Practice.' This called the attention of managers in general to such matters as the significance of business as a public organ, the importance of their awareness to their responsibilities to shareholders, employees, consumers and the general public, as well as to practical means for fulfilling them.

It is now evident that Japanese businessmen have a new attitude towards the objective conditions of their position. They are not satisfied with the concept of business as a purely private affair, proclaim its public importance and look forward to its establishment as an integral part of society as a whole. These progressive ideas are, of course, a direct result of the enlightened philosophy of management which was brought over from the United States after the war; how far they have permeated is examined in what follows.

Pre-War Japanese Business

The ideological background of industry in pre-war Japan could be said to be devoid of such concepts as an independent sense of responsibility or of social mission among businessmen. That this was so may be ascribed to the fact that the capitalism of Japan had always been firmly based on government intervention and the control of financial cliques. Coming into the industrial world far later than other advanced countries, Japan had largely to depend on government protection or support to overcome her backwardness. Typical examples of government intervention were the various factories set up in the early days of the Meija Era (1868-1912) and later sold to private interests, the munition and arms factories built and operated by the government till the closing years of the Taisho Era (1912-26), the counter-measures taken by the government against the panic which took place at the beginning of the ensuing Showa Era and the enforcement of a controlled economy during the last war. For some years after the end of war, the government had to adjust the demand for and supply of food in a market disturbed by its shortage.

These historical facts not only distorted the development of free enterprise but also greatly affected the outlook of businessmen. Independence and self-criticism were weakened, and it became natural to compromise or to depend on government control or intervention. To be fair, however, businessmen had little choice but to come to terms with a pattern of government control which sprang from the nationalism and militarism prevalent in Japan at the time.

For many years before the war, the financial combines—monopolistic bodies based on family and social relationships—set up holding companies in order to establish affiliated firms through which they could exercise their influence or control. Just before their break-up after the war, the four biggest combines (Mitsui, Mitsubishi, Sumitomo and Yasuda) possessed 24.5 per cent, and the big ten combines, including these four, 32.2 per cent of total paid-up corporation capital. Moreover, they had absolute control of the majority of such important industries as heavy chemicals, shipping and mining, of finance and of foreign trade. The entire Japanese financial world was, to all intents and purposes, under their dictatorship. According to the report of the Holding Company Liquidation Commission, the four giants alone had 49.7 per cent of the paid-up capital in finance; 32.4 per cent in the heavy chemical industry; 60.8 per cent in shipping; and 12.9 per cent in commerce.[6] In such a situation, the medium-size and small firms under the control of the combines also developed as 'family' organisations. Thus, the basis of many pre-war enterprises was similar to a family constitution—an enterprise was identified with a family. The businessman sought to run his company in rather the same way as he saw to the continuity and prosperity of his family—and he and his employees were considered members of one and the same family. Such an attitude certainly fostered habits of loyalty but something of family selfishness and paternalism lurked behind it. At any rate, it had nothing in common with modern ideas of service to the community.

It does not follow, however, that there existed no 'business ideal' to stand in contrast against the principle of profit for profits' sake in pre-war Japan. Particularly in the Meiji Era, profit-making was regarded as despicable. The tone was set by the same Confucian principles which had formed the basis of the four classes in feudal Japan—knights, farmers, artisans and merchants—and by the industrial development policy pursued by the government in a spirit of patriotism. It is true that patriotic sentiments soon afterwards become powerful in the nation as a whole; but such high-mindedness was more something of a defence mechanism against excessive government control or intervention and, as far as businessmen were concerned, was an outward gesture rather than a spontaneous expression of their sense of responsibility.

The expression *uchi no kaisha* ('my home company') is still quite often heard in modern Japan—not just from executives but also from ordinary employees. A symbolic phrase of this sort is a relic of the idea of the business as a family affair and, indeed, of 'family' structures applied to all aspects of social life in pre-war Japan. In other words, the head of a business was considered the patriarch of a family and its employees as blood relations. The capital/labour relationship was summarily dealt with by the paternalism of the employer and the slavish fidelity of his employees. The benovolent paternalism of the employer became formalised in welfare and recreation facilities for employees and the system of grading wages by seniority. The employee's loyalty became devotion to one job for life and a fatalistic attitude of compliance. Thus, the relationship between the entrepreneur and his employees was vertical or, in other words, feudalistic.

The dissolution of the financial combines and the rapid unionisation of industrial workers which accompained the wholesale democratisation of the economy and industry of Japan marked the end of the traditional business system based on the family. The relationship between capital and labour emerged as a negotiation between equals and businessmen acquired an entirely new conception of their role. Naturally enough, many Japanese businessmen now devote much energy to the promotion of the welfare and recreation of their employees; but these efforts are now motivated rather by economic considerations, to supplement, at the company's expense, the inadequate benefits of a national social security system that is still in its infancy.

Attitudes of Modern Japanese Businessmen

What do the Japanese businessman of today think about their management responsibilities? Some insight into this has been given by a survey commissioned by the Keizai-Doyukai, based on questionnaires sent to 1,447 large firms. The rather poor response rate of about 27 per cent may perhaps reflect a certain reluctance to think deeply about the principles of business. The results of the survey are summarised in the paragraphs that follow.

In the traditional view, the pursuit of *profit* is considered to be the main purpose of any business. According to the survey, only 35.7 per cent of the respondents still thought this to be so. The others allowed profit a functional value as a measure of the contribution a company may make to the national economy or to some loftier purpose. In other words, they valued profit only for the secondary service it performs, not as an end in itself. This is a clear result of the separation of ownership and management. The point is further clarified by the attitude towards *shareholders.*

27.2 per cent of the respondents considered that the shareholders were the owners of a company, and that it was the duty of management to act in such a way as to secure the maximum profit for them. 33.0 per cent thought that managers sometimes behave as though they disregarded the shareholders, in the apparent belief that they were promoting the latter's long-term interests. 33.8 per cent replied that, though it was true that shareholders were the owners of a company, their importance was becoming relatively less and their interests could be considered only in a wider context. Thus, the percentage of respondents who considered their duty to shareholders as an absolute imperative was lower than that of those who still claim to regard the pursuit of profit as the ultimate business objective. From this it may be inferred that the shareholder is no longer an entrepreneur, but merely a lender of fund like a banker. Thus, the immediate purpose of a dividend policy is to maintain the market price of shares at a level high enough to prevent shareholders from parting with their stocks. It is also evident that, for managers, the profit motive, as an incentive to enterprise, is declining in importance.

On the question of *'social welfare,'* only about 3 per cent of the businessmen in this sample thought it would be automatically realised if every company devoted itself wholeheartedly to the pursuit of profit. As many as 93 per cent considered it could be realised only when it was a conscious aim and that this aim would be pursued only when businessmen become aware, by their own efforts or under external pressure, of their social responsibility. The remaining 4 per cent held the view that social welfare would be promoted only when private enterprise was directly guided or encouraged by the government or other public authorities. (The question of course arises of what is meant by 'social responsibility' and by the social duties of businessmen 'Society' seems to be interpreted in two ways in discussions on this subject. It is taken to mean either a comparatively small group of people directly interested in the company—shareholders, employees and customers, or a local community— or a much larger community such as the nation, in which business plays an important economic role. The questionnaire concentrated on the first definition).

As regards attitudes toward *employees,* as many as 95.7 per cent of the sample said they felt responsible not only for the payment of wages but also for the provision of facilities to raise their employees' living standards and improve their welfare in general.

Indeed, concern on this point could be rated very high but it is doubtful whether this should be taken as evidence of a full appreciation of 'social responsibility' in a modern sense. As already explained, Japanese business still remains powerfully influenced by paternalistic sentiments derived from the idea of the company as a family, an attitude quite different from that in modern Europe and America. The traditional motives of this sort encourage Japanese firms to provide housing, dormitories and medical services for their employees. Moreover, since the social security system is underdeveloped by comparison with that in European countries, businessmen consider it a managerial necessity to grant their employees various fringe benefits at their own expense, in order to secure and retain sufficient labour.

The survey, when considering the interest of *consumers*, did not take up the question of price but limited itself to such topics as 'model change' and the 'merits or demerits of certain types of advertising'. Nearly all businessmen assert the social importance of non-price factors and dwell enthusiastically on such matters as the enlightening effect of commercial advertising and 'model change' as vital factors in economic development. Few, on the other hand, will willingly reduce their prices. They may constantly complain of the anarchic state of *competition* but will still treat price as something for themselves to settle on their own. These attitudes testify to the oligopolistic state of Japanese industry and to the shift from price competition to non-price competition.

It has already been pointed out that in pre-war days government intervention in private enterprise was so deep-rooted, and the monopolistic influence of the financial combines so extensive, that the attitude of businessmen to free enterprise and consequently their conceptions of competition, the essence of the free market, were quite ambiguous. After the war, the old financial combines were disbanded and the excessive concentration of economic power was abolished by the anti-monopoly law. But a lingering fear of excessive competition remained. (There has been, of course, a tendency in the last few years to adjust or combine business interests with the object of reorganising industry in order to make a good showing against *international* competition). The survey we are considering showed that 64.2 per cent of the respondents were in favour of competition because it is the 'mother of progress'; 30 per cent were somewhat defensive as they considered competition likely to bring disorder and confusion; and 4.5 per cent believed that competition aggravated unfairness, as different companies start their business in different conditions. Thus, as many as a third of those who replied had a negative attitude to competition. Even those who were more positive did not necessarily support free competition in the sense of the classical economists. Their support, in other words, was conditional and different in degree according to the level of concentration in their particular industry.

The survey also revealed that more than 80 per cent of the respondents considered 'restriction of competition' was unavoidable if the development of industry was to be stable. 84.4 per cent thought that competition should be restricted by cartels and two out of three that government intervention was necessary for the effective operation of a cartel. More than half favoured restrictions on price formation, more than a quarter on plant investment. 23 per cent on the volume of production and 17 per cent on exports. Price restriction, direct or indirect, is obviously generally supported by the Japanese businessmen in this sample. Most of them would like to see such cartels run by employers' organisations probably because the latter worked well before the war under government protection. It seems, however, that views on this point differ according to considerations of scale: generally speaking, the large companies put a high value on employers' organisations whereas the medium and small firms have complaints and criticisms about them. Under the present anti-monopoly law, cartels are illegal with the exception of those that are particularly provided for in legislation. Consequently, businessmen in the main consider the law to be an undesirable restriction. Hardly any respondent to the survey thought it should be made stricter or be applied more strictly. Only about 15 per cent were in favour of maintaining the status quo and more than 82 per cent thought the law should be moderated or its application made more lenient.

These complacent attitudes to cartels appear inconsistent with the ideas of social responsibility to which businessmen have recently given so much support. Moreover, Japan has now emerged into a world of free international trade and free capital movements. The arguments for and against the antimonopoly law are therefore in the melting-pot. Our own view is that the law will lose the respect of informed public opinion if it is amended in a manner that narrowly favours the interests of individual firms. The business world must put forward far more comprehensive and persuasive arguments for the adjustment of the law, if it wants the public to believe its talk of social responsibility to be sincere. Under the prevalent oligopolistic economy the open establishment of cartels would be a drastic measure. Prices would no longer be 'given' but arbitrarily administered by a corporation and its allied interests. Such a situation would naturally call in question the social responsibility of the company concerned. The firm would therefore have to clarify its price-setting policy so that the public would be convinced of the reasonableness of its decisions.

Before concluding, it may be useful to consider some other points of view on these questions. The Sohyo, for instance, the largest of the Japanese trade union federation is traditionally marxist. It wishes to continue to fight the class war and is therefore hostile to attempts at a redefinition of the businessman's role in society. (It declined to take part in the survey just summarise.) It goes along with marxist social scientists who utterly refuse to admit the facts of the separation of ownership and management and of management control and regard such expressions as 'the awareness and practice of social responsibility by businessmen' as meaningless. Such people have no doubt at all that a handful of capitalist financiers controls the business world with the banks as citadels for economic exploitation. They even think that the dispersal of shares, far from effecting a separation between ownership and management, makes it easier for capitalist financiers to exert their influence. If marxists admit that the operation of business has been transferred to professional administrators, they still consider the latter's power as being limited to the mass of small shareholders while the administrators themselves remain completely subordinated to the giant financiers.

Scholars who support private enterprise have given a warm welcome to the new willingness of businessmen to shoulder social responsibility. By studying the latest trends in management thinking as developed, for instance, by Berle and Drucker, they are trying to lay down some theoretical foundation for the businessman's social role. Their work would be stronger, however, if it paid more attention to modern large-scale private enterprise as represented, say, by firms of national dimension; it is too often limited to small Japanese communities consisting of a variety of interested groups, and their concern, as far as managerial policy goes, seems mainly to be with the distribution of surpluses within these groups. On the union side, the Sohyo's main rival, the Domei, long ago discarded Marxism and exemplifies the new labour movement matching the endeavours of employers to keep up with modern economic developments at company, industry and national level. Recently, however, it has not been eager to participate in affairs at the level of the firm, preferring to be involved in planning at industry level as seen in the broad context of the national economy. Such as attitude, it may be observed, seems entirely unacceptable.

There are two main currents of thoughts among orthodox economists, or modern economists who are not influenced by marxism. Some of them oppose the view that businessmen should be aware of a social role and should accordingly pay attention to objectives other than profit-making. They believe such an attitude to be contrary to the principle of the social distribution of work and harmful to the efficient running of business. (In this they are, curiously enough, in line with the marxists.) They put their trust in the power of competition and the free price mechanism. They are, as it were, the Japanese counterparts of the Chicago School of Hayek and Freudman. The economists of social-democratic persuasion, on the other hand, recognise the significance of the separation of ownership and management and put a high value on the incipient awakening of a sense of social responsibility among businessmen—indeed, they look forward to fostering it still further. Their interest, they believe, should not be confined to the problems of economic distribution in a small community but should extend to industrial structure, economic growth and national stability. They place great emphasis on the importance of the role to be played by large companies and the relevance of the latter's sense of social responsibility as related to such questions as national industrial planning, investment and employment. Moreover, they believe that business responsibility will be guaranteed if consumers' organisations as well as trade unions are represented within the enterprise and are permitted to take part in planning and policy decisions.

Conclusions

There is no denying that a new type of businessman has emerged in Japan, aware of the important role he is expected to play and conscious of his social responsibility. His attitudes are, however, still tinged with old, paternalistic ideas, particularly with regard to labour relations and competition. His confusion of thought may be traced to the confrontation between a distorted economic system, which had laboured under government intervention and the monopolistic control of financial combines, and the new freedoms encouraged after the war. Consequently, many Japanese businessmen have still not yet succeeded in acquiring a vigorous feeling of independence and in cultivating an ethical sense of responsibility. There is still to much easy-going reliance on government direction and mere lip-service to a social role. There is an urgent need to enquire into business philosophy or ethics to provide a base for the practical fulfilment of social responsibility. (In Europe and America, Christianity seems to go a long way in answering such a need).

Judged by the results of the survey summarised above, Japanese businessmen appear inconsistent in their understanding of social responsibility. This inconsistency seems to spring as much from inadequate training and practical experience in new managerial techniques as from ideological or cultural confusion. It is only during the last decade that the science of management has been introduced into Japan from the United States and that firms have begun, consciously and publicly, to base their policies on these new techniques. We look to the future for better things. Japanese businessmen must now clearly explain to a critical public, both at home and abroad, how they propose to put their 'social responsibilities' into practice.

2. INDIA

Introduction

The historical roots of present-day Indian thinking about the corporate sector of the economy lie in the socio-economic ideology of the Congress Party, evolved during the most acute phase of the struggle for independence some thirty-five years ago. The basis of this ideology was the essentially egalitarian concept of economic order, then held by the dominant leaders of the liberation movement, which was later to be formalised as the 'socialist pattern of society.[7] The beliefs of the Congress leaders were subsequently backed up by considerable practical evidence that, in the circumstances then prevailing, the resources of organised trade and industry could best serve the fuller and more balanced development of the national economy by large-scale state initiative and the active participation of the state in economic enterprises.

The early company law reformers grew up with these ideas. They were not, however, concerned with making any basic changes in the 'classical' concept of the joint-stock company or the tradition of company law which they had inherited from the Anglo-Saxon world. Although many of them might have shared, in an abstract philosophical sense, the views of the dominant section of the Congress Part on the future economic order, and on the role of trade and industry in the development and modernisation of the national economy, their primary anxiety at that time was how to deal with the growing mal-practices of company management which had become serious during the inter-war years.[8] They sought to do this by providing structural and procedural checks and balances in the organisation and working of joint-stock companies without impairing the classical framework of Anglo-Saxon company law. Most of the reformers were keen adherents of the traditional liberal faith in disclosure as an effective restraint on reprehensible and anti-social conduct; but, apart from aiming at increased publicity for major company decisions, they also devised measures to ensure greater powers for the general body of shareholders, and closer supervision by the latter over decision-making by the management.

The leaders of the reform campaign at this stage were confined to a few shareholders' associations (notably the Bombay Shareholders' Association which was a pioneer in the struggle for the recognition of shareholders' rights and privileges), a few leading company lawyers and commercial journalists in Bombay and Calcutta and some leading members of the Congress Party.

The first glimmerings of the 'new thinking' on joint-stock companies and company law were discernible in the report of the Company Law Committee which the Government of India set up in 1950 with Mr. C.H. Bhabha—a distinguished commercial banker—as Chairman and the present author as Member-Secretary. Chapter II of this document, halting and hesitant as it was in outlining the main points of the report, appears nevertheless to have been of germinal importance and to be worth recalling even now. The following passages illustrate the Committee's approach:[9]

'Some witnesses.... seem to assume that our task necessarily presupposed that we should take a view of the role of private enterprise in the economic development of the country.... and then formulate our recommendations.... Other witness suggested more explicitly that our recommendations should conform to particular economic policies which, in their opinion, represented the avowed aims of the present Government and the welfare state, while still others pleaded for recognition of the importance of particular interests, e.g. labour, in the administration of the Companies Act.

'For the reasons which we explained ... we have not adopted any such an a priori approach.... The truth is that the Company Law is primarily concerned with means and not ends.... One should recognise the limitations of an enquiry such as ours which is concerned primarily with the mechanics of company management and not with the basic economic logic underlying it.

The operation of private enterprise under current conditions must, however, be subject to the acceptance of certain broad social objectives and of some recognised standards of behaviour.... The working of Company Law in any country must take not, of this factor, which will become increasingly important in future.'

It is clear from this chapter (and, indeed, from other parts of the Report) that the Committee, although it was pressed to take a wider view of company objectives and management behaviour than was traditionally accepted, felt that this was too unorthodox a departure from the classical view to deserve serious notice. Hence its recommendations, though far-reaching and in many ways much in advance of the classical attitude, scarcely deviated from the basic framework of traditional thinking on companies and company law.[10]

The Companies Bill 1953 faithfully followed the recommendations of the Company Law Committee. During the parliamentary stages of this Bill in 1954-55, however, its provisions underwent some major changes and it is in many of these that the slowly emerging outlines of the 'new thinking' may be discerned. This was reflected not only in the large-scale structural changes which were incorporated in the Bill at its Select Committee stages but also in the reshaping of the traditional aim of many of the procedural provisions of the law.

The distinguishing features of this 'new thinking' were the statutory recognition given in the new Companies Act to the concept of the 'public interest' in company management and the concern felt for the twin goals of a reduction of inequality in incomes and of the concentration of economic power, in so far as these were affected by company management and practice. The present author has attempted elsewhere[11] to expound these aspects at some length. There is no need to dwell on them here but it should be mentioned that, although this 'new thinking' influenced many operative provisions of the Companies Act 1956, and was officially accepted in the formulation of basic government policies for the Act's administration and enforcement, neither its underlying aims and objects nor its administrative implications can be said to have won the willing allegiance of the business community. The important issues raised are still matters of continuing argument and debate.

It may be gathered from this brief account that only a few narrow sectors of Indian society were actively involved in the origin and growth of the new ideas. The major impulse came from some leading members of the ruling political party, a few members of the government and a group of senior civil servant associated with them in policy-making, legislation and the setting up of appropriate administrative institutions. The radical wing of the Congress Party created the political conditions necessary for putting the 'new thinking' into practice when, under the leadership of the late Pandit Jawaharlal Nehru, it resolved at its annual meeting in January 1955 to accept the 'socialist pattern of society' as the ultimate goal of the country's economic and social policies. This policy was formally ratified by the Indian Parliament shortly afterwards.

In spite of doubts and hesitations expressed in some quarters, a broad (albeit formal) cosensus on the new policy emerged in the other dominant sectors of Indian society. The Federation of Indian Chambers of Commerce and Industry (the leading representative body of trade and industry) adopted a resolution at its annual conference in 1955 endorsing the declaration. Many other professional institutions recorded their formal approval. Although subsequent events after 1959-60 were to reveal that this consensus was largely superficial, it provided the necessary climate for the basic legislative and administrative measures adopted during the years between 1955 and 1960 which gave shape and direction to the new ideas. It may be worth while to add that although wide differences of views later became apparent even between senior members of the government—particularly after 1959-60—the Cabinet as a whole had endorsed all these major decisions which were implemented in the earlier years of the acceptance of the 'socialist pattern of society'. The few senior members of the civil service who were concerned with the problems of joint-stock companies not only played a leading part in the formulation of the policies underlying these measures but had also to carry the burden of enforcing the policy decisions. As was to be expected, the atmosphere in which they had to work from 1959-60 onwards became severely strained, and the enforcement of policies and administration of the law could not but be affected by the gradual erosion of the consensus on basic policies.[12] Whatever impact the 'new thinking' may have had on management practice during the life of the 1956 act has arisen mainly from the commitment of a few civil servants who had been entrusted with the administration of company law to the policies underlying it and to the values which these policies represented. An appreciation of their role is necessary for a proper understanding of the forces at work at that time. They not only pioneered but also promoted the new ideas. It was the privilege of the writer to head this small group, drawn from different service cadres and belonging to different professions, from 1953 to 1963.

The new outlook on company affairs continues to be an active concern of the radical sections in Congress (now perhaps in a minority), of several left-wing opposition parties and of the Department of Company Affairs in the Government of India. However, the old sense of urgency which inspired the radical elements of Congress has largely abated. The interest of the opposition parties on the left has become increasingly political and combative, in contrast with the zeal for reform and reconstruction which they displayed in the years between 1953 and 1960. The voice of the Department of Company Affairs has been progressively muted and the sense of commitment of its senior members to the basic values underlying the 'new thinking' has been continually diluted. Nevertheless, these circles maintain a degree of their former active interest in the implications of the new ideas for company affairs in general.

The legal profession, on the other hand, had remained largely unaffected, with a few notable exceptions, particularly in the Calcutta and Madras areas. Most company lawyers have continued to adhere to 'classical' tradition and attitudes, typified by their predominantly legalistic view of managerial behaviour and company practice, and their purely formalistic opinions on many basic provisions of the new company law.

No substantial enquiry into the structure of working of company law has been held since the company Law Committee reported in 1952,[13] although a number of *ad hoc* committees of enquiry have expressed views on many aspects of management and practice. The most important of these was the Commission of Enquiry on the Administration of Dalmia Jain Group of Companies,[14] presided over by a distinguished former Judge of the Supreme Court of India, which in the course of its detailed investigation into the affairs of these companies recommended further amendment of the Companies Act 1956. These recommendations were intended primarily to close loopholes in the Act, which in the view of the Commission permitted the abuse of some of its provisions, and the indulgence by some groups of companies in dubious practices which the Act had attempted to control. More recently two other Committees were set up to examine the incidence of monopolistic and restrictive practices in the corporate sector[15] and to consider the future of the managing agency system,[16] the traditional form of company management in India. Important as were the recommendations of these two committees, they did not impinge directly on the structure or working of the Companies Act, being concerned with two major aspects of company practice and management which had been the subject of continuous and widespread debate since 1952-53.

Other professional people—accountants, executives and company secretaries—though relative newcomers and (with the exception of the accountants) not yet fully institutionalised, have taken a much more lively interest in the 'new thinking' than their colleagues in the very much older legal profession. Their views have, however, been largely confined to professional issues of accountancy, management and the mechanics of company administration. From time to time, however, they have shown a perceptive understanding of and interest in the impact of these issues on the relationship between company practice and society in general.

Trade unions and other workers' movements played a significant role in the evolution of the new ideas in the formative stages of the new Companies Act between 1950 and 1955. Indeed, several provisions of the Act, particularly those relating to company management, owe a great deal to the constructive suggestions and recommendations of trade unions.[17] In recent years, however, union interest seems to have shifted more to industrial relations, to wages and participation in profits, not to mention their unending competitive struggle to secure the allegiance of workers. The earlier demands for participation in management voiced by some sectors of the union movement now seem less insistent. Employers' organisations, banking and other investment institutions have clung tenaciously to the classical tradition and have shown little interest in innovation.

The contribution of social scientists has been conspicuous by its absence. Apart from economics, the social sciences in India have yet to reach the necessary degree of sophistication. Senior Indian economists, following the example of their British colleagues, have till recently taken little interest in the study of analytical institutional economics. Furthermore, neither the economists nor the other social scientists have so far learned to regard the joint-stock company as the most dominant socio-economic institution in the organised sector of the Indian economy, much less as a significant system of power. It is only during the last ten years or so, as a by-product of the interest taken in company affairs by legislators and administrators, that some statistical and descriptive studies have been undertaken.[18] It is to be hoped that, with growing interest in the study of corporate economics, these pioneering efforts may stimulate further studies in depth and provide the essential raw material for a more meaningful investigation into corporate management and practice in the future.

The only significant public opinion groups which can claim to have made any contribution to the new developments are shareholders' associations in the leading centres of commerce and industry. The most important of these and one which has to its credit a remarkable record of constructive effort over many years is the Bombay Shareholders' Association. In recent years its influence has somewhat declined, mainly because of the many stockholders who have joined this association, and whose interests and points of view do not always coincide with those of shareholders. As a result, its approach and attitude towards company matters and company law has become somewhat blurred and less cohesive.

The press and other mass media might have been expected to influence thinking on company matters but the conditions in which the Indian press functions, and its close links with trade and industry, make it difficult for it to express any views which might appear to be critical of the practices of leading businessmen or business houses, on whose support it still leans heavily. Besides, economic journalism, even of the generalised type, is still in its infancy in India. Professional journalists by and large lack the specialised and sophisticated training needed for component study and analysis of company practice and finance and their relationship to society, and a specialised cadre of journalists who can be expected to handle with knowledge and confidence company data and the statistics of finance and investment has yet to emerge.

Corporate Distinctions

Different Forms of Private Enterprise

The two major classes of companies recognised in the Indian, as in the English,[19] Companies Act are (i) private companies and (ii) public companies. Like the English Act, it also provides for a class of non-profit-making companies, i.e. companies whose objects are limited to the promotion of commerce, art, science, religion, charity or any other useful object and which intend to apply their profits, if any, or other income, in promoting their object and which prohibit the payment of any dividend to their members. There is no distinction, as in English law, between exempt and non-exempt private companies. On the other hand, the Indian Act (Sec. 43A) recognises a new type of private company, popularly known as a 'deemed public company'. In private companies of this category not less than 25 per cent of the paid-up share capital is held by one or more bodies corporate For all practical pruposes the duties and responsibilities of such companies are the same as those of public companies and the provisions of the law relating to public companies broadly apply to them.

Indian law also recognises a class of 'Government Companies' (similar to the so-called 'Crown Companies' in some other parts of the world), in which not less than 51 per cent of the paid-up share capital is held by the Central Government or by one or more state governments, or partly by the Central Government and partly by one or more state governments. Subsidiaries of a government company so defined are included in this category. The three principal distinguishing features of these companies are: (i) they are not under managing agents; (ii) the standard audit provisions of the Companies Act, which apply to all other companies, do not apply to them in as much as the audit of their account is carried out by auditors appointed by the Central Government under the general supervision and direction of the Comptroller and Auditor-General, whose instructions they must carry out; and (iii) that the Comptroller and Auditor-General is entitled to supplement the audit of the accounts of these companies and in fact does so in much detail.

The line drawn between private limited companies and public limited companies so far as their objects, constitution, management and external control are concerned follow broadly the distinction between such companies in the English Act,with certain modifications. For example, the Indian, unlike the English, Act requires the accounts of all private companies to be audited by qualified auditors. On the other hand, the control provided for by the Act over the management of public companies or the remuneration of different classes of executives does not apply to private companies, nor do these sections intended to regulate the contracts, inter-company loans, and investments of public companies and their subsidiaries.

The 'deemed public companies' under Sec. 43A of the Companies Act were a conceptual innovation, meant to bring the two principal classes of limited companies somewhat closer together as regards their status, privileges and liabilities. The amendment arose from the growing dissatisfaction with the use of private limited companies as a device for getting round the restrictive provisions applying to public companies and as channels of undesirable investment by public companies, whose freedom to invest and engage in financial transactions not directly connected with their interests had been severely restricted by the Act of 1956.

The general theory underlying the differentiation in the Act between private and public limited companies (the two principal classes) is that the public interest in the organisation and working of the latter justifies the exercise of a much wider and tighter supervision and control than is needed in the case of private limited companies in whose operations, it is assumed, the public are not normally so interested or concerned. This theory, inherited from the classical Anglo-saxon tradition of company law, has, in the light of the Indian experience (and presumably that of other countries), become increasingly difficult to support. During the discussion on the amendment of the Companies Act in 1960, several prominent members of the Joint Select Committee of Parliament argued that the distinction between the two classes of companies as laid down in the Act of 1956 was unrelated to actual contemporary developments in company method and practice, served to useful purpose and should be abolished. These would-be reformers maintained that if there was to be any distinction between different categories, it should be between relatively small and larger companies, as, for instance, between the German AG and GmbH. The Minister in charge (the late Shri Lal Bahadur Shastri) favoured a classification based on size but eventually no action was taken because it was felt that to amend the law in this way would involve too drastic a departure from long established legislation and practice. Be that as it may, many contemporary students and experts believe that it may now be time, in the public interest, to take a further look at this question. Experience of Indian company legislation and the working of joint-stock companies leads the present author to share this view and to feel that a good case can be made out for the rationalisation and simplification of the law, involving the abolition of the distinction between private and public companies in favour of a classification based on more relevant criteria, such as size or other related objective facts.

As far as enterprise in the private sector are concerned, the choice as to the form in which they should be organised is, of course, left to promoters and investors and the provisions of the relevant laws have nothing to say about how this choice should be exercised; in practice, however, apart from the sprawling unorganised sector of the Indian economy, with its many 'self-employed' business, the choice in the organised sector is between partnerships and limited companies. Because of the increase in the scale of business, in both manufacturing and trading, the number of companies has grown enormously. After the end of the second world war, many large partnerships were converted into private limited companies, particularly in the years between 1946 and 1950. The principle of limited liability was a very important factor, next only to the taxation laws, in this change-over.

This choice between private and public limited companies is largely determined by a complex of considerations in which fiscal laws, the size of the company, the nature of its business, the manner of its financing, the extent to which it is likely to depend on internal or external sources of finance and to which it has to apply to semi-governmental or private financial institutions and, above all, the stock exchange requirements, play a decisive role.

Public and Private Enterprise

The debate on the form of ownership of public sector enterprise goes back to 1950.[20] Shortly after Independence the issue assumed considerable practical importance as a result of the new government economic policy of establishing key and basic industries, often very large, in the public sector. Several committees and commissions debated the pros and cons of the different forms of organisation suitable for public enterprises, and a number of official and unofficial *ad hoc* studies were made of the practice in other industrial advanced countries. Opinion on this subject has varied from time to time and it is unnecessary in this context to go into the history of this debate. The present thinking seems to be broadly as follows. (*a*) If an enterprise is closely integrated with and forms part of the operational activities of a government department (e.g. a factory building coaches or locomotives for the Department of Railways), it may be carried on either as an independent wing of the department concerned or as a government company, depending on the comparative advantages of the two forms of organisation as seen by the departmental authorities. (*b*) For business or industrial undertakings which provide goods or services in the nature of public utilities (e.g. civil aviation) or relating to the infrastructure of trade and industry (e.g. electricity or road transport), the form of a public corporation might be desirable. (*c*) For other businesses or industrial undertakings which are engaged in the production and sale of goods and services—particularly where collaboration with private capital or private management is desired—the company form of organisation would ordinarily be considered to be the most suitable.

The differences between public and private enterprises organised in the form of companies do not arise from the provisions of the Companies Act—except in regard to audits (se above)—but from policies and attitudes towards their responsibilities. These differences are reflected in the articles of government companies'. As a rule, these provide, *inter alia,* for the appointment of the chief executives by or with the approval of the government and for government approval of contracts above certain ceilings (the latter fixed by the government), of the appointment of executives above prescribed salary levels, of capital increases, of the raising of loans, of capital expenditure beyond a prescribed ceiling and of the allocation of profits. Government companies are also subject to parliamentary control and to scrutiny of their accounts and other activities by the Public Accounts Committee of Parliament and the special Parliamentary Committee on Public Undertakings set up a few years ago.

Most people believe that the main differences between public and private enterprises arise from their objectives, how they operate and the different degrees of public control exercised over them. It is implicity held that public companies must have wider business objectives than the maximisation of profits, that they should aim to earn no more than an optimum return from their investments, consistent with their responsibilities to their employees, the local community and the public interest, which may involve quite legitimate expenditure out of their income. Their constitutions and ways of organisation also provide, if not expressly at least by implications, that they must accept the obligation to follow national policies on the appointment and recruitment of personnel and appropriate levels of remuneration for top management, with due regard to the latter's competence and technical qualifications. It is also the prevailing view that public enterprises are under a special obligation to subject themselves to the public gaze and assume the liabilities imposed on them by the need for scrutiny of their accounts and of policies, both managerial and financial, by Parliament or any central public agency set up by Parliament. It is clear that people expect from public enterprise what the best undertakings in private enterprise would do of their own accord. In other words, the view taken in India of the attitudes, motivation and behaviour of public enterprises seems to approximate to the 'ideal' organisation and working of firms in the private sector—a point of view not very different from that observable in other advanced countries.

The Objectives of the Company

It has been increasingly recognised in recent years that, irrespective of legal provisions, the responsibilities of a company are not merely to its shareholders and creditors but extend to employees, customers and suppliers, and embrace within their scope also the interests of the local community and the national economy. The Companies Act 1956 was the most important single factor in developing this attitude. Other important influences have been the gradual development of professionalism in management; the example of the industrially advanced countries of the world, reinforced by that of foreign collaborators in Indian joint ventures; an increasing anxiety among large firms to project an acceptable 'image'; the gradually increasing impact of the new schools of management set up in different regions during the last decade; and the competitive effect of the broader social objectives officially accepted by companies in the public sector. It would be unrealistic to claim that such enlightened views are held by more than a few progressive businessmen. Most companies have yet to translate them into appropriate action.

The economic environment since the second world war has not been helpful. War-time controls and their aftermath, followed by continuing shortages and consequent restraints on trade and industry, both internally and externally, have ensured a highly sheltered domestic market. Foreign competition has been virtually non-existent and internal competition relatively weak except in a few consumer industries such as cotton textiles. The size and the productive capacity of the internal market has steadily increased but effective demand has at the same time continued to run ahead of production and supply. Indian management has never been forced to accept the usual social obligations to customers or partners in production, nor to strive for the high standards of performance which would help to transform the strictly economic process of marketing and distribution into socially responsible business.

The Consumer

The desirability of reducing the cost of goods and services, while improving their quality and providing marketing facilities normally available to consumers in industrially advanced countries, is widely recognised and accepted by far-sighted business leaders. The urgent need to secure for Indian trade and industry a better reputation abroad has been emphasised, not only for the sake of the growth of Indian business but as an essential aspect of public relations in contemporary society. Little, however, has been done. Businessmen complain that they are hampered on all sides—by shortages of materials and equipment, the poor quality of labour in some industries and above all by taxation. Frustrated consumers argue that the government must intervene. But there are hardly any consumers' associations worthy of the name, even in the industrial and commercial centres, and the few that do exist in the name lack the leadership and expertise necessary for dealing effectively with the problems.

The Shareholder

There is at present hardly any statutory control over dividends or other monetary benefits to shareholders except in the case of one or two utilities such as electricity generation. Studies on income and price policy are still in their infancy.[21] There are, however, other factors which exercise some indirect control on dividends. A major provision of the Companies Act 1956 (Sec. 205) prohibits the declaration of a dividend by a company which has not made any provision for depreciation in its accounts. This gives statutory backing to the orthodox view, hallowed by many court decisions, that dividends may be paid only out of profits and not out of capital. The other indirect control is the demand of employees for a share in company profits, which in Indian industrial parlance goes by the name of 'bonus'. Both the industrial courts and the Bonus Commission,[22] appointed by the government to go into the matter and lay down norms for the determination of profit-sharing, have accepted the legitimacy of this claim under certain conditions and up to certain limits. The recommendations of the Commission have been embodied in a statute. No other definitive proposal has so far been made for the regulating of dividends and other benefits to shareholders.

The Employee

The wages of industrial labour and the conditions governing their fixing and regulation are dealt with in the labour laws and labour codes. The remuneration of other employees (middle management, for example) is also for all practical purposes outside the provisions of the Companies Act and is indeed free from all legal restraint.

The 1956 Act, however, deals at length with the remuneration of managing agents, directors and the most senior executives.[23] Very briefly, the position is broadly as follows. The aggregate marginal remuneration payable by a public company (or a private company which is a subsidiary of a public company) to its directors, managing agents, secretaries and treasurers and to its general manager may not exceed 11 per cent of annual net profits, exclusive of fees paid to directors for attending board meetings. If profits are nil or inadequate, minimum remuneration of not more than Rs. 50,000 a year, in aggregate, may be paid to top managerial personnel, whether they are directors, managing agents or the general manager. Compensation in excess of these two overall limits must meet with the approval of the company, conveyed through a special resolution, and/or with the approval of the Central Government. Within the limit of 11 per cent of annual net profits, further ceilings on the remuneration of managing agents and whole-time directors have been imposed administratively; the law also specifically provides that the remuneration of an individual director may not exceed 5 per cent of annual net profits.[24] These provisions are more than twelve years old and have been administered in consultation with and on the advice of a small body of eminent persons drawn from some of the major interests concerned in the working of joint-stock companies. Nevertheless, business is still not reconciled to their underlying objectives and fitfully continues to voice its opposition.

Recent studies in several western countries, and particularly in the USA, have shown that the problems of top managerial remuneration do not arise merely from the issue of legitimacy, but even more importantly from the fact that there is no competitive market in the higher echelons of the management procession, partly because of its characteristics and partly because of the methods of appointment and the conditions of employment. These non-competitive aspect are aggravated in India by a number of factors—the tardy growth of professional management, the prevalence of caste and family considerations in many private firms, the persisting hereditary character of top management in disproportionately large segment of trade and industry, and the dominance of the ideological concept of equality on the part of elites generally, irrespective of their socio-economic or party affiliations. The provisions in the 1956 Act represent a rough and ready approach to this difficult problem and should be considered in the light of what has been said.

Development Expenditure Within the Firm

The Indian Companies Act, like its English prototype, is neutral towards all internal development expenditure, whether destined for capital investment, research and development, employee training or the improvement of organisation and methods.

Expenditure under the last three is given some indirect encouragement by liberal tax reliefs. Fiscal policy has varied from time to time but has never been deliberately designed to encourage the ploughing-back of profits rather than their distribution. Nor has the state ever made any claim to a share in ploughed-back profits, although, as already mentioned, the claim of employees to a share in earned profits, whether they are distributed or not, has been recognised following the recommendations of the Bonus Commission. (Towards the end of 1955, the then Minister of Finance, Shri T.T. Krishnamachari, proposed a Compulsory Reserves Scheme, under which companies would have been required to obtain Central Government approval for the use to which they put their reserves. The scheme was poorly conceived and was soon found to be unworkable. It was abandoned by Shri Krishnamachari's successor.)

The need to increase company expenditure on research and development, and also on employee training, has been much emphasised in recent years and it is possible that such outlays will receive greater fiscal encouragement. However, the pace of to technological advance and the scale on which industrial research has to be undertaken make it unlikely that the great majority of Indian companies will be able to take advantage of probably limited tax incentives. For many years to come, small and medium-sized firms will have to be assisted by industrial research in government or semi-official research institutes.

External Expenditure

Expenditure incurred by companies in their relations with trade and research associations qualifies for tax relief but is relatively small as few associations offer costly services. By and large, trade associations function as if they were employers' trade unions and are mainly concerned with negotiating tax concessions and similar advantages. Apart from the research institutions organised and financed by the associations of leading export industries, several new research institutes have been set up by other associations of predominantly domestic industries during the last fifteen years. Progress in this area has been slow but steady. With regard to expenses incurred in relations with distributors and suppliers, it should be borne in mind that one of the earliest concerns of the Indian company law reformers was to try to prevent the marketing and distribution functions from imposing needlessly onerous burdens on consumers and the community. The 1956 Act lays down certain procedures for regulating the appointment of sole selling agents and their remuneration and also of buying and selling by managing agents of companies or their associates.[25] The Indian marketing and distribution system will have to be modernised before a more liberal view of expenditure on this account can be taken by either the government or other concerned.

Services to the Community

Most large-scale industrial investment since 1951 has been covered by the Five Year Plans and has had to conform to Plan requirements both as to location and size. In some cases certain obligations on pricing policy have been imposed but only on the advice of a competent statutory body like the Tariff Commission and always with recourse to administrative arbitration. Any non-commercial services which companies may be asked to render to the community, either under the national plan or otherwise, are regulated through administrative machinery. Firms are not, for instance, generally required to accept unremunerative or not fully remunerative public service responsibilities except in emergencies. In normal times leading businessmen frequently serve as voluntary part-time members of government commissions and committees and as paid members of the boards of public sector enterprises. These duties are more often regarded as a recognition of merit than as a burden and it is rare for either the companies or the individuals involved to be called upon to make much sacrifice. Business donations for education, research and charity are usually granted to institutions directly or indirectly controlled by the donor but other unconditional gifts are made from time to time. The record of a small number of Indian firms is not unworthy in this respect. Few business houses have so far set up non-family trusts or foundations, whose policy and management is not directly or indirectly influenced by their leading members, and it is only in rare cases that such organisations are run by competent independent trustees.

The Legal Definition of Objectives

Following its English prototype, the Indian Companies Act of 1956 merely required the inclusion in the memorandum of association of a brief statement of the company's commercial objectives and the ancillary or incidental powers necessary to give them effect. An amendment[26] has provided that the objects clause should specifically distinguish between main objects, objects incidental or ancillary to the attainment of the main objects and other objects. It seems doubtful whether the purpose underlying this amendment, which clearly was to check indiscriminate diversification, will be achieved. The suggestion originally made by George Goyder in his book *The Responsible Company* that every company 'should be required by statute to add to its Memorandum of Association a general purpose clause expressing its purpose in terms of its obligation towards the shareholders, customers, workers and the community affected by the enterprise' has been considered at various seminars and conferences in India. The most important of these, held at the India International Centre in March 1965, was concerned with the social responsibilities of business. Mr. Goyder and several other foreign scholars participated. The seminar broadly endorsed his views but expressed some scepticism as to the effectiveness of a general purposes clause of this type. It was thought that any such clause, phrased only in general terms, was likely to remain merely a statutory declaration of good intent. To achieve anything more, the proposed new obligations would have to be translated into operational terms and appropriate changes in company law (based on the operational concept of these aims and objects) made both in the substantive and the procedural provisions of the Companies Act. To a limited extent, the present Indian Act has done something of this kind with regard to remuneration of directors and senior management.

The doctrine of *ultra vires* has been invoked only in a few cases but nevertheless dominates the thinking of lawyers and judges, probably because of the influence it has enjoyed in the United Kingdom. If the objects clause of the Companies Act is extended in the manner proposed by Goyder, and suitable substantive and procedural amendments are made in the law, the purpose underlying the doctrine would appear largely to have been served. This would be particular true if the policy-making organs of a company included representatives not merely of shareholders but also of employees, customers and the general community, and if the law provided for consultation with these outside interests before a company took decisions which might directly concern them. Such developments, however, would have more to do with the 'new thinking' on the wider objectives of a company than any revision of the doctrine of *ultra vires*.

Company Organisation and Control

The Powers and Accountability of Chief Executives

When the 1956 Act was under discussion there was some debate about the powers of boards of joint-stock companies and the merits and demerits of both the Anglo-American and Federal German systems. The government undertook a tentative study of the latter, chiefly in the context of the relationship of labour to internal company management. In recent years, even in trade union circles, interest in the German model has noticeably declined. This does not mean that the unions considered the Anglo-American to be altogether satisfactory but by and large they now incline to the view that corporate accountability is best secured by their own activities, backed up by effective and vigilant shareholder participation and government control over decision-making in the more important areas of company management, such as trading and financial policies, managerial remuneration, investment and disclosure.

One particular aspect of the management structure of Indian companies, peculiar to the country, has received much attention in recent years. This is the 'managing agency' system, up to now the dominant form of company management. It involved a two-tier constitution, with the board of directors at the head of the hierarchy and 'managing agents' forming an inner core of management, theoretically under the control and supervision of the board but in practice leading them in decision-making. The system has been under attack for nearly twenty years and has been the subject of many investigations.[27] The latest official report[28] recommended its abolition in several well-established industries, but supported its retention in some others for the time being. The government, however, decided to do away with managing agencies altogether and, under the Companies (Amendment) Act, 1969, the system is completely abolished as from April 1970.

The Indian Companies Act deals elaborately with the appointment and dismissal of chief executives, whether they be managing directors, managing agents or general managers. By and large the terms of such appointments are set by company boards, subject to the provisions of the Act with regard to directorial and management remuneration which have already been described. Contemporary thinking on managerial remuneration has become much less rigid than it was at the time the Act came into force—largely, perhaps, because of dissatisfaction with the somewhat haphazard administration of the law and also because of the growing professionalisation of company management.

The traditional hierarchical system of management and the fact that major decisions still remain in the hands of managing agents, managing directors or general managers (many of whom, over a large area of Indian business, still constitute fairly well-knit family or caste groups) mean that the powers of chief executives in relation to third parties and their accountability for the actions of their subordinates are not live issues. The legal responsibility of directors (including managing agents and general managers holding directorial positions) for the major decisions of a company are, however, recognised in Indian company law in much the same way as in English law.

The representation and Protection of Interests within the Company

Disclosure

Even before 1956 the attitude of Indian company law towards disclosure went far beyond the traditional limits of its English prototype. Indeed, several provisions of the Indian law, particularly those relating to company accounts, were much in advance of similar English and other foreign legislation. This was recognised by the Company Law Committee.[29] Until the period of 'new thinking', the law on disclosure was intended primarily to benefit shareholders and creditors. At first, shareholders' associations, the legal and accountancy professions and other bodies combined in their demands for greater disclosure, on the ground that it was in the interest of their clients. The concept of disclosure in the interest of employees and the national economy emerged later as a by-product of economic planning in the 1950s. The Act of 1956 greatly enlarged the scope and limits of disclosure, particularly with regard to company accounts and increased supervision of decision-making by the shareholders—the 'democratisation of management'. Many important areas of management and company practice, previously left entirely to the judgment of the board, were brought by the Act under the surveillance of the general body of shareholders, either through ordinary resolutions or 'special' resolutions needing a three-quarters majority of shareholders present at a meeting. It was also laid down that copies of all special resolutions and of certain categories of ordinary resolutions must be forwarded to any member of the company who might ask for them (on payment of a nominal fee) and also to the Registrar of Joint-Stock Companies. In this way much detailed information about the working of joint-stock companies was now readily available not only to the shareholders but also in offices of public record.

In recent years the business community has voiced even louder demands that these requirements be relaxed, on the grounds that they are costly and time-consuming; that most shareholders make little use of the resolutions they ask for; that neither the employees nor government departments make much use of the information contained in these records; and that the added publicity may sometimes needlessly expose companies to malicious attacks by hostile individuals or groups. No proposals, however, have been made for amending the legislation and it is doubtful whether the burden on companies is really still felt to be onerous. The question, nevertheless, remains whether much use is being made of the newly available information (even on company accounts) by any one, including the government. If it is not, is it worth while indefinitely to retain the present requirements of the law? In a sense, the answer would depend on the government's future attitude to company management and administration and on the public's attitude to private enterprise.

The Shareholder

Before considering the position of the shareholder under Indian company law, it will be useful to recall a few points made earlier in these pages and developed more fully elsewhere[30] by the present author. (*a*) In several important areas management decisions are subject to the consent of the shareholders, by ordinary or special resolutions, depending on the nature and importance of the decisions. This control is, in particular, exercised with regard to the appointment, reappointment and remuneration of managing agents, managing directors and top managerial personnel, and in respect of contracts and other financial transactions of the management, especially inter-company contracts entered into between companies belonging to a group controlled by the same management. (*b*) Competition and other market forces do not operate effectively in the managerial field in an economy such as that of India. (*c*) The organs of public opinion and other forms of communication, many of which have close thinks with the higher ranks of business, cannot adequately protect the interests of shareholders and others. (*d*) Business must increasingly conform (within the pragmatic limits of administrative enforcement) with the basic values implicit in the accepted goals of national economic and social policy.

The Companies Act 1956 greatly extended the scope and range of *shareholders' meetings* and created conditions in which active shareholders could play a useful part and also exercise an indirect influence on company practice by taking advantage of the disclosure rules. Experience has shown, however, that the company reformers' naive faith in 'shareholder democracy's has largely vanished. Like any other form of democracy, it needs to be backed up by the continuous vigilance of a few men with enough time, money, trained assistance, knowledge and experience to build up the organisations necessary for shareholders' meetings to have any effective impact. (The present writer had personal experience of these problems when, shortly after the passing of the Act of 1956, he and some of his colleagues tries to revitalise a number of the existing shareholders' associations and to encourage the establishment of new ones.) Efforts have been made to devise other political or economic substitutes to offset the powers of company management, such as joint advisory boards consisting of representatives of management, shareholders, employees and public authorities, or 'local meetings' open to representatives of consumers, workers and the community, including the local authorities.

Indian company law does not contain any special provision for the representation on company boards of any class of *capital suppliers*. Such an arrangement has not so far been thought necessary despite the increasing reliance of firms on external finance for their short-term as well as long-term capital requirements during the last decade or so. These requirements have in the main been met by the commercial banks and several public and specialised financial institutions, the most important of which are the Industrial Finance Corporation of India, finance corporations operating at state level, the Life Insurance Corporation of India, the Industrial Credit and Investment Corporation of India and the more recently established Industrial Development Bank of India. These institutional investors have not had to resort to statutory board representation in order to protect their legitimate interests and safeguard their investments in joint-stock companies. When one of these bodies grants financial assistance to a firm it usually enters into a specific agreement which, apart from the normal contractual safeguards (including the power to foreclose in an extremity), permits it to be represented on the board of the company to which a loan has been made. It is then left to the management and shareholders of the beneficiary firm to accommodate the representatives of the lending institution within the limits of their articles of association, which are amended, if necessary, for this purpose. These institutional investors have, like their British counterparts, on the whole refrained from taking any active interest in the management or control of any company, except when gross mismanagement may have threatened their investment. There has been little demand from any other source for the representation of capital suppliers on company boards. It has been generally assumed that the attitudes and values of institutional investors towards economic and social matters would inevitably lead them to take a limited view of their duties and responsibilities even if they were represented on boards.

The Act of 1956 hardly recognises a distinction between *committed and uncommitted investors.* Before 1956, special classes of investors could influence or control companies by holding shares with disproportionate voting rights, variously described as founder's share, deferred shares, etc. The new Act provided that the share capital of companies limited by shares formed after it came into force could be of two kinds only—equity or preference. Ordinarily only equity shareholders have voting rights, in proportion to their holdings. Preference shareholders normally have no such rights, except when their dividends fall in arrears for two years. The Act also laid down (*a*) that no company formed after its coming into force could issue any equity shares carrying voting or any other rights as to dividend, capital or otherwise, disproportionate to the rights of holders of other equity shares; and (*b*) that existing disproportionate voting rights should be terminated within one year of the Act coming into force. Although the Central Government took powers to exempt companies from this provision in the public interest, or in that of the company, or any group of its shareholders or creditors, it has exercised this power in one or two instances only.

The Act does not contain any special provision[31] for *minority rights* except in cases of oppression or gross mismanagement of company affairs by the majority, likely to jeopardise the interests of the minority. In the latter case the more important of certain elaborate provisions are contained in the following sections of the Act. Sec. 233A enables the government to order a special audit of a company's affairs, when the latter is not managed in accordance with sound business principles, or is run in a manner likely to cause serious injury or damage to the interests of the trade, or when its financial position is such as to endanger its solvency. Sec. 388B empowers the government to bring to the notice of a tribunal constituted under this section the conduct of the management of a company, and to ask for an enquiry into the fitness of the management to carry on the business, in the event of fraud, malfeasance, persistent neglect, or default in carrying out the obligations of company law; or where the company is not being managed in accordance with sound business principles or is being run in a manner which is likely to cause serious injury or damage to the interests of the trade. Sections 297 and 398 deal with the powers or the courts and the government to intervene in the event of oppression of its members, gross mismanagement or serious prejudice to its interests of prejudice to the public interest. Sec. 408 empowers the government to appoint not more than two suitable persons to the board in order to prevent the affairs of a company from being conducted in a manner which is oppressive to any section of its members, or is prejudicial to its interest or that of the public.

It should be said that, in the Indian context, these apparently drastic powers have not so far been regarded either as oppressive or constraining. They have been used effectively in a few cases only, and the leaders of the business community (and others close to the business world) have reluctantly recognised them as a necessary check upon certain elements which can still cause much damage to the reputation of business.

The Employee

The old demands of left-wing trade unionists for employee representation on boards and other internal company organs, which received some support in recent years in official labour circles and from left-wing intellectuals and economists, appear to have been much less loudly voiced lately. Greater reliance is now put on institutions such as works councils and committees, joint consultative or advisory bodies within a firm, and on normal external union activities for the protection and advancement of workers;' interests. Most of those directly or indirectly concerned with labour problems agree that, given the traditional organisation and structure of company management, this is the best way for labour to safeguard and advance its legitimate interests with the support of suitable legislation. The government appointed a National Commission at the end of 1966 to undertake a comprehensive reappraisal of current labour legislation. This Commission has now reported but it is unlikely that early action will be taken on its wide-ranging recommendations, some of which concern very controversial issues.

The Consumer

Although under Indian law there is no representation of consumer's interest within the firm, several provisions of the 1956 Act were intended to afford indirect protection to these interests within the limits of statutory provisions. These provisions concern such matters as the purchase and sale of goods and services by managing agents; the appointment of sole selling agents by directors; and contracts for the sale and purchase of goods by directors and managing agents.

The prevailing view is that consumers would be better protected by direct legislation on product price and quality and, to a lesser extent, by legislation directed against mergers, amalgamations, combinations and restrictive practices which are held to be contrary to the common good. (The difficulties of strengthening the bases of market competition have already been discussed.) Some legislation on quality and other services to which consumers are morally entitled was passed several years ago but it has by and large proved inadequate and ineffective. Because of this, more and more support has been given to consumers' associations and co-operative stores, particularly in metropolitan areas. These, however, have been severely hampered by continuing shortages of goods and services (and especially of basic consumer goods), in the face of accelerating demand. This is a major issue of economic policy and administration which can be hardly dealt with through company law or practice as such. Enlightened management could do a great deal to improve matters but unfortunately any sign of leadership on this score has been slow to emerge.

The Public Interest

A feature of the 'new thinking' on company management, practice and law has been the formal recognition given to the concept of the public interest, not only in several provisions of the Companies Act but also in the official formulation of policy relating to company affairs. In an essay written some time ago the present author pointed out that the more important sections of the 1956 Act which specifically mention the concept of public interest are generally in those areas of law where even conventional legal wisdom was disturbed at the likely consequences of the unhindered exercise of private rights by management or stock-holders. Indian law has now formally recognised the fact that there are circumstances when the joint will of management and stock-holders may have to give way to the requirements of public policy. This recognition may be traced in numerous sections of the 1956 Act—for example those requiring compulsory provision for depreciation before dividends on shares or stocks can be paid; those dealing with the form and content of the balance sheet and the profit and loss accounts and those concerning the presentation of these-documents; and those dealing with the compulsory amalgamation or merger of companies in the public interest. The concept has been spelled out in such a way as not only to provide in certain circumstances for special procedures and action but also to authorise exemption from the general rules laid down in the Act.

An institutional step was taken in a recent amendment of the Companies Act, which set up the office of Public Trustee in order to enable the Trustee to take over the voting rights of shares and debentures held in trust from their trustees to be exercised in such manner as he may determine. The object of this amendment was to ensure that voting powers attaching to funds held in trust for the community or the public were exercised to promote the public interest and not to further those of private individuals who had formed tax-free trusts, ostensibly for 'public motives.' Whatever the theoretical justification for this amendment, however, it has so far had hardly any impact on company practice and is unlikely to have any in the near future.

The Location of Interest Representation

Contemporary Indian thinking has not seen boardroom as a suitable forum for the representation of the various interests involved in the conduct of a company's business. The increasing professionalisation of management is one important factor. It has already been mentioned that greater reliance is likely to be laid on new institutions to be set up within or outside the organisation of a company, integrated with the organisation on an advisory or consultative basis. Hence an important future task of management will be to assimilate the views expressed in these new institutions into the processes of policy formulation and execution. At the seminar mentioned above, much emphasis was given to this integrative role of management, as the following extracts from the Declaration adopted at the seminar will show:

'It should now be clear that it falls to management to see that the multiple social responsibilities of business are fulfilled. Each of the parties involved in business has no more than a partial interest in the enterprise; only management entrusted with its governance carries the overall responsibility for its success and growth. Management must be freed from one-sided dependence on any single interest, if its has to take a broad enough view of its obligations. Hence, our proposals for extending its formal accountability, but they will not in themselves suffice.

'With the growth of large-scale enterprise, management under any system of accountability and control necessarily acquires a high degree of autonomy in its decisions. While it must in practice reconcile the sometimes conflicting claims made on the enterprise by various interests groups, it is not merely their servant but has creative powers of initiation and innovation. How these powers are used depends essentially on the prevailing philosophy of management and the capacities and convictions of managers.... We want to promote a more enlightened philosophy of management which encourages responsible participation of all employees by respecting their dignity as human beings.'

Partly or Quasi-Independent Units of the Firm

The special problems of dependent units would *prima facie* appear to arise from the fact that, in law, they are formally under the control of their parent firms. The managements of these companies are, therefore, formally subject to the overriding control and direction of the management of the parent companies, should the latter decide to exercise their rights. A similar problem used to arise with companies managed by the same managing agents. It was not unusual for as many as twenty or thirty companies to be managed by one or more associated managing agents, although the 1956 Act attempted in many provisions[32] to deal with these problems of agglomeration and the attendant and inevitable complications.

Indian thinking on subsidiaries and other quasi-independent units has, however, chiefly confined itself to the limited issues of the concentration of power. It is widely accepted that, whatever the legal or formal status of subsidiaries and other quasi-independent units, the objects which their management should pursue should be the same as, or similar or ancillary to, those of their parents; but their status should not have any effects, either in law or in practice, on the freedom of initiative or action, or the accountability, of their chief executives. Likewise, if the constitutions of the parent companies provide for the representation of all the participating interests, there is no good reason why the constitutions of the subsidiaries or other units under their control should not provide for similar representation.

Public Control

The conviction that all companies set up under the terms of a public franchises, and dealing with the public in some form or another, and especially public limited companies as defined in law, are institutions in which the public are both directly and indirectly interested is central to the 'new thinking' on company affairs. Hence, the boardroom decisions of such firms should not merely conform to the technical requirements of the law but also take account of public requirements. It follows that all their major policy decisions should be based on the value implicit in the ultimate goals of national economic and social policy. Thus, in the Indian context, 'public interest' means not merely that of the national economy, as defined by state policy or legislation, but embraces all the other interests (quite apart from those of managers, shareholders and financiers) which are directly or indirectly affected by the operations of firms. It has never been suggested that this concept of 'public interest' implies that the 'external' interests are as relevant or as close to the day-to-day running of a company as are the more direct interests. It has merely been held that management should integrated all these diverse interests in a systematic and coherent manner, and take decisions founded on an integral and not a partial concept of the managerial function. How this is to be done is not a matter of law but of empirical judgment on the part of management.

In practice of course, it is not always easy to define the area of 'public interest' in individual decisions. Ordinarily, therefore, both law and practice leave it to the management of companies to act in the spirit of the law. But when a particular decision is clearly and seriously against the public interest, the administration has pointed out to the company management how they have failed to measure up to legal requirements. In situations like this the administration has taken its line from several sources, among them the following: constitutional provisions concerning the goals of Indian economic and social policy; authoritative statements on 'economic and social policy approved by Parliament; the advice of statutory advisory commissions and committees, in cases where these have been set up to assist the administration; competent expert advice on good company practice relation to managerial, investment and financial problems; and the advice and opinions of trade and industrial organisations.

There has consequently been much more supervision of company management than is usual in the administration of similar measures in Britain or America, for instance. It has often been asked why India has chosen to follow this method of detailed regulation. The present author has endeavoured on many occasions in the past to explain the underlying theory of the Indian approach and will now limit himself to recalling some observations made by the late Shri Lal Bahadur Shastri (then Minister of Commerce and Industry and later Prime Minister), during the debate in the Indian Parliament at the time of the enactment of the Companies Amendment Act 1960.

Shri Shastri emphasised six main points. (i) Principles of social responsibility have won no more than limited acceptance—and that only comparatively small section of the

Indian business community. (ii) The average company management has been rather slow in acquiring a sense of fiduciary responsibility. (iii) There is a lack of strong and well-organised financial institutions, with long traditions of public service and reputations to lose, for overseeing company flotation and management and, to some extent, thereby making the statutory regulation of company practice less urgent. (iv) The financial and economic press is weak and not wholly independent. (v) A vigorous and well-developed public opinion, such as would not tolerate unwarranted deviations from the accepted forms of company behaviour and practice, is also lacking. (vi) Comparatively slow progress has so far been made towards the professionalisation of management. Shri Shastri contrasted this situation with situation with that in Britain, the USA and other Western countries, in which far-reaching changes in the character and quality of company management have evolved.

There is another aspect of this mater which should be mentioned.[33] Much debate took place in 1952 and 1955 on the institutions which were to be entrusted with public control over firms. Earlier, the Company Law Committee had expressed its preference for a statutory corporation on the lines of the American Securities and Exchange Commission, rather than ministerial or department control. The government, however, finally accepted the recommendation of a Joint Select Committee of Parliament that, in order to exercise the wide range of control necessary in the Indian context, the authority should be a duly constituted department of government, under a minister. The minister in charge of the Companies Bill pointed out that the type of control over company affairs envisaged in the new Act would involve judgment on important public issues, many of which would go to the heart of the country's economic and social policy, and that it was therefore desirable for the government itself to assume direct responsibility. In the light of what has happened since, in is now possible to take a different view and, on balance, more people are inclined to do so. Their opinion is backed up by the fact that control over companies involves detached understanding and neutral and informed judgment with regard to company affairs, qualities not often found in civil servants (executive or judicial) and even less frequently in politicians.

The prevailing attitudes to the question of public control of companies in India may be briefly summed up as follows. The government and the Civil Service are in a sense committed to established policy, however much certain individuals may deplore the circumstances which made statutory controls necessary and however much they see the need for changing many of the provisions of the present law, particularly those which appear to serve little practical purpose. Business opposition to public control is sometimes based on ideological grounds—never very forcefully expressed—but is more often realistic and complaints that the present legal and administrative requirements are complicated, time-consuming and irksome. There is, however, little inclination to challenge the basic philosophy underlying the present policies, much less to repudiate it altogether. Professional people are less vocal. Lawyers and accountants from time to time point out the system's defects and deficiencies and plead for simplifications. Shareholders' associations seem no longer to take a strong line either way. Many of them now perhaps understand quite well that their members' interests cannot be protected merely by means of legal provisions and that they have to rely almost wholly on the administration to enforce the law, particularly when their interests are most closely affected. Public opinion is by and large indifferent to business affairs except when a scandal is in the news. Most of the organised political parties (except, perhaps, a section of the Swatantra Party whose economic and social views are not recognisably different from those of late nineteenth century liberalism) accept the need for the provisions of the Companies Act and their vigorous enforcement by the administration. In general, the whole question of company management and practice is no longer the live issue that it was in the 1950s. It is now the problems of growth and development, and the hardships and frustrations caused by failure to move ahead fast enough, that appear to hold the centre of the stage.

Social and Efficiency Audits

The idea of an 'efficiency audit' has been much discussed in recent years but little has emerged in the way of concrete and detailed proposals as far as the private sector is concerned. There has been some practical interest in public sector companies but progress has been hampered even here by the inability of the accountants and the management's financial advisers to work out the full implications and put a system to the test. Experiments have usually been no more than variations on the audit system operated in government departments under the control and guidance of the Comptroller and Auditor-General. An amendment of the Companies Act (Sec. 233B) provides that the government may order the audit of a company in suitable cases, but only if the company has been officially asked to record additional information in its books and accounts, with particular reference to the utilisation of material of labour and/or to other cost items as may be prescribed. Although this amendment was made about five years ago, no administrative orders have so far been issued. It would therefore seem to be primarily an expression of intent on the part of the then minister which does not appear to have been followed up.

The concept of a 'social audit' received a good deal of support at the India International Centre seminar already mentioned and the Declaration then adopted[34] recommended that a social audit should be introduced (on a voluntary basis at first) so that a factual assessment could be made by trained and professional observers of companies 'social performance'. Such an assessment would, however, be meaningful only if undertaken by people trained not only in the social sciences but also in the mechanics of company management and finance, since they would be called upon to do for the 'social' performance of a company what they financial auditor already does for its financial. Since the recommendation cannot be implemented unless efforts are made to build up, from scratch, a force of auditors specially trained in the social sciences, it is hardly surprising that both business leaders and accountants have looked askance at this suggestion. It is nevertheless worth mentioning that several companies in the public sector have been already subjected to detailed study and assessment of their performance (in regard to matters such as prices, wages, research and development, public and human relations and employment stabilisation) by the Committee on Public Undertakings set up by the two Houses of the Indian Parliament some time ago.[35] The studies on several government enterprises undertaken by this Committee (and such staff as it has been able to command) cannot yet be said to constitute a real social audit, but they do contain much valuable raw material for such an audit and point to a possible institutional innovation which might help to strengthen the social outlook of management.

Rights of Appeal

The Indian Companies Act provides for a right of appeal by shareholders to the Central Government and the courts and in this respect goes further than its English prototype. Under Indian law, this right is not confined to cases of fraud, malfeasance, mismanagement or oppression of minorities but extends, for instance, to the cases covered by Sec. 233A of the Companies Act. Furthermore, as has already been pointed out, the government has taken additional powers in Sec. 388B of the Act to refer to a tribunal the cases of individual managerial personnel who are *prima facie* deemed to be guilty of malpractices or gross mismanagement, in order to seek their dismissal. Action under these two amendments can be taken only by the Central Government and cannot be initiated by shareholders or any other group. Nevertheless, the fact that the Act has provisions which go beyond the traditional limits of punitive action by governments or any central authorities, such as the American SEC, has damped down any demands for additional rights by either shareholders or employees. Many responsible people believe that the present powers are not only adequate but border on the excessive and that institutional changes should be made to ensure that they are used only in the public interest and not at the whim of an interventionist civil servant or minister.

Conclusions

This chapter has attempted to set out the views of those who take an active interest in company affairs in India. It should be stressed, however, that big business still remains a distant and, in many ways, a somewhat esoteric element in the modernised sector of the Indian economy. There remains, in many parts of the country, a gulf between businessmen and educated and thoughtful people, especially intellectuals. An important consequence of this psychological and moral alienation has been the lack of any close involvement on the part of intellectuals and others in business affairs and a corresponding failure to take a constructive interest in business problems and particularly in the organisation and working of firms. The ideas behind the 'new thinking'—largely worked out by sophisticated politicians, civil servants and professional people aided by the writings of Western scholars and the example of the best foreign corporate practice—have yet to impinge upon the average businessman whose conventional wisdom is still derived from the old-world practices of craft and marketplace. Only when this happens will there be a hope of building a bridge of understanding and assimilation between the two points of view.

Until recently, no scheme for the general reform of company law has so far been seriously considered in India and there have been no more than the suggestions for limited changes in particular aspects of the law, as outlined in this chapter. In 1967, however, a Working Group on Company Law Administration (under the chairmanship of the present author) was appointed by the Administrative Reforms Commission which was itself set up by the Central Government in 1965. This Group undertook a rapid survey of the whole field of the administration of company law in India and suggested some far reaching changes to improve its working and relate it more specifically to economic policy as pursued since the enactment of the basic legislation of 1956. No action has yet been taken on the Group's recommendations[36] but they cover such a wide field, of both law and administration, that it seems likely that, together with other suggestions for reform, they will form the basis of any future scheme (which cannot be delayed much longer) for the general reform of company law in India.

REFERENCES

1. Kuniyoshi Urabe, *Kigyo-keitairon (The Structure of the Enterprise)*, Moriyama-shoten, 1958.
2. Statistics from Research Department, Nikyo Securities Co., and Ministry of Finance.
3. Ibid.
4. Kosei Torihiki Iinkai (Fair Trade Commission), *Nihon no Sangyo Shuchu (Industrial Concentration in Japan)*, Tokyo Keizai Shimpo-sha, 1964.
5. The Keizai-Doyukai was founded in 1946. Businessmen join it as individuals and a large part of the membership is youthful and at middle management level. It serves as a meeting-place and study centre. The other main business organisations in Japan are more formal in character. The most important are the Keidamen (Federation of Industry), the Nikkei-res (Federation of Employers' Organisations) and the Nihon-shoko-kaigisho (Japan Chamber of Commerce and Industry).
6. Hitoshi Misono, *Nihon no Dokusen (Monopoly in Japan)*, Shisei-do, 1960.
7. The famous resolution adopted at the annual session of the Indian National Congress at Avadi in January 1955 declared that 'planning should take place with a view to the establishment of a socialistic pattern of society, where the principal means of production are under social ownership and control'. (Indian National Congress, *Resolutions*, 1955-56, p. 1). This resolution followed a series of policy declarations by the All-India Congress Committee, the National Development Council and the government in Parliament during the second half of 1954. It must not be forgotten, however, that there declarations saw in important role for the private sector in the national economy. The Avadi resolution laid it down that 'the private sector or the non-state and voluntary enterprises...will continue to have importance', and, in the course of his report as the outgoing President of the Indian National Congress, Prime Minister Nehru himself started that '...the main purpose of a socialised pattern of society is to remove the fetters to production and distribution.... It becomes therefore necessary to have a private sector and to give it full play within its field.' Throughout these statements runs a curious blend of ideology and pragmatism—the hall-mark of India's mixed economy.
8. Many authoritative enquiries and committees which reported between, 1947 and 1952 deplored the weakening of business morality since the end of the war. See, for example, the reports of the Fiscal-Commission (1949-50); the Industrial Finance Corporation (Second Report); the Income-tax Investigation Committee; the Planning Commission (First Five Year—Plan), etc., and also N.K. Mazumdar (Special Officer, Ministry of Commerce, Government of India), Memorandum on the Indian Companies Act (1949).
9. Government of India, *Report of the Company Law Committee*, 1952, pp. 10-11. This passage refers to the evidence of some well-known trade unions and professional associations, of which the following are typical. (i) 'Company law partakes of the character of both public law and private law, of substantive law and adjective law. It regulates the commerce and industry of this country and therefore vitally affects the public interest. It imparts rights and imposes

responsibilities on private individuals and their associations and controls the economic system. Its contents will, however, differ with the character of society, past and present, or the one to be shaped in the future.' (Hind Mazdur Sabha, a leading trade union in Western India.) (ii) We are of opinion that labour is a partner in any business or industry in which it is employed. Though it does not contribute capital, it performs its functions by contributing labour which is as essential an ingredient as capital in the production of goods or rendering of service.' (Indian National Trade Union Congress.)

10. Ibid., p. 13. 'It is not, however, the province of company law to anticipate what economic policy should be, and we fully endorse the observations of the Cohen Committee' (On the Cohen Committee, see Introduction, p. 26 above.)
11. D.L. Mazumdar, *Towards a Philosophy of the Modern Corporation*, Bombay, Asia Publishing House, 1967, pp. 54-66.
12. See *Annual Reports on the Working and Administration of the Companies Act, 1956*, particularly for the years ending 31 March 1957 (pp. 1-2), 1958 (p. 1) and 1960 (pp. 1-2).
13. But see 'Conclusions', p. 319 below.
14. Government of India, *Report of the Commission of Enquiry on the Administration of Dalmia Jain Companies*, 1963 pp. 797-815.
15. Government of India, *Report of the Monopolies Enquiry Commission*, 1963.
16. Government of India, *Report of the Managing Agency Enquiry Committee*, 1966. (On the managing agency system—abolished as from April 1970—see p. 308 below.)
17. The far-reaching amendments to Chapter III of the Companies Bill, 1953, on managing agents, introduced at the session of the Joint Select Committee of Parliament held in August and September 1954, were inspired by a resolution passed at the 1954 annual session of the Indian National Trade Union Congress.
18. See P.S. Lokanathan, *Industrial Organisation in India*, London, Allen and Unwin, 1935, and D.H. Buchanan, *The Development of Capitalistic Enterprise in India*, New York, The Macmillan Co., 1934. The more important of relatively recent publications are: M.M. Mehta, *Combination Movement in Indian Industry: A Study in the Concentration of Ownership, Control and Management in Indian Industry*, Allahabad, Friend's Book Depot, 1952, and *Structure of Indian Industries*, Bombay, Popular Book Depot, 1953; N. Das, *Industrial Enterprise in India*, Bombay, Calcutta and Madras, Orient Longman, 1956; *Concentration of Economic Power in India*, Allahabad, Chaitanya Publishing House, 1962; R.K. Hazari, *The Structure of the Corporate Private Sector*, Bombay, Asia Publishing House, 1966. See also the publications of the Research and Statistics Division of the former Department of Company Law Administration, of which the author of this Chapter was Secretary between 1955 and 1963. The more important of these are *Managing Agencies in India (First Round: Basic Facts)*, 1958 and *The Corporate Sector in India*, 1960.
19. It should be noted that this chapter was written in the light of English law before the British Act of 1967 came into force. Reference may be made to the British sections in the earlier parts of this book for the changes introduced by the Act of 1967.
20. See Government of India, *Report of the Indian Fiscal Commission*, Vol. 1, 1950, pp. 219-221. The debate continued intermittently until the Congress Parliamentary Committee under the chairmanship of Shri V.K. Krishna Menon reported in 1960.
21. See Reserve Bank of India, *Report on a Framework on Incomes and Prices Policy*, 1967. The report was prepared by a steering committee of economists and other employed in Central Government departments and in the Reserve Bank of India, under the Chairmanship of Dr. B.K. Madan, until recently Deputy Governor of the Bank.
22. Government of India, Ministry of Labour and Employment, *Report of the Bonus Commission*, 1964, pp. 107-120.
23. See Government of India, *Annual Report of the Company Law Advisory Commission for the year ended 31 March 1957* for a detailed summary of these provisions and of the principles evolved by the Commission, constituted under Sec. 410 of the Companies Act, on whose advice alone the government were competent to take decisions on these matters.

24. In an earlier publication (*Towards a Philosophy of the Modern Corporation*, Bombay, Asia Publishing House, 1967, pp. 18-19 and 155-156), the author of this chapter has gone into the reasons for these unusual provisions in the Act of 1956. It is not necessary to discuss them again. However, as the Indian law represents a major departure from the classical tradition of the Anglo-Saxon countries, it may be worth while to reproduce the following brief extract in order to explain the nature of Indian thinking.

'All these provisions of our new Companies Act have been the subject of much comment not only in this country but also abroad. They have been attacked on the grounds that it is for shareholders to fix the remuneration of the management of companies and that administrative interference with managerial remuneration may be arbitrary, and may adversely affect the incentives to effort and risk-taking. And yet perceptive observes of the corporate scene in this as well as the Western countries have always recognised the fact that this problem of managerial remuneration or compensation, as it is called in some of the latter countries, provides a classic example of the unregulated use of corporate power, in the sphere of decision-making which calls for some effective measure of internal and external control. In a fairly well-publicised book on the Western methods and practices of corporate management in the USA, called *The America Stock-holder*, the financial commentator of a well-known Philadelphia journal attempted an analysis of the social consequences of the inevitable erosion of shareholder power on corporate management. "Executives", he commented, "had become an over-privileged class in a democratic society." The gravamen of his charge was that "with the restraining hand of shareholders atrophied, a tax-sheltered elite was inexcusably setting its own extravagant compensation [and that] the most serious consequence of this policy was not the diversion of corporate funds to personal use, but the impact which unduly high executive reward had upon the rest of society". In the light of this comment from a well-informed and sober critic of corporate methods and practices in this field, the provisions of our Companies Act, 1956 relating to managerial remuneration may well be said to blaze a new trail in thinking on the problems of corporate management in modern society.'

25. Sec. 294(1) and (5) of the Companies Act, 1956, require that the appointment of sole selling agents must have the prior approval of the company in general meeting and authorise the government, if necessary, to call for information about such agents. Sections 356-360 attempt to regulate the appointment of managing agents or their associates as selling or buying agents and also the terms and conditions on which managing agents or their associates can enter into selling or buying agency contracts with the managed companies.

26. See Sec. 13 of the Companies Act, 1956, as amended in 1965.

27. The managing agency system is easily the most distinctive Indian contribution to the formation of institutions in the corporate sector and the greater part of the meagre Indian literature on the subject relates to it. The most comprehensive factual study of the system before the passing of the 1956 Act was undertaken by the Research and Statistics Division of the former Department of Company Law Administration (within the Ministry of Commerce and Industry). The study was supervised by Dr. R.K. Nigam, under the instruction and guidance of the author, then Secretary of to the Department.

28. Government of India, Ministry of Law, Department of Company Affairs, *Report of the Managing Agency Enquiry Committee*, 1966.

29. See p. 113 and pp. 467-472 of the Committee's report.

30. Mazumdar, op. cit., pp. 31-32 and 51-53.

31. Nevertheless, Sec. 265 of the Act does give a company the option of adopting proportional representation for the appointment of directors. This compromise between English law and the compulsory provisions of company legislation in several states of the USA was embodied in the Act of 1956 after an amendment to provide for compulsory provisions of the American type was defeated at Select Committee Stage.

32. The more important of these are Sections 332, 370 and 372, which deal particularly with problems of management and investment.

33. This debate began with the recommendations of the Company Law Committee (see *Report*, pp. 193-195) and continued until the conclusion of the parliamentary discussions on the Bill in the middle of 1955. (See Government of India, Department of Company Law Administration, *Selections from the Debates of the Report on Company Law*, 1955, pp. 51-55.)
34. The text of this Declaration has been reproduced in the *Report of the Seminar on the Social Responsibilities of Business*, Manaktalas, Bombay, 1966, pp. 25-32.
35. This Committee, comparable with the British Select Committee on Nationalised Industries, has already completed studies on a large number of government companies. Its reports are published by the Lok Sabha Secretariat, New Delhi.
36. *Report of the Working Group on Company Law Administration*, Administrative Reforms Commission, Government of India, 1968.

2

International Business Fragmentation Versus Globalisation

Since World War II, growth in international trade has exceeded world economic growth by a substantial margin, national economies have become increasingly dependent on world trade. Up to 50 per cent of the gross national product (GNP) of small European countries is traded internationally, whereas only about 25 per cent of GNP in larger European countries and 10 to 15 per cent of GNP in the comparatively isolated large economies of the United State and Japan is traded internationally. Markets for many industrial good have become increasingly homogeneous. Simultaneously, foreign investment has grown rapidly, both in developed and in developing countries.[1] Not only has the total stock of capital grown rapidly, but, more significantly, there has been growth in the number of subsidiaries of multinational companies (MNCs); growth in the number of countries in which specific firms were active; and increasing diversity in the products manufactured and sold abroad through subsidiaries of MNCs (Vernon and Davidson, 1979).

As both international trade and investment grew rapidly, international competition became more intense, and many national industries became global industries. Similarity of markets in different countries and intense global competition drove international competitors to coordinate their market and competitive strategies between countries more actively. The relevant scope of strategy thus shifted from discrete national markets to global markets, and coordinated worldwide competitive actions between the various subsidiaries of MNCs became more important.

As national competition shifted to global competition, foreign investment also shifted. Protectionism in the 1930s, the trauma of World War II, and national reconstruction policies led the early multinational investors to fragment their operations into discrete market-servicing, self-sufficient investments with little interdependence between operations in separate countries. The developing countries' import substitution policies had similar effects. With freer trade and more intense competition, both the possibility of, and the need for, sourcing investments in manufacturing arose: International corporations started to specialise and rationalise their plant to exploit national comparative advantages.

Even where economic and technical condition prohibited such specialisation—for example, for cement, glass, or industrial gases—competitive actions became coordinated across subsidiaries a the companies realised they were competing in a very concentrated global oligopoly. As a result, portfolio foreign investments, where only intangible assets are leveraged, gave way to strategically coordinated integrated operations worldwide, exploiting comparative advantages of different countries for various types of activities. Labour intensive activities were sited in locations where labour costs were low and from which the world markets were served. Such advantages were most often exploited by owned subsidiaries—through "internalisation"—rather than through subcontracting or licensing.[2] This, in turn, led to the development of intrafirm international trade. Such trade may be intraindustry (e.g., the processing of semiconductors overseas for reimport into the United States) or intrafirm but interindustry (e.g., General Electric "off-setting" the sale of jet engines to the Canadian Armed Forces with exports of consumer goods from Canada).

With some significant exceptions—usually government imposed—the trend toward industry globalisation and toward MNC integration has affected most countries and most internationally traded goods. The proportion of internationally traded goods in the GNP of countries also increased substantially, so that by 1980 internationally traded goods with substantial trade levels comprised more than 80 per cent of the industrial sectors in Western Europe (Orlean, 1986). This trend was particularly strong between 1968 and 1978.

Since the late 1970s, however, three sets of factors have come to limit such globalisation. First, the technology no longer always drives toward globalisation: New manufacturing techniques may reverse the trend toward "world-scale" plants and allow differentiation an segmentation with smaller cost penalties. Second, protectionism is on the rise and limit the strategic freedom of global competitors. Protectionism applies not only to trade in goods, but also increasingly to trade in knowledge, technology in particular. Third, the organisational and strategic capabilities of global competitors often lag the competitive opportunities available to them, and many firms are less than fully successful in exploiting their opportunities.

The impact of the three sets of limiting factors mentioned above deserves more attention. This chapter reflects this interest, beginning with a selective review of the abundant, if still fragmentary, evidence on the trends toward market homogenisation, industry globalisation and firm integration, and the underlying forces that drive them. These issues are discussed at three complementary levels of aggregation: the international economic relations framework; individual industries and their competitive dynamics; and the logistics, organisational structures, and management processes of individual firms. Finally, the recent evolution of the three sets of moderating factors—technologies, government policies leading to growing protectionism, and the limited organisational capabilities of firms—and what their effect may be on the fragmentation or globalisation of international industries are analysed.

GLOBALISATION OF INDUSTRIES

Enabling Conditions

Globalisation is rooted in several key enabling conditions: the homogenisation of markets, the decreasing costs of transport and communication, decreasing trade barriers, and the competitive pressures from new competitors. First, national markets have become increasingly similar in taste as income distributions in industrialised nations have equalised. The result has been the development of relatively homogeneous market segments that cross borders (Levitt, 1983). Though national markets may have been more similar in the past than was generally recognised (Helleiner, 1981), the media (mainly television), international travel, and the action of active multinational marketers have contributed to the homogenisation of markets across national boundaries. Furthermore, global market segments appear in industries as different as automobiles (to the advantage of BMW or AMC's "Jeep") and beer (to the advantage of Hieneken and a few others). Higher disposable incomes also encouraged the development of a market for fashionable "world products" in a number of countries, be these products such as British raincoats, Italian sweaters, Swiss watches (Rolex or Swatch), French wines, or Japanese consumer electronics.

Lower communication and transportation costs—the second enabling condition—also made serving these homogenous markets from centralised locations economical, even for relatively bulky products such as cars. Real-time low-cost communication also made the coordination of a complex worldwide logistics system feasible. The globalisation of manufacturing in certain industries where products are complex and differentiated might not have happened without the drastic reductions in transportation and telecommunication costs between 1950 and 1980.

That trade barriers were removed between the 1950s and the 1980s is well known and needs no detailed analysis here. The removal of these barriers provided a third enabling condition of the globalisation of industries. Only in some industries where government-controlled customers predominate, and where national defense considerations are relevant, did trade barriers stay in place (Doz, 1986). Specific trade agreements (e.g., the Lome convention), as well as the extension of credit to developing countries, allowed these countries to participate in this move toward free trade, initiated by traditional industrialised countries. The recognition that across-the-board import substitution measures usually fail, and the successful example of the newly industrialised countries (NICs) also provided an incentive for developing countries to participate actively in the world economy.

A fourth enabling condition, usually at the level of individual firms, was the existence of the organisational infrastructure for globalisation. In the mid-1960s, when trade liberalisation was initiated and national markets started to coverage visibly, many MNCs were already in place, with their infrastructure of sales subsidiaries and foreign plants. This gave them the capability both to gather data worldwide and to respond quickly—at least in theory—to globalisation trends. Global information networks and means of global market reach were already in place, decreasing the cost of transition from national to global competition for the major competitors. Experience in handling foreign manufacture, new product introduction, and technology transfer facilitated a prompt response to industry globalisation by MNCs (Vernon. 1979). Where such networks and means did not exist, helping hands could be found. Initially, for example, Japanese exporters relied on Japanese trading companies, importing countries' mass merchandisers (e.g., Sears in the United States), mass buyers (e.g., TV. rental companies in the United Kingdom), and original equipment manufacturer (OEM) customers (e.g., for computer peripherals). This allowed the new competitors to skip both the market intelligence tasks (Sears, for instance, specified the TV sets it wanted) and the initial market access cost and delay. More complex, more fragmented, less transparent, and less willing distribution structures would have been a formidable barrier to globalisation and, where present, remain a source of asymmetry in globalisation (witness the painful efforts of many European and American firms to establish a significant market presence in Japan).

Driving Forces for Sourcing and Marketing Globalisation

The enabling conditions summarised above were necessary, though not sufficient, for industry globalisation to take place. They had to be exploited by firms trying to gain a permanent competitive advantage. The intense competition created by these firms was in most cases the main driving force for integration and globalisation to actually take place. Intense competition itself dependent on the opportunity for substantial gains through globalisation, the existence or the creation of destabilising conditions, and the presence of competitors with the strategic intent and capabilities to exploit destabilising conditions to their advantage.

Growing economies of Scale in R&D and in production provided the most frequent opportunity for increased profits through globalisation. Changes in product and process technology have increased the minimum efficient size of production in a variety of industry, such as cars, chemicals, consumer electronics, semiconductors, and machinery. Combined with the emergence of smaller differentiated global segments, this is a powerful incentive to pool demand from a variety of national markets and serve such demand from large, optimally sited specialised plants. New product development costs have also risen considerably in a range of industries, the best-known of which are aircraft, telephone switching, cars, and semiconductors. These higher costs have created a strong incentive for industries to serve the world market to spread R&D costs over a larger production. There is a further incentive to serve the world market quickly to minimise the finance cost of the initial investment and the competitive risk of technological obsolescene (Hamel and Prahalad, 1985).

In some capital goods industries, such as papermaking machinery, electrical equipment, and railroad equipment, the cyclicality of domestic demand and the uncertainty of future domestic orders have led to chronic overcapacity and to the need for national firms to diversify their customer base by selling abroad. Intense competition, though, is the key driving force. In Europe, following the European Economic Community's (EEC) lowering of trade barriers, little change toward a more efficient industry structure took place unless triggered and stimulated by intense competition (Owen, 1983).

The emergence of a period of intense competition was facilitated by technological or market discontinuities that destabilised the existing market and industry structure. Increases in energy costs, for example, destabilised the structure of such industries as automobiles and papermaking machinery, making it possible for new global competitors to emerge. Shifts from electromechanical to electronic technologies in industries ranging from watches to digital switching system and avionics have similarly allowed new competitors to establish themselves and occasionally to render a whole industry obsolete (e.g., the mechanical Swiss watch industry). Wide fluctuations in exchange rates have occasionally had significant effects, helping new competitors to penetrate mature industries, even in the absence of new technology or changing economies of scale. In 1983 and 1984, for example, the overvaluation of the U.S. dollar helped Komatsu gain overseas customers at the expense of Caterpillar (Bartlett, 1985).

Ambitious competitors, with a vision of how to turn situations to their advantage, were also, needed to make competition more intense. These competitors, such as Komatsu, have the long-term strategic intent to dominate their industry, and they are able to exploit opportunities as they arise. While the new competitors have usually been Japanese, they are also occasionally European (e.g., Leroy Somer in small electric motors) or American (e.g., Otis in the small-elevator industry). Confronted with intense competition from new competitors intent on exploiting economies of scale, new product and process technology,and other destabilising factors such as exchange rate fluctuations, established competitors have typically reacted in two complementary ways: (1) reducing costs through the exploitation of economies of scale or through economies of location; and (2) gaining worldwide market access through their own efforts or through networks of partnerships and coalitions.[3] First, many companies attempted to reduce costs by exploiting potential economies of large scale, typically by integrating and rationalising production in a region (e.g., Philips rationalising its television tube and receiver plants in Europe and Ford doing the same with cars). Companies also-searched for lower factor costs and other locational advantages (e.g., the moves offshore in the U.S. electronics industry in the late 1960s and 1970s, or the relocation of the aluminum smelting industry). Demands for cost competitiveness led to sourcing globalisation. This practice was sometimes encouraged by governments, either through factor subsidisation (small open countries such as Ireland or Singapore) or by the imposition of export performance requirements in exchange for access to local markets, typically in large "promising" countries such as Spain, Brazil, and recently India (Guysinger et al., 1984).

Managing costs is not enough, however, as companies have also come to recognise the value of worldwide market access (Hamel and Prahalad, 1985). Such access is becoming critical not only as a response to rising R&D costs but also as a way of providing potential for competitive retaliation. Goodyear responded to Michelin's inroads into the U.S. tire market by competing more actively in Europe, where Michelin was dominant, thus depriving Michelin of the cash flow it needed to continue its investments to gain market share in the United States. A fight confined to the U.S. market would have been more costly for Goodyear than for Michelin. Similarly, IBM fights Japanese computer manufacturers not so much in the United States, where it would hurt itself, as in Japan, where IBM hurts its Japanese competitors most at the least cost to itself (New Scientist, 1985). U.S. markets of consumer electronics had no such option and fell almost defenseless to the Japanese and to Philips.[4]

Where firms were not yet global enough and could not establish market presence quickly (either because of government restrictions, or because distribution channels are hard to penetrate, or both), strategic partnerships and coalitions developed in industries that were becoming global. The primary motive of most partnerships and coalitions is to shore up market presence and technological competence to establish quickly a defensible position in a global industry. While these do provide a viable option, the sharing of strategic control over competitive actions by several partners usually results in tensions as soon as the external technological and market conditions evolve or the relative strategic importance of the joint activities to the various partners changes. This is probably the single largest cause of mortality in collaborative agreements. Even when the collaboration endures, conflicting priorities may result in delays that blunt its competitiveness (e.g., the 2-year delay in the launch of the A-320 airplane by Airbus Industries and the continuing tensions between the main partners on future product policy and on acceptable financial performance).

Empirical Evidence

Although anecdotal evidence of industry globalisation and MNC integration abounds, systematic measurable data on their extent remain scarce and fragmentary. Some industries are well documented (e.g., automobiles, textiles, electronic components, aerospace) through numerous industry studies, but most others are much less well analysed.[5] Aggregate statistics using proxies such as intrafirm trade also suggest that integration of operations within MNCs is important, with 20 to 30 per cent of the international trade of countries such as the United States, the United Kingdom, and Sweden being intrafirm trade. Intrafirm trade seems to be more prevalent in R&D-intensive industries, with high wages and large plants, which is consistent with the driving forces hypothesised above (Dunning and Pearce, 1985; Lall, 1978; United Nations Center on Transnational Corporations. 1983). Yet, even the most detailed studies are fraught with problems in the availability and interpretation of data (Hood and Young, 1980). There is a convergence between findings from studies that start with trade statistics (e.g., based on the U.S. Department of Commerce Annual Survey of U.S. corporations), those that start with a survey of large samples of firms (e.g., Dunning and Pearce, 1985), and those that start with an analysis of the strategic behaviour of firms (e.g., Hood and Young, 1980). The more anecdotal evidence from individual "case" studies and from industry-specific studies also points in the same direction.

Industry studies also provide evidence that even in industries that are traditionally nationally fragmented, pressures for integration and globalisation are being felt. In the furniture industry, for instance, companies such as IKEA or Habitat-Mothercare are exploiting economies of scale in purchasing, subcontracting, advertising, and brand image, shifting the bottom end of the furniture market away from a fragmented national structure to an integrated multinational one. Similar moves are made at the top end of this market with international designers' brands and with global distributors, such as Roche-Bobois. Even where national prestige, national defense, and strategic independence have traditionally weighed more heavily than competitiveness in industrial choices, original patterns of globalisation and integration develop. By and large, European integration in aerospace is making progress under tight supervision from governments. The failure to agree on a single design for a future fighter plane may ultimately be beneficial in offering two complementary products and maintaining spirited competition for export orders: Britain, Italy, Germany,and Spain joined forces and will compete against France and smaller countries. Similarly, the European microelectronics industry is evolving out of a stalemate. We see cooperation between large firms that traditionally were competitors as in the joint development of "megachips" by Philips and Siemens, and we see new ventures occasionally being funded by old firms, as when European Silicon Structures is financed by a group of large European electronic industry firms to make semi-custom chips economically in Europe. Although these collaborative ventures may not operate under the best possible conditions, and their cost of coordination is high, they at least overcome the worst aspects of fragmentation.[6]

Besides the turnaround in many governments in favour of government-sponsored transnational cooperation, it is also important to note that pressure groups that might have tried to block globalisation and integration by and large have failed. Although in the early 1970s it seemed plausible that unions would gain a strong say in MNC management, they have now been ruled out as a severe barrier to globalisation and integration. This is the result of a combination of factors, namely, the change of attitude in Europe (both the effect of the unemployment crisis and also of an ideological shift away from statism and socialism), the failure of unions to lock MNCs into transnational bargaining, the lack of support provided by governments (e.g., the inability to get the Vredeling proposal off the ground), and the divisive aspects of MNC integration itself on international labour corporation. Where unions succeeded in gaining a say, as they did with the German codetermination laws, their representatives quickly aligned their positions on those of management.

Economically weak but politically strong national industrial companies could also be barriers to globalisation, but by and large they fell to competitive pressures in Europe. Only in a few partly competitive but largely government-controlled sectors, such as electrical equipment for railroads; do the old industry structures survive largely unchanged. Even in some of these industries, there are encouraging signs of possible rationalisation, such as the investments by Compagnie Generale d'Electricite into Ateliers de Constructions Electriques de Charleroi. Computer manufacturers are victims of probably the worst stalemate along these lines in Europe. Britain, Germany, and France each have their "national champion," hopelessly small for global competitiveness, and unable to renew its product line without much outside help—usually Japanese. Yet each of these national champions is well enough ensconced in its national political and economic environment to survive, to prevent its merger into a transnational alliance, and to block the development of new, more entrepreneurial national or international competitors. First-class customers desert European suppliers—mainly to IBM—despite the switching costs involved, and the technical capability of European computer companies is withered by their Japanese partners, who provide them with components, critical subsystems, and peripherals. The continuation of this stalemate threatens the European computer industry with extinction. In Europe, though, this is more the exception than the rule, and in most industries—aerospace, chemicals and plastics, pharmaceuticals, and even now automobiles—are taking on the challenge of global competition with a fair measure of success.

Research and Development

Unlike marketing and manufacturing, research and development have not been significantly affected by globalisation and have remained principally home-country activities. In a world of sequential market development, where new products and new processes were first developed and put to use on the domestic market or in the home plants, home-country R&D made good sense. As foreign markets developed to resemble the domestic markets, or as foreign plants were built, new products and technologies were transferred abroad once they had been proved domestically. Foreign R&D was mainly devoted to the adaptation of transferred products and processes to local conditions such as taste, product features, norms and standards, and climate (Fischer and Behrman, 1979; Hirschey and Caves, 1981). The role of foreign subsidiaries was not to innovate on their own but to absorb and apply technology developed in the parent company's laboratories. Technology was in fact global from the start, but research was centrally performed and leveraged internationally through product life cycle phenomena or through transfers to foreign subsidiaries. Even a group such as Brown Boveri, which epitomised the nationally responsive—and fragmented—MNC, leveraged its Swiss-developed technology in its foreign operations (Doz, 1978).

In a more complex world, where the United States no longer clearly leads in product innovation, nor Europe in process innovation, centralised R&D is less effective. First, the leading users—those who can contribute their experience to the success of an innovation—are no longer necessarily available in the domestic market. Although this is truest for MNCs in small countries (e.g., Holland, Sweden, Switzerland, Korea), it is also applicable to U.S. or Japanese companies. Leading markets for medical electronics, for example, may be in the United States and in Japan and Sweden for factory automation, in France for nuclear engineering, and in Britain for consumer electronics. Second, key scientists, like the leading users, are potentially more dispersed geographically than they have ever been. Some European pharmaceuticals or electronics firms find it easier to locate laboratories for new technologies such as genetic engineering or microchips in the United States than in Europe. Conversely, India may offer the potential for a large number of inexpensive software specialists and Italy for creative ones. Several U.S. electronics companies, such as Control Data, Motorola, and Texas Instruments, are setting up software R&D centers in India and Italy. Exploiting a larger pool of talent and avoiding the cost of expatriation are strong motives to locate R&D in various countries. Third, locating R&D in host countries may also help placate their governments' desires for more higher skilled jobs (see Branscomb in this volume).[7] (It may also make the firm eligible for national R&D subsidies or access to national collaborative projects. Finally, the mobility and transfer of knowledge within MNCs is neither easy nor costless (Teece, 1977).

Despite these trends, the forces favouring centralisation of R&D remain strong. First, as markets become increasingly homogeneous, the need for specific local product adaptation or for autonomous product development is lessened. Second, the benefits of close proximity of researchers are strong. Although estimates of the distance beyond which easy informal communication between scientists breaks down range from a few yards to a 1-day plane commute, observers agree that the scattering of related research activities is detrimental to their effectiveness (Allen, 1977). Third, there are often economies of scope in R&D, particularly where technologies are interdependent, which make the scattering of R&D laboratories costly since they cannot be made self-contained. Fourth, considerations of political risk seem to have limited the willingness of major firms to be dependent in their home markets on technologies developed abroad.

It is thus no great surprise to observe that, with a few notable exceptions, the performance of the R&D function in firms has neither been globalised nor integrated to any extent comparable to that of manufacturing and marketing. The results of R&D are global, not the performance of the R&D tasks. With a few significant exceptions, R&D remained centralised, at least in the technology-intensive sectors. Foreign R&D labs do mostly product development and adaptation to local conditions, or sometimes basic research, but seldom have broad research mandates, except in some of the most mature MNCs (e.g., IBM, Dow Chemical Company, and Ciba Geigy). Further, few firms seem to have developed systematic processes for the coordination of R&D activities across regions of the world, again with a few notable exceptions, such as IBM.

Yet, as the home market can no longer be equated with the lead market, centrally performed R&D needs to be responsive to the needs of distant potential users. This may be easy to achieve for engineered commodities, such as consumer durables, photocopiers, and typewriters, but it is more difficult where needs can be defined only in close conjunction with users rather than through market research (von Hippel, 1982). Whereas Japanese successes have been confined mainly to engineered commodities, European exporters and MNCs cover a wider spectrum of products. Large European companies have particularly difficult problems with their U.S. subsidiaries. Their products are often developed with too much of a "technology-push" by central labs whose scientists and managers may have gained a sense for European needs but are insensitive to U.S. needs. In some cases, they seem to be following what they think is the "right" path from a technological rather than market standpoint without considering the lead users' needs. As a result, it is not uncommon for U.S. subsidiaries of European groups to avoid marketing products developed in Europe, thus ensuring that their volumes will be too low to break even. Instead, they develop new products at great cost, take a license from a competitor, or buy the products directly on an OEM basis.

The issue is not who is right or wrong between the U.S. subsidiary and headquarters, but the fact that a European group facing such a situation gains little competitive advantage from being in the United States at all. The converse example, of insensitivity by U.S.-based companies to non-U.S. market needs in their product development, is better known and more easily explicable, given the historical dominance—in the operation of most U.S. MNCs—of the U.S. market over smaller fragmented national markets. Faced with the dilemma between economies of centralisation and the market access advantages of R&D dispersion, MNCs have occasionally done both; some U.S. MNCs have maintained central laboratories but located the primary labs for a set of products in the lead market away from headquarters.

In summary, R&D activities have not changed as dramatically over time as manufacturing and marketing: Their activities have remained largely centralised—most often in the home country—and their output leveraged through transfer to foreign subsidiaries or through embodiment in exported products (Hirschey and Caves, 1981). For most MNCs, the arguments for centralisation seem to have outweighed those favouring geographical fragmentation.

Summary Observations

Although it has to remain impressionistic, since detailed data are lacking, the analysis of the balance between forces of global homogenisation and integration and forces of fragmentation clearly shows the balance tilting toward globalisation. The removal of trade barriers, and the growing similarity of national markets created the potential for globalisation of markets and competition. The development of MNCs, or of global networks allying independent firms, and the technology of cheap effective transportation and communication provided the practical means necessary for the integration of supply. These conditions were necessary, through not sufficient. Intense competition in most industries was the driving force necessary for integration and globalisation. During the same period, actors who might have stalled globalisation either did not act or acted ineffectively.

Thus, homogenisation of markets has increased, industries have globalised, and firms have responded by geographic integration of their activities. Such integration took place (1) for sourcing—usually driven by manufacturing cost-reduction opportunities stemming from growing economies of scale and from economies of location; (2) for marketing—usually driven by a mix of economies of scale in distribution and manufacturing; and (3) by the competitive leverage brought by market scope. Coalitions and partnerships of all kinds provide an attractive low-cost alternative to single-firm manufacturing and market access investments. They do not, however, provide the strategic freedom and control available through a company's own investments.

Research and development activities have typically remained in the home country.

However, as more and more products are developed for world markets, usually for simultaneous rather than sequential introduction, the need for a better integration of foreign subsidiaries and domestic labs has arisen. Evidence from specific product innovation studies in the United States and in Europe tends to suggest that this need for integration is now well met. Conversely, there is little to suggest that MNCs successfully apply innovations that originate in one subsidiary outside of that subsidiary.

The next section discusses three sets of factors that suggest the trends toward homogenisation, globalisation, and integration may slow down of even reverse themselves in the coming decade. Some of the underlying conditions or driving forces will have run their course, and new limits may appear.

LIMITS TO GLOBALISATION

Manufacturing Technology

The evolution of manufacturing technology—in particular the increase in economies of scale in manufacture—has been one of the key conditions in favour of market globalisation and MNC integration in a number of industries. Several factors may now slow down this trend. First, new technology has been so successful at reducing manufacturing unit costs that these costs now account for only a small proportion of total delivered costs. Further reduction of manufacturing cost will be of lesser impact than in the past, as other elements of cost play a much greater role, namely overheads, R&D recovery, and distribution.

Second, economies of scale may no longer increase in the same way as in the past. Some new technologies may abruptly decrease economies of scale. New multipurpose smaller processors in the chemical industry are an example of this type of technology. Even in the absence of genuinely new technology that would reduce economies of scale, the advantage of manufacturing systems—from the well-known materials and resource planning systems to the embryonic "factory-of-the-future" concepts—are based on cost reduction from better managing the manufacturing system rather than from increasing the plant size or the length of the production run. Better manufacturing processes allow more flexibility in production. For instance, multiple car models can be produced in varying proportions on the same assembly line with relatively little cost penalty. This could allow car manufacturers to move back from large single-model factories serving multicountry markets to multimodel factories serving single-country markets. Although there may still be some cost penalty to setting up a flexible factory rather than a narrowly focused one, at least the trade-off between increasing flexibility and decreasing costs can be explicitly considered.

The impact of flexible manufacturing on the trade-off between integration and fragmentation of manufacturing is still unclear, however. Greater flexibility allows producers to cater to shifts in consumer preference—as their discretionary income increases—from cheap standardised goods toward customised products. Flexible manufacturing systems may allow both product customisation—at least so long as such customisation can be achieved through featurisation around a common core—are low cost. These systems may shift the basis for cost advantage from scale to scope and thus make it possible for an integrated manufacturer to serve differentiated worldwide needs.

Third, the "just-in-time" manufacturing concept works best with the colocation of various facilities into an integrated system. This polarises globalisation and integration to the extremes: either a series of small "local-for-local" plants, each by and large self-sufficient, or, at the opposite extreme, a single integrated source for everything (e.g., Toyota City, or to a lesser extent, Boeing around Seattle, or Caterpillar around Peoria). A widely dispersed integrated manufacturing network (such as Ford of Europe), where plants are distant and supply each other with components and subassemblies, is least amenable to just-in-time manufacturing management. Buffer inventories must be kept to allow for transportation delays, localised strikes and disruptions, and slowdowns in custom clearance. This would suggest that the initial patterns of integration within MNCs, particularly in Europe, may not endure. Either the advantages of colocation and flexibility will be such that we will witness a return to largely local plants, or the advantages of focus and specialisation will continue to exceed those of flexibility, and the advantages of collocation will lead to even further centralisation of manufacturing.

Fourth, the trends toward vertical deintegration may allow more creative combinations between independent firms at different stages in a value-added structure. This would allow producers to continue to draw benefits from economies of scale for components and to gain flexibility for end products. Large-scale component manufacturing can be delegated to independent suppliers serving multiple smaller-scale assemblers, for instance. This may lead to different balances between integration and fragmentation at various stages of the value-added chain in the same industry.

Most industries and firms are not yet affected by all of these trends, but economies of scale in production are unlikely to be the opportunity they were in the 1960s and 1970s. As a result, economies of scale will no longer be a driving force toward globalisation and integration. Choices for MNC managers will be more complex than just building up the largest plants with the aim of regaining competitiveness. Most companies are likely to end up with a mix of plants of various sizes and locations, and with various degrees of focus or flexibility.

Economies of location are also likely to become less important. With a few exceptions—such as aluminum—economies of location derive mainly from labour cost advantages. Several observations can be made. Not only has manufacturing cost decreased in relation to delivered cost for a whole range of industrial products, but also labour costs will decrease in relation to manufacturing costs with any shift toward more capital-intensive technologies. Stable or increasing real wages in Europe, despite the recent recessions, have accelerated the substitution of capital for labour. Even with relatively low wages, the product quality provided by automation in consumer electronics, for instance, may lead to rapidly decreasing labour content and to the repatriation and automation of plants previously dispersed from developed countries.

Locations with low labour costs also tend to catch up with locations with higher costs if only because skilled labour is scarce and the general wage structure moves up. Location advantages based on cheap labour are thus often temporary. Although labour may remain cheap in countries where political risks, government policies, or financial problems deter foreign investors—and thus limit the competition for labour-countries such as Singapore, Korea, and Taiwan, which have been hosts to massive foreign investments, have often seen their real-term wage rates increase significantly. In some industries—such as garment production—firms may shift their manufacturing locations in a search for cheaper labour. Where developed countries' firms subcontract to local producers—a prevalent practice for garments—shopping around for cheaper subcontractor is easy; when the foreign MNC sets up its own sourcing plants, however, closing down and relocating elsewhere is a much more costly and difficult process.

Differences in the cost of capital between countries also tend to decrease as the world's capital market becomes more integrated and as MNCs cross-finance themselves on multiple markets and arbitrage between them. Although domestic firms may still benefit from favourable institutional arrangements, e.g., the institutional structure of Japanese capitalism, or from specific government assistance, e.g., European exporters, these advantages are limited, not always accessible to MNC subsidiaries, and not often sufficient to justify location.[8]

Finally, exploiting economies of location also entails certain risks, for instance, exchange risks. If the mix of manufacturing locations differs significantly from that of selling locations, the firm is exposed to currency risks. Whereas this can play in their favour occasionally (e.g., the hefty margins made by European companies exporting to the United States in 1984-1985); it can also play the other way around as in the plight of U.S. exporters. Various hedging approaches can be adopted, but they usually either run counter to the search for economies of location, or they result in the creation of abundant "buffer" excess capacity. Instability of the exchange rate only increases the difficulties and costs of these approaches.

Protectionism

Since 1975 protectionist pressures on the U.S. Congress have increased largely as a result of the globalisation process. Outright protectionist bills have been avoided only by successive administrations' careful negotiation of selected "voluntary" protection. Examples include the "Orderly Marketing Agreements" for TV sets and the "trigger prices" for steel or other commodities. Proposals such as the Burke-Hartke Act, which would have considerably limited the opportunity for U.S. firms to import goods made by their overseas subsidiaries, have been turned down, but at an increasing political price. The overvaluation of the dollar in 1983-1985, and the huge U.S. trade deficit only made matters worse. In the fall of 1985, only the shift in the U.S. position toward an active intervention policy to devalue the dollar staved off strong protectionist measures.

Europe, while making only slow progress toward a true free internal market, has resorted to protectionism toward a variety of industries, particularly those threatened by Japanese imports. Government purchasing policies that favour national suppliers also endure and close whole industries to foreign suppliers. Whether the Japanese market is closed or just hard to enter is an old debate, but it is clear that market access to Japan in critical industries is extremely difficult.

What is important here is not so much the exact extent of protectionism, but that recent evolutions do not allow managers to make a safe assumption about freer trade. The risk of a widespread return to protectionism puts a damper on globalisation strategies that imply high levels of trade and adds fuel to strategies that return to traditional foreign investment as a way of overcoming trade barriers. Indeed, the purpose of many of the Japanese investments in Western Europe and in the United States is to overcome trade barriers, or at least to serve as "insurance" against new trade barriers, should they be implemented.

Among the less-obvious aspects of protectionism that may hamper MNC integration strategies are the issues of data flow across borders. Several countries have argued that data should be likened to raw material and processed locally rather than internationally. The issues are manifold and vary from country to country. Among the most prominent are (1) the importance of local data processing for stimulating the national demand for electronic data processing hardware and services and for telecommunication services: (2) the disadvantage of local firms and governments in relation to MNCs and their access to global market information; and (3) the threat of more centralisation of decision making in MNCs, a process directly related to integration strategies. Canada has clearly articulated concerns about transborder data flows. Brazil and France have followed suit, with somewhat different concerns and priorities. Although policies on data flow are often lent moral legitimacy by being amalgamated with a series of regulations to protect the privacy of individuals, economic and political considerations drive the development of such policies. Countries do compete for the location of date processing centers by MNCs, and they also compete for internatioal data transmission and value-added services. A few countries, including the United States and Britain, have taken an aggressive commercial position by lowering packet-switching charges, for example, and others try to regulate data flows. Although the current impact of data flow regulations is limited, it is a concern for at least some firms.[9] In addition, regulation of data flows may also be a way to ensure that critical knowledge exists within the country. One widespread concern, for instance, is that some U.S. suppliers of computers keep debugging software at home, where it can only be accessed by telephone lines from Europe. Should denial measures be taken by the U.S. government, whatever the reasons (as was done in 1982 in the Dresser case), such critical software might no longer be available.[10]

More broadly, protectionism in technology has become a major issue. In the 1980s the U.S. government, as well as several U.S. firms, became worried about the transfer of technology to Japan and to the USSR. This concern arose as the extent and success of efforts by Japanese firms and the Soviet government to appropriate Western technologies became clear. With regard to Japan, the issue is competition, particularly in industries such as semiconductors. In this industry, in particular, manufacturing equipment is critical to success, and the U.S. industry became concerned that process technology was transferred too easily to Japan. The concern was heightened as Japan came to be seen in the United States as an "unfair" competitor. Similar concerns have been voiced in other industries, such as aerospace and computers, as evidenced by IBM's actions against Mitsubishi and Hitachi.

With regard to the USSR, the issue is twofold: first, to deny the USSR access to the core technologies of military systems, a priority widely shared in the West; and second, to limit the USSR's access to technologies that may allow faster economic growth and thus make large military expenditures more affordable to the Soviets. The second point is a matter of debate between U.S. government hard-liners and more liberal circles in the United States and among European governments. The issue gained prominence with the discovery, probably by French counterespionage in early 1982, of the magnitude of the Soviet effort to spy on the West, and of the success of that effort.[11] Later updates, based on captured Soviet documents, kept the issue salient. Also giving prominence to the issue were several instances of discreet reexport of classified U.S. equipment via Sweden and Austria and several cases of industrial espionage in major West European and American companies, including MBB, Dassault, and Hughes. Although studies suggest that the Soviets are not able to absorb and finance the use of the new technology they obtain from the West, legally or otherwise, the Reagan administration took it to heart to stem the flow of technology to the Soviet bloc (Bornstein, 1985).

The Export Administration Amendment Act of July 1985 extends the list of goods subject to U.S. export licenses to "dual-use" equipment, civilian in principle, but using technologies or components with potential military use. The U.S. policy of reexport control also considerably limits the mobility of components to be incorporated into systems assembled in another country, and sold in yet another. European integrated MNCs, such as Philips, suffer great logistic complications from this new set of laws (Dekker, 1985). This leads them to substitute, where possible, non-U.S. for U.S. components and subsystems. Although such substitution is a boost to some European industries, it leads to an inefficient duplication of effort between the United States and Europe.

Protectionism in technology—be it through limiting the transfer of data or through restrictions on exports of goods possibly related to the manufacture of defense-related equipment—makes it difficult for technology-intensive MNCs to adopt integration strategies, since the various parts of the company need to be technologically autonomous. It also makes it difficult for U.S. firms to cooperate with foreign partners on joint R&D and casts doubt on the ability of European firms to use technology they would have acquired through collaborative efforts with the United States or with U.S. government support. Although Japanese firms are more strongly encouraged than their European counterparts to participate in U.S. defense projects, the same issues arise between the United States and Japan as between the United States and Europe. Conversely, IBM's or

Texas Instruments' access to the results of joint Japanese research projects is a difficult issue.

These concerns have prompted Europe into action, first with the European Strategic Programme for Research and Development in Information Technology (ESPRIT) and with specialised projects, such as Research in Advanced Communications in Europe (RACE) and more recently with a programme called EUREKA. ESPRIT's relative success was a surprise, but by the end of 1985 about 195 projects shared 1.4 billion European Currency Units, and many of them looked promising. EUREKA, launched as a civilian equivalent to the U.S. Strategic Defense Initiative, is still embryonic and funding is uncertain. Despite widespread skepticism, it may take hold and lead to interesting projects. This direct subsidy approach addresses only one facet of European competitiveness, however, and may be not the most important: European firms show inferiority not in the development of new technology but in its exploitation. Technology may not be the critical issue. Market structure and management are. Although much attention in Europe is focused on making Europe a true "common" market, remarkably little attention is devoted to managerial limits to the successful exploitation of global technological and competitive opportunities.

Organisational Capabilities

The various elements discussed above suggest that large international competitors will face a world of neither fragmentation nor global integration, but a mixture of both, with many shades of gray and complex patterns of internatioal operations that are unlikely to fall neatly into any category. Thus, there will be many trade-offs between industry fragmentation and globalisation and strategies of integration and subsidiary autonomy, and they will vary by function, country, and business. Differences between industries, between segments within the same industry, and even between stages in the value-added chain are going to be important. This will introduce considerable variety in the situations faced by MNCs. Further, strategies will vary from free and competitive to negotiated and collaborative through complex networks of collaborative agreements, coalitions and joint ventures among firms, and occasionally between them and governments (Doz, 1986).

Not all global competitors are able, organisationally, to cope with such diversity. Most started as national companies (e.g., most Japanese competitors) or with fragmented organisational structures loosely "federated" by headquarters. Such fragmented structures, leaving a lot of autonomy to individual subsidiaries in various countries, fit well with the fragmented environment faced by MNCs prior to the 1970s.

The initial transition from autonomous subsidiaries to coordinated international strategies and integrated manufacturing and marketing networks has been a traumatic experience for many companies. The process has been slow (typically 3 to 7 years), painful, and not always successful (Doz and Prahalad, 1981; Prahalad and Doz, 1981). For a while in the mid-1970s, matrix organisations were seen as the answer to complex trade-offs between integration and fragmentation. Though a matrix organisation may achieve such trade-offs, it achieves them well only if a number of conditions are met.

First, a matrix organisation is not merely a different form of organisation. Rather, it is a different mode of making decisions and ensuring that relevant data and perspectives are brought to bear on the choices, that trade-offs are made explicit, and that well-considered decisions are reached. This requires both a well-developed management system infrastructure, the involvement of top management, and much attention to the quality of the executive process. Observations of many companies suggest that not all are able to meet these conditions. Hence the widespread disillusionment with matrix organisations (Prahalad and Doz, 1987).

Although the "ideal" MNC organisation is easy to spell our in principle, it is difficult to put in place and make work. Yet, as discussed in the earlier sections, the conflicting demands for flexibility and responsiveness, on the one hand, and for global competitiveness and integration, on the other, call for complex trade-offs. Such conflicting demands thus further limit the capabilities of firms to succeed in global industries.

Moreover, in many industries, speed and interdependence in action become increasingly critical. Product cycles are shorter, and the maintenance of competitive advantage requires coordinated policies across product lines and business units, both for technology development and for market access (Hamel and Prahalad, 1985). The growing number and variety of collaborative arrangements also make it more difficult for companies to maintain conventional configurations of strategic control, as can be more easily done with fully owned operations (Doz, 1986). As a result, a gap develops between the demands put on companies by global competition and the capability of their organisations and management to meet them.

Conclusion

The three sets of factors outlined above—manufacturing technology, protectionism, and organisational capabilities—may limit the growth of integrated multinational companies and tilt the balance again toward fragmentation. Collaborative agreements and strategic partnerships may increasingly represent an alternative to direct investment for gaining market access, achieving volume production, or leveraging technology. These may deeply modify the nature of global competition and international industries by creating a series of intermediate positions between national and global competitors.

NOTES

1. For summary data, see Dunning and Pearce, 1985; Stopford, 1983; Vernon, 1977; Franko, 1976. See also, for U.S. multinationals, U.S. Bureau of Economic Analysis, 1986.
2. For a summary of the internalisation argument, see Casson, 1979; Rugman, 1981; Dunning, 1979. Many authors draw on Hymer, 1976.
3. For a general argument on the dynamics of global competition, illustrated with the example of color television sets, see Hamel and Prahalad, 1985.

4. See Hamal and Prahalad, 1985, for a summary argument. For a more detailed anlaysis, see Millstein, 1983.
5. For a series of industrial studies, see Zysman and Tyson, 1983; Hochmuth and Davidson, 1985.
6. For an early analysis of these problems in collaborative ventures, see Hochmuth, 1974.
7. The argument cuts both ways, though, as it may be argued that local scientists or technicians employed by MNCs develop knowledge, the economic benefits from which may well accrue to another country where the MNC operates, whereas local firms would have a greater propensity to export innovative goods and processes, thus creating more value for the country.
8. For a more detailed discussion of the limits to the competitive advantage that can be obtained from multinational resource deployment, see Doz and Prahalad, 1986.
9. For a summary analysis, see Kane, 1985, and United Nations Center on Transnational Corporations, 1982.
10. For a detailed discussion of the Dresser case, see Bettis, 1984.
11. Although not publicly available, the various CIA reports to the U.S. Congress did much to increase the political salience of the transfer of technology to the Soviet Union.

REFERENCES

Allen, T.A. 1977. The Flow of Technology, Cambridge, Mass.: MIT Press.

Bartlett, C. 1985. Komatsu Limited Harvard Business School Case Study. HBSCS 0-385-277.

Bettis, R.A. 1984. Dresser Industries and the Pipeline. Southern Methodist University Case Study.

Bornstein, M. 1985. East-West Technology Transfer: The Transfer of Western Technology to the USSR. Paris: Organisation for Economic Cooperation and Development.

Casson, M. 1979. Alternatives to the Multinational Enterprise. London: Macmillan.

Dekker, W. 1985. The technology gap: Western countries growing apart. Speech presented at the Atlantic Institute for International Affairs, Paris, December 5, 1985.

Doz, Y. 1978. Brown Boveri and Cie. Harvard Business School Case Study, HBSCS 4-378-115.

Doz, Y. 1986. Government polices and global competition. In M.E. Porter, ed., Competition in Global Industries. Boston: Havard Business School Press.

Doz, Y., and C.K. Prahalad. 1981. Headquarter influence and strategic control in multinational companies. Sloan Management Review 23(1).

Doz, Y., and C.K. Prahalad, 1986.Quality of management: An emerging source of global competitive advantage? In N. Hood and J.E. Vahlne, eds., Strategies in Global Competition. London: John Wiley and Sons.

Dunning, J. 1979. Explaining changing patterns of international production: In defense of the eclectic theory. Oxford Bulletin of Economics and Statistics 41 (November): 269-296.

Dunning, J.H., and R.D. Pearce. 1985. The World's Largest Industrial Enterprises, 1962-1983. New York: St. Martin's Press.

Fischer, W.A., and J.N. Behrman. 1979. The coordination of foreign R&D activities by transnational corporations. Journal of International Business Studies 10-3 (winter): 28-35.

Franko, L.G. 1976. The European Multinationals. Stamford, Conn.: Greylock.

Guysinger, S., et al. 1984. Investment Incentives and Performance Requirements. Washington, D.C.: The World Bank Mimeographed Report.

Hamel, G., and C.K. Prahalad. 1985. Do you really have a global strategy? Harvard Business Review (July-August): 139-148.

Helleiner, G.K. 1981. Intra Firm Trade and the Developing Countries. New York: St. Martini's Press.

Hirschey, R.C., and R.E. Caves. 1981. Research and the Transfer of Technology by Multinational Enterprises. Oxford Bulletin of Economics and Statistics 43(2): 115-130.

Hochmuth, M.S. 1974. Organising the Transnational: The Experience with Transnational Enterprise in Advanced Technology. Cambridge, Mass.: Harvard University Press.

Hochmuth, M.S., and W. Davidson. 1985. Revitalising American Industry. Cambridge, Mass: Ballinger.

Hood, N., and S. Young. 1980. European Development Strategies of U.S. Owned Manufacturing Companies Located in Scotland Edinburgh: Her Majesty's Stationery Office.

Hymer, S. 1976. The International Operations of National Firms: A Study of Foreign Investment. Cambridge, Mass: MIT Press.

Kane, M.J. 1985. A Study of the Impact of Transborder Data Flow: Regulation on Large U.S.-Based Corporations Using an Extended Information Systems Interface Model. Ph.D dissertation. College of Business Administration, University of South Carolina.

Lall, S. 1978. The pattern of intra firm exports by U.S. multinationals. Oxford Bulletin of Economics and Statistics 40(3): 209-223.

Levitt, T. 1983. The Globalisation of Markets. Havard Business Review (May/June): 92-102.

Millstein, J.E. 1983. Decline in an expanding industry: Japanaese competition in color television. In J. Zysman and L. Tyson, eds., American Industry in International Competition. Ithaca, N.Y.: Cornell University Press'.

New Scientist. 1985. IBM being sits Japanese assault. (17 October): 22-23.

Orlean, A. 1986. "L'insertion dans les echanges internationaux: comparison de cinq grands pays developpes. Economic et Statistiques 184 (Janvier): 25-39.

Owen, N. 1983. Economies of Scale. Competitiveness and Trade patterns within the European Community. Oxford: Clarendon Press.

Prahalad, C.K., and Y. Doz. 1981. An approach to strategic control in multinational companies. Sloan Management Review 22(4): 5-13.

Prahalad, C.K., and Y. Doz. 1987 (forthcoming). The Multinationals' Mission. New York: The Free Press.

Rugman, A.M. 1981. Inside the Multinationals: The Economies of Internal Markets. London: Croom Helm.

Stopford, J.M. 1983. The World Directory of Multinational Enterprises, 1982-83. London: MacMillan.

Teece, D.J. 1977. Technology transfer by multinational firms: The resource cost of transferring technological know-how. The Economic Journal 87 (June): 242-261.

United Nations Center on Transnational Corporations. 1982. Transnational Corporations and Transborder Data Flows: A Technical Paper. New York: United Nations.

United Nations Center on Transnational Corporations. 1983. Transnational Corporations in World Development: Third Survey. New York: United Nations.

3

Indian Economy: Towards Liberalisation and Open Market

ECONOMIC REFORMS REVIEW

The wide-ranging structural reforms initiated in July 1991 have placed the Indian economy on the path of sustained high growth to integrate it with the global economy. The positive results emerging from three years of structural reforms have been reassuring. There is near unanimity that the reform process is good for the country in the long run. Even as far as the short-term is concerned, there is general agreement that there is little alternative to the course of action now being pursued.

Nevertheless, the painfulness of the process of change is not underrated and it is felt that speed is of less importance than the manner in which the reforms are implemented. The enthusiasm for reforms varies in the degree that the section of the society are affected. In the public sector, there is a perception that the reforms are creating a lot of difficulties. On the other hand, the private sector is unanimous that the reforms are good, even if some sectors are adversely affected in the short run.

There is a general feeling that little is being done about financial sector reforms, the exit policy, agricultural subsidies, infrastructure development and administrative reforms.

The economy has emerged decisively from the crisis of 1990-91. The crisis reached its peak in the summer of 1991 when foreign currency reserves had plummeted to about $ one billion, inflation had soared to an annual rate of 17 per cent, industrial production was falling and overall economic growth had declined to 1.1 per cent (1991-92). The economic reform measures put in place in 1991-92 brought down the rate of inflation to seven per cent and took economic growth to 4 per cent in 1992-93. Foreign currency assets were restored to over $ 16 billion in July 1994 and exports experienced strong recovery. With the comfortable foreign exchange reserves and the accelerated pace of exports, the government plans to roll back the restrictive import policies and make the rupee convertible on the current account in two years time.

The foreign exchange reserves including foreign currency assets, gold and SDRs totalled over $ 20 billion in July, 1994. The major reforms include a new industrial policy, phased devaluation of rupee, pruning of the import list, invalidation of FERA, dismantling the cumbersome and abuse-prone industrial licencing and liberal policy towards foreign investment.

The average rate of growth of industrial production during 1993-94 was 3 per cent, as compared to 2.1 per cent in 1992-93 and a zero growth rate in 1991-92.

Inflation was the most serious problem in 1991-92, having reached a peak level of 17 per cent in August 1991. It had declined to 7.1 per cent in July 1993. However, the year ended with double digit inflation and the inflationary pressure continues to remain strong.

After successfully bringing down the fiscal deficit from 8.4 per cent of GDP in 1990-91 to 5.9 per cent in 1991-92, the Government, however, seems to have lost control over fiscal discipline, with the fiscal deficit placed at 7.3 per cent of GDP for 1993-94 as against the stipulated target of 4.7 per cent. The target for fiscal deficit has been fixed at 6 per cent of GDP in 1994-95.

Critics argue that some dangerous aspects of reform are leading the nation into a debt trap and impeding indigenous technological development. Besides, the social costs of the reforms are mounting. It has been estimated that the number of persons in poverty increased by 10.7 million, according to NSS data, and by 6.10 million, according to CSO figures, between 1990-91 and 1991-92.

Unemployment threatens the educated and the ignorant alike. There are more than four million job-seekers on the rolls of employment exchanges. To achieve full employment by the end of the century, the employment growth rate, currently 1.5 per cent, will have to be 4 per cent. In the coming years, a large number of workers are likely to be displaced by the introduction of sophisticated and modern technology in the industrial sector.

Imbalance

Sixty per cent of the industrial investment in the country is going to only four states — Maharashtra, Gujarat, Uttar Pradesh, and Madhya Pradesh. In contrast, the eastern states of Bihar, Orissa and West Bengal have together been able to attract only about five per cent of investment since the liberalisation of the industrial policy.

According to a document prepared by the Department of Industrial Development, Ministry of Industry, investments (actual and cleared) worth Rs. 177,120 crore have gone to the four states out of a total investment of Rs. 296,167 crore between August 1, 1991, and June 30, 1994.

The gross imbalance in distribution of investment following liberalisation of the industrial policy has also led to proportional imbalance of employment generation in various states. More than 50 per cent of the total employment generation as a result of the above-mentioned investments would take place in Maharashtra, Gujarat, Uttar Pradesh and Madhya Pradesh.

This has led to serious concern in the government about the possibility of eruption of social unrest in the near future unless the trend is checked through official intervention.

The latest data of the Industry Ministry show about 10 states accounting for 90 per cent of the total investment and employment generation. The data are based on industry enterpreneurial memorandums (IEMS) filed and cleared between August 1, 1991, and June 30, 1994.

Apart from the top four states, the others which are able to attract sizable investments and employment generation are Tamil Nadu (5.05 per cent investment and 6.04 per cent employment), Haryana (3.92 per cent and 6.01 per cent), Punjab (3.63 per cent and 9.15 per cent) and Rajasthan (4.46 per cent and 6.22 per cent).

States like Andhra Pradesh with 7.42 per cent of investment and 5.92 per cent of employment and Karnataka with 3.84 per cent and 2.69 per cent are also better placed.

The worst sufferers since liberalisation seem to be Orissa and Bihar. Of the total investment of Rs. 296,167 crore during the period, Bihar has been able to attract only Rs. 3,906 crore. This has a corresponding employment generation element of a meagre 20,094, which is 0.73 per cent of the total employment generation of 27,69,495 in the country in the given period.

Orissa is even worse off with investments of only Rs. 2926 crore and employment of 38,201. West Bengal, another badly-affected state, has drawn investments of Rs. 7,392 crore and employment of 108,064.

The other states that are finding it hard to woo investors are Tripura, Meghalaya, Sikkim, Jammu and Kashmir, Assam and Kerala.

The Ministry has also compiled data on scheduled industry-wise distribution of IEMs. According to this, sectors attracting the highest attention in investment and generating the most employment are metallurgical, chemicals, textiles, vegetable oils and vanaspati and food processing.

(Annexure-I gives distribution of investment and employment generation).

The new economic policy has opened up the road for a freer flow of foreign investment and a bigger role for the multinationals in the Indian economy. According to some international financial experts, India is now rated ahead to China and Mexico in terms of foreign investment.

Earlier, Indian businessman had been critical of government controls and had been asking for a liberalised economy to expand and strengthen India's competitive position. The opening up of the country's economy has provided this opportunity, but it has also led to foreign companies not only controlling a large equity in Indian companies and controlling them through portfolio management. There are also several instances of outright buying out of Indian companies by multinationals. All this is upsetting the calculations of Indian businessmen, who had thrived on sheltered markets.

Level Ground

The Government is now being criticised for laying out a "red carpet" for foreign investors without providing a level ground where these investors and the Indian companies could operate on equal terms. A major complaint from the Indian side is that there is no "level playing ground" for the foreign and Indian companies because the cost of money is much lower abroad and India still has the highest rate of interest as also a much higher rate of taxation — both corporate and individual — as also capital gains tax. The other areas of uneven ground are low productivity, one-sided labour laws and trade union leaderships which are more politics-oriented rather than welfare-oriented.

It is not possible to have a level ground without a change in work culture. The economic reforms also throw out a challenge to Indian business and labour leaders to change their outlook and shed their complacency and to squarely face a highly competitive and technologically efficient world.

Strategies

In the new world economic order, India will have to compete with similar developing economies like Brazil, China, Mexico and Russia for a share of world trade. Competition will be between countries and will call for country strategies developed jointly between Government and Industry.

The experience of the last 45 years has shown that no single country can do everything well by itself. Factor advantages, innate skills and a number of other variables generate competitive advantage in specific areas. Countries that are able to identify and focus on their areas of potential competitive advantage will emerge as winners.

India's GDP is 1/25 that of the US', whose GDP exceeds $ 6000 billion. On a per capita basis, the difference looks even more startling, with India's per capita GDP of $240 being 1/100 th of the US's $ 23,800.

Closer home, the developing Asian economies of Thailand and Malaysia respectively have per capita incomes 8 times and 14 times larger than India's. These economics are growing at rates of 7 to 8 per cent a year, compared to India's 4 to 5 per cent. Their population is increasing annually at around 1 per cent compared to India's 2 per cent. The economic gap that is already awesome, will only widen in the years to come unless drastic remedies are taken. If India's per capital income is to catch up even in the next 25 years with Thailand's — one of Asia's relatively less developed economies — given Thailand's rate of growth of 7 per cent, and the present rates of population growth, India's GDP needs to grow by an astounding 18 per cent per annum for the next 25 years! Even assuming India's population growth is held at 1 per cent instead of 2 per cent per annum, to catch up with Thailand it needs a growth rate of 15 per cent year on year for the next 25 years!

India needs to make substantial progress on several fronts at a frenetic pace and at the same time. It first need a large infusion of technology and capital very quickly. This is best achieved by opening up the economy to the world and inviting foreign companies to boost the economy by participating in the huge Indian consumer market. It also needs to nurture Indian companies to grow and be able to compete globally, evolving into India's MNCs in the next few years. Besides several private sector companies having such capability, the huge public sector also holds enormous potential, already having 4 companies in the list of Fortune Global 500 companies. The public sector needs to be energised effectively and freed to compete successfully in the world markets.

Reform Giants

India's economy is seemingly riding the crest after three years of reforms. The average index of Industrial Production for 1993-94 was 225.4 which was 3 per cent higher than the average index of 218.9 for the previous year.

The biggest turnaround has been in the field of exports. From a negative growth in 1991-92, exports in dollar terms increased by 3.8 per cent in 1992-93, and spurted to 20.4 per cent over 1993-94. With exports of $22.13 billion was thus actually over-achieved. It is significant that export growth of this nature has occurred against the background of recession in many of India's traditional markets.

Inflation too has been brought down. It declined from 17 per cent rate in 1991, to no more than 7.2 per cent last year. The worry, however, is that inflation has again attained double digit figures and the rate is hovering around 10.5 per cent.

Numerous measures have been taken to dismantle previous controls on investment, and to open up most areas of the economy to the private sector. The power sector is, for example, open for 100 per cent private investment, and the banking sector is also being opened up gradually.

In manufacturing, a sector for which licences are still required and which adds up to less than 15 per cent of manufacturing value added (MVA) for Indian nationals; foreign investment is permitted up to 50 per cent. Investment approvals have also been sharply on the uptrend, and the January 1993 amendment to the Foreign Exchange Regulation Act (FERA) has ushered in a semblance of equality between foreign and Indian investors.

Foreign investment in the mining sector is also allowed up to 50 per cent. And even a higher equity participation is possible on a case-by-case basis. (This contrasts with investment in the mining sector in most East Asian countries, where it is mostly reserved for domestic residents.)

Overall, companies in India with foreign equity participation — both majority as well as minority — can now invest in all sectors that are open to purely domestic companies.

There are also been a comparable derestriction and delicensing of the trade regime. Cuts this year have reduced maximum tariff levels from 400 per cent at one time to 65 per cent. Import-weighted tariff has been reduced this year from 87 per cent (1990-91) to 33 per cent. Near-full current account convertibility for the rupee, which was floated in March 1992, has also been attained.

Financial Sector

In the financial sector, liberalisation measures include greater independence for financial institutions, since CRRs and SLRs have both been reduced to 14 per cent and 25 per cent respectively.

Priority sector lending rated too have been rationalised and increased over a broad front. These, along with a relaxation of credit norms, have meant that the cost of such lending activities is now lower. The Reserve Bank of India has instructed banks to create conditions that will enable them to attain Basic Accord capital adequacy standards by 1996.

There are also plans to reduce official recourse to RBI financing through the issuance of ad hoc treasury bills (T-bills). The government has itself decided that the net amount of financing that it gets in this manner should not exceed one per cent of GDP, for any continuous period in excess of 10 working days; over the year as a whole the amount should not exceed 0.66 per cent of GDP. These are expected to liberate the RBI and assist in its ability to formulate a more independent monetary policy.

For the first time, scheduled banks are now having to conform to more exacting prudential standards which is part of the reason why they showed losses in 1992-93.

Not only are weaknesses in banks' capital bases getting clearer thereby, official steps have also been taken to enable public banks to mobilise resources directly from the market. Some other nationalised banks are expected to approach the capital market by the end of this financial year.

Meanwhile, banks will also have to gear up for greater competition. Nine additional banks, three of them foreign, have already been granted permission to set up shop in India, according to the RBI's December 1993 guidelines. Alongside these, the government is also well advanced in the process of reducing its own equity shareholding in Indian financial institutions such as IFCI and ICICI. Private ownership in banks up to 49 per cent is also being introduced to assist in the objective of recapitalising them.

Tax Reforms

On the fiscal front, the government has begun implementing tax reforms based on the recommendations of the Tax Reform Committee. The 1994-95 budget saw some acceleration in these reforms. Tariffs are on their way down. Taxes on corporate income also have been reduced, while excise reform has transformed such (indirect) taxation closer to a modified value added tax (MODVAT). This, for the first time, also includes a number of manufacturing sectors so far excluded, as well as a number of services.

This shift towards ad valorem taxation will impart greater buoyancy and bring about a reduction in the number of rates, besides placing greater reliance on invoices for the determination of value.

But the efficiency of tax administration, and some tense questions surrounding revenue sharing between states and the centre still remain unresolved. At the state level, the issues which remain include sales tax, and also the imposition of octroi between states; the latter for example poses an impediment to the emergence of a really unified economic area within the country.

PSUs

There are almost 1,000 public sector undertakings (PSUs) within the country — of which no less than 700 are owned by state governments. These are important as they represent an important weight in terms of capital stock; they also contribute about one-quarter of non-agricultural GDP.

The government's strategy for reform includes the dereservation of areas within which the PSUs operate, and non-access to budget and banking sector resources. There were ideas too, to restructure those that had potential, to close down the rest, and to let redundant workers avail themselves of a safety net programme. Finally, PSUs were given more autonomy. There are many with whom memorandums of understanding (MoUs) have been concluded; these MoUs leave the PSUs independent to conduct their own affairs without government interference, and divestment is often the final stage after that.

Broadly, therefore, apart from the recourse the MoUs, the government strategy in relation to PSUs also includes the elimination of format barriers to entry into the sector by others. Thus competition is already on the rise. This is supplemented by the reduction of trade barriers — which had been another source of protection. A National Renewal Fund (NRF) has also been set up, and there are greater numbers of PSUs being referred to the Board of Industrial and Financial Reconstruction (BIFR). The process has been further eased through a December 1993 amendment to the Sick Industrial Companies Act (SICA); which means that companies which have not been making cash losses can also now approach the BIFR. All that would be required is that they have negative net worth and a minimum five year (seven earlier) registration period.

The bottom line remains that although PSUs still lack the substantive ability to restructure where it hurts, they do not yet possess the means to restructure their labour force. For example, they have been unable to seriously undertake corporate reorganisation, sell off assets (like land and units), or enter into joint-ventures with private partners.

Often, therefore, the reforms have translated into no more than attempts either to increase prices, or to minimise operating costs through lower capacity utilisation. These have occurred especially since the PSUs have been made partially independent through the MoU route, and budgetary subventions too have been cut-off.

There is a sound case, therefore, for arguing that those additional reforms that are hanging fire should be speedily got over with. There should especially be greater alacrity in the matter of implementing the Rangarajan Committee recommendations—disinvestment of up to 49 per cent of equity in areas still reserved for public investment, and over 74 per cent in other areas. What has been said in general for the central PSUs applies also for the state-level ones; these number 700 odd, and include a number of state electricity boards.

Foreign Investment

The economic reforms process has succeeded in bringing about the much-needed external financial flows.

There has been a welcome improvement in the country's external accounts (both current and capital) which have exceeded the most optimistic forecasts.

The impressive export performance of 20 per cent in dollar terms in 1993-94, a modest growth, of imports and improvement in the 'invisibles' account have helped in reducing the current account deficit to $0.8 billion in 1993-94 from $10 billion in 1990-91.

The opening up of the capital market to foreign investors and other liberalisation measures like reducing tariffs, simplifying import licensing requirements and easing rupee convertibility norms increased the foreign investment flow to $4.7 b in 1993-94. As a result, India's foreign exchange reserves rose from $ 1 b in June 1991 to $ 15 b in March 1994 and to $20 b in July 1994.

The economic necessity for foreign investments flows into India can hardly be exaggerated, considering the fact that the debt route in exhausted, with an external debt burden of $85 b (1993). While the country cannot afford to borrow more, It needs massive external funds not only to take care of the balance of payments gap, but also as a source of capital, technology and management systems.

The series of measures undertaken during the past three years are now bearing fruit in promoting confidences among foreign investors to invest in India. The opening up of the stock market has definitely made the Indian economy more viable and truly global with easy movement of funds into and from the country. Foreign investors are now changing their minds about India and are far more confident of good returns.

In September 1992, the government decided to open the capital market to Foreign Institutional Investor' (FIIs). With the foreign investors confidence growing in the Indian economy, Indian companies raised funds abroad by floating Euro issues. Indian companies raised nearly $ 2.5 billion by floating Euro issues in 1993. India can raise easily over $ 10 billion every year from overseas markets, according to international fund managers.

Foreign investment flows have increased from just 0.3 billion in 1992-93 to $ 4.7 billion in 1993-94 and are expected to more than double to $ 9.0 billion in 1994-95.

In the case of foreign direct investment, approvals so far have exceeded $5.0 billion while actual inflows are only $1.5 billion. However, the FDI approvals continue to grow at the pace of more than 6 per cent month. An encouraging feature is that 90 per cent of the approvals are in infrastructure sectors like power, telecom and transportation and in high technology areas.

Portfolio investment gathered momentum towards the end of 1993-94. Out of the total investment of $ 2.5 billion, nearly $1.5 billion was concentrated between September 1993 and March 1994. The inadequacy of custodial services effectively reduced investment to a trickle thereafter. The stock markets are once again picking up with return of foreign institutional investors. The prospect for FII in 1994-95 depends to great extent on the custodial problem which is being resolved through the entry of other banks offering custodial services and the creation of jumbo shares which will reduce the transactions costs of large traders. In addition to the earlier two custodians i.e. Hongkong Bank and Citibank, FIIs are making use of SBI, ICICI, Standard Chartered Bank and IFCI.

Infrastructure

The latest World Development Report (1994) has focused on infrastructure as a critical input for the growth of developing economies. It has brought a painful awareness that in the past the growth experiment in many countries including India did suffer bottlenecks as a result of the lopsided development of infrastructure. Both at the policy as well as the operational level, most economies did not do full justice to this vital sector in terms of investment and organisational structure. In most countries, infrastructure has remained a public sector domain with the consequent inefficiency, wastage and delay. The World Bank report has said that Asian economies have lost some $ 178 billion in undercharging and technical inefficiencies, including over-staffing as well as poor maintenance, transmission and distribution. The major cause was the lower price of infrastructure services that failed to cover their costs.

This scenario fits the Indian case very well. The major infrastructural segment has done rather poorly in recent years. In energy coal output has gone up from 211.7 million tonnes in 1990-91 to 246.0 million tonnes in 1993-94, a rise of 16 per cent. Of the electricity generated, thermal accounted for 78.3 per cent, in 1993-94.

Thermal electricity has risen from 192.7 bn. kwh in 1990-91 to 253.0 bn. kwh in 1993-94. Hydel electricity has in fact declined fractionally from 71.5 bn. kwh. to 70.3 bn. kwh in the same period. Not much can be said about the petroleum sector either. Crude oil throughout declined from 33.0 million tonnes in 1990-91 to 27.0 million tonnes in 1993-94. The refinery throughout showed a marginal rise to 54.3 million tonnes in 1993-94, up from 51.8 million tonnes in 1990-91, a huge rise in the imports of petroleum products in recent years to keep the wheels of the economy running betrays a helplessness as well as policy failure in this regard.

There is little to be proud about in the progress of other sectors. The railways hauled 362.1 million tonnes of goods in 1993-94, up 13.7 per cent from 318.4 million tonnes in 1990-91. Cargo handled by Indian ships rose from 152.9 million tonnes in 1990-91 to 166.7 million tonnes in 1992-93, hardly a commendable performance.

In this dismal scenario, the only sector that seems to have registered some progress is telecommunications. Telephone connections increased from 4.85 million in 1990-91 to 9.86 million in 1992-93. The new Telecommunications Policy has an ambitious programme of providing a telephone connection on demand by 1997. Private sector participation is invited on a big scale. Other infrastructure facilities too have not done as well as expected.

A major reason has always been the inadequate allocation of funds to the infrastructural sectors. The planned outlay has gone up 71.5 per cent to Rs. 1,00120.2 crore in 1993-94 over Rs. 58,369.3 crore in 1990-91. The total outlay in the Eight Plan has risen by a hefty 141.2 per cent to Rs. 4,34,100 crore from Rs. 1,80,000 crore in the Seventh Plan.

India has a long way to go as regards social infrastructure. The Human Development Report (1994) has ranked India 135th among 173 countries in the Human Development Index (HDI) as known life expectancy, infant mortality, population with access to safe drinking water, underweight children, adult literacy, health, water, sanitation and food security (in terms of nutritional requirement) in India are way below those in other countries. This underscores the need for toning up social infrastructure if the growth rate, as well as the quality of development, are to improve in future.

As the World Development Report (1994) puts it, "Infrastructure represents, if not the engine, then the wheels of economic activity". Unfortunately India is trying to push the engine of economic growth on rickety wheels. The recent reforms of the Indian economy have raised high hopes about achieving a target of 5 per cent GDP per annum. A few other studies point out that a 6 per cent growth rate is quite possible. But the caveat is infrastructure which needs a new and fresh look. The new Asian tigers as well as China have scored better than India in this regard. Therefore, the WDR calls for improving the quality of infrastructure as the quantity improvements are essential to modernise and diversify production, help countries compete internationally; and accommodate rapid urbanisation.

Noted economist Prof. Jagdish Bhagawati in his latest book 'Indian in Transition: Freeing the Economy' (Clarendon Press, 1993), has among other things, blamed the inefficiency of the public sector utilities and infrastructure as causing low productivity. The point is the inefficient working of the public utilities and the low priority to the infrastructure in the planned period have weakened the base of the Indian economy. The opening up of the infrastructure to the private sector in recent years has sought to remedy this defect. It is difficult to see how, in the absence of a permanent framework of policies, the mere recognition of the neglect and the ad hoc measures to remedy these weaknesses can put the economy on a sound base.

The government has reduced capital and social expenditure in its anxiety to cut the deficit. Apparently the thinking is that such expenditure does not yield quick results in the short-term. Yet this policy does not augur well for a country that is set on a course of long-term growth by achieving a minimum of five per cent growth in this GDP to eliminate poverty and unemployment. As the Asian Development Bank Outlook (1994) puts it: "Politically these expenditures (capital and social) are the easiest to reduce, but in a country whose infrastructure is still poorly developed they are also the expenditures that are most likely to yield the highest social returns".

The worst part of the story is that the poorest are the worst hit because of the low infrastructure. With the incessant pressure of the World Bank and other bodies on the government to dispense with the subsidy in every sector, and the infrastructural area being thrown open to the private sector, the market may act to the disadvantage of the weaker sections. It is only if the government balances the private sector efforts with its own spending on infrastructure is there hope for a modicum of facilities to those who need it most, i.e. the weak and the meek.

Prices

Whatever the gains of the three-year-old reforms programme in terms of a more liberal economic environment and a dramatic uptum in forex reserves, the common man has nothing much to feel elated about, thanks to the continuing rise in prices.

The general index of wholesale prices (with base year as 1981-82) has risen to about 265 in June from 198.4 in June 1991 — an increase of nearly 84 per cent in three years. This is higher than the inflation rate of 26.2 per cent computed by the World Bank for the period June 1991 to December 1993 in one of its recent reports. Worse still, the upswing is continuing at a double-digit pace.

In fact, there has been no respite for the common man from the high inflation rates for the past five years. After recording a moderate increase of 5.7 per cent in 1988-89, the annual average index of wholesale prices rose by 9.1 per cent in 1989-90, 12.1 per cent in 1990-91, 13.6 per cent in 1991-92 and about 10 per cent in 1992-93. Although by mid-1993, the inflation rate had declined to 7 per cent, it started rising again, rather menacingly, in the latter half of that year and touched 10 per cent in early 1994.

Since March, the double-digit inflation has again become the norm, with the monthly index ruling above 10 per cent over that in the corresponding month of last year.

Although the present inflation rate is lower than the peak of 17 per cent reached in August-September 1992, the common man has little comfort to draw from this statistical fact, given the fairly high rate of rise in prices of several essential commodities.

TABLE 3.1

Statewise Distribution of Jobs, Investment

State	*No. of cases*	*% of total*	*Investment (Rs. cr)*	*% of total*	*Jobs Numbers*	*% of total*
Maharashtra	2994	20.67	60721	20.50	516381	18.65
Gujarat	2052	14.16	49142	16.59	376635	13.60
Uttar Pradesh	1567	10.82	35421	11.96	290517	10.49
Tamil Nadu	1025	7.07	14957	5.05	167340	6.04
Haryana	951	6.56	11601	3.92	166526	6.01
Madhya Pradesh	928	6.41	30836	10.41	234765	8.48
Punjab	860	5.94	10762	3.63	253321	9.15
Rajasthan	844	5.83	13208	4.46	172259	6.22
Andhra Pradesh	778	5.37	21977	7.42	161170	5.82
Karnataka	512	3.53	11370	3.84	74387	2.69
West Bengal	487	3.36	7392	2.50	108064	3.90
Delhi	329	2.27	5200	1.76	38344	1.38
Dadra and Nagar Haveli	248	1.71	3503	1.18	30337	1.10
Daman and Diu	154	1.06	1629	0.55	12836	0.46
Himachal Pradesh	143	0.99	4390	1.48	44752	1.62
Bihar	133	0.92	39.06	1.32	20094	0.73
Kerala	118	0.81	2800	0.95	24070	0.87
Pondicherry	96	0.66	503	0.17	9954	0.36
Orissa	94	0.65	2926	0.99	38201	1.38
Goa	86	0.59	1885	0.64	10920	0.39
Assam	34	0.23	401	0.14	3152	0.11
J & K	22	0.15	117	0.04	6738	0.24
Chandigarh	12	0.08	121	0.04	3604	0.13
Sikkim	8	0.06	22	0.0	680	0.02
Andaman and Nicobar	4	0.03	261	0.09	2180	0.08
Meghalaya	3	0.02	38	0.01	482	0.02
Tripura	3	0.02	1038	0.35	1345	0.05
Arunachal	1	0.01	35	0.01	23	0.00
Nagaland	1	0.01	1	0.00	140	0.01
Lakshadweep	1	0.01	4	0.00	278	0.01
Total	**14488**		**296167**		**2769495**	

From 1.8.91 to 30.6.94

Finance Minister Manmohan Singh had recently held out the promise of bringing inflation down within this year. But he did not indicate any precise target. Nevertheless the failure of the government to use the hefty foreign exchange reserves and the huge foodgrain stocks to stem the rising tide of prices does not lend credence to any sanguine projections on the price front.

Though some seasonal decline in prices in the post-monsoon season cannot be ruled out, there are other factors mitigating any real thaw: These include the high fiscal deficit target of 6 per cent of the GDP set for the current year, the inevitable increases in foodgrain procurement and issue prices, the continuing inflows of funds from abroad and the weaker-than-expected industrial recovery.

It is estimated that about half the current inflation is on account of the successive hikes in administrated prices. It may, thus, be considered an inevitable fall-out of the reform programme.

However, while the increases in administered prices are supposed to strengthen the public sector's financial position, the resultant inflation may erode much of the gains on this count unless steps are taken simultaneously to cut costs and enhance efficiency all around.

It is also open to question whether the procurement and issue prices of foodgrains need to be raised just because their international equivalents have risen following the devaluation of the rupee.

RUPEE CONVERTIBILITY

The Indian rupee has been made fully convertible on the current account from August 20, 1994. The Reserve Bank of India (RBI) has notified the relaxations in the exchange control regime, promised earlier by the Finance Minister in the Budget for 1994-95. With this, India complies with the conditions laid down in Article VIII of the Articles of Agreement of the International Monetary Fund (IMF).

The decision to make the rupee convertible on the current account and to permit repatriation of income earned on investments by non-resident Indians and overseas corporate bodies announced by the RBI is a reflection of the confidence gained from the inflow of foreign exchange reserves, which had crossed $ 17 billion by the end of July 1994.

The RBI's acceptance of the commitments contained in Article VIII of the IMF against imposing restrictions of making payments and transfers for current international transactions makes it clear that it no longer has any fears about a run on the exchange reserves. The commitment also implies acceptance of the IMF's right to exercise firm surveillance over the exchange policies of the member countries. Since the rupee has fared creditably in relation to other currencies after it became partly convertible on March 1, 1992, India could have no objection to agreeing to this commitment.

The RBI's decision to permit repatriation of income on non-resident investments should generate more confidence and hopefully induce more investment inflows into the country. The RBI has hastened slowly by restricting the remittances to one-third and two-thirds of the annual income earned for 1994-95 and 1995-96 before permitting full repatriation in 1996-97. Obviously, it would be sometime in 1997 that the Government would let a full float of the rupee, making the latter convertible on capital account also. The nation must wait for the 1997-98. Union Budget for the Government to take the final plunge. A comfortable foreign exchange reserve has led many to prescribe adoption of capital account convertibility. But there are many steps between convertibility on the current account and on the capital account.

In the early 1980s, the European countries had freed all controls on the capital account, but they soon found cross broder capital transactions too hot to handle and quickly reimposed controls. India has a long way to go before it can allow unfettered cross border movement of capital. The point is to set the fundamentals of the economy right and complete financial sector reforms. Until then, Safeguards are necessary. Not surprisingly, the IMF also recently cautioned India against any immediate steps towards capital account convertibility.

Limits

The "indicative limits" within which authorised dealers can make foreign exchange available for purposes of travel, studies and medical treatment should be sufficient for meeting most of the legitimate requirements. The restrictions which are still in force do not put India in the same class as the developed countries or newly industrialised economies of South East Asia. If the headway made on the export front and in the expansion of direct foreign investments is sustained it should in the not too distant future enable the lifting of all restrictions.

The Government has placed reasonable restrictions to ensure that full convertibility on the current account is not misused and leads to a larger than normal outflow of foreign exchange form the country. The government would remain on guard against any possible capital outflow in the guise of a current account transaction. There are checks and balances to ensure this and transactions of certain nature will be monitored in future.

Partial Convertibility

Earlier, under the partial convertibility of the rupee, all foreign exchange remittances, whether earned through exports of goods or services or by way of inward remittances from Indians working abroad, were converted into rupee in the following manner — 40 per cent of the exchange was converted at the official exchange rate and the remaining 60 per cent at a market determined rate. Exporters had the benefit of the premium on 60 per cent of their earnings, in the foreign exchange market.

After the unification of the exchange rate from March 1993, and a somewhat staggering build-up of foreign exchange reserves which posed problems of management, extension of rupee convertibility to current transactions, besides trade, had become logical.

The structural transformation of the Indian economy was launched in July 1991 with a hefty devaluation of the rupee, followed by a dual exchange rate system — based on official and the unification of the exchange rate in March 1993.

The exchange rate, determined by forces of supply and demand, has remained stable and helped in the impressive export growth of 1993-94. Continuing capital inflows of a significant order will, however, exert pressure on the rupee at a time when the country's still high inflation rate remains unchecked, jeopardising its export competitiveness.

The RBI has been doing its utmost to maintain a realistic exchange rate by making heavy purchases of US dollars, the intervention currency, while additions to the reserves are contributing to money supply expansion.

There are several options open to the Government as an adequate level of reserves could take care of sudden sharp fluctuations without aggravating inflationary pressures. While import liberalisation seems to be the easy way out, little headway in seen in translating the flows into investments in the economy, which is yet to grow out of a low-growth syndrome.

The balance of payments outlook has certainly improved for the immediate future, with non-gold foreign exchange reserves at $17.5 billion at the end of July. Foreign portfolio investments are also steady, having crossed $2.4 billion by the end of July.

The current account deficit, which was at a record low of $230 million in 1993-94, will certainly widen this year with the expected surge in imports, and exports (so far) not doing as good as last year.

Despite the comfortable reserve position, India's external viability cannot be taken for granted until the fiscal deficit is controlled, inflation lowered and pending reforms completed, leading to higher growth and larger exports.

In the latter half of the 1980s, India relied heavily on NRI deposits for balance of payments support by offering them higher rates of interest. The realisation that these deposits were in the nature of "hot money" came later, and by then, NRIs had begun to withdraw part of the deposits.

However, there are still NRI deposits of over $ 7 billion which are intended to be retired. No fresh deposits of three-year maturity will be accepted under the Foreign Currency Non-Resident Account (FCNRA) scheme and the Government will not bear the exchange rate risk on such deposits. This will mean the virtual winding down of FCNRA.

In terms of the IMF stipulations for qualifying for Article VIII status, the RBI has also made interest on deposits under the NRI non-repatriable rupee deposit scheme eligible for repatriation.

Foreign exchange allowance for travel, education and medical expenses had already been liberalised by the RBI. Indicative limits ($2,000 per person for travel) for various purposes have been set within which authorised dealers can make available foreign exchange without RBI approval. Income on investment by NRIs has now been made repatriable in a phased manner.

India has done away with practically all exchange control restrictions, barring the movement of capital, but convertibility on capital account may not be achievable in the near future, at any rate until the economy becomes strong and beings to build substantial current account surpluses.

According to IMF economists, current account convertibility reduces distortions associated with foreign exchange rationing, contributes to increased productivity by opening the domestic market to increased competition, improves access to imported inputs and capital goods and facilitates the international transfer of technology.

RBI Announcement

The rupee achieved full convertibility on current account with the RBI announcing major relaxations on current account transactions from August 20, 1994.

RBI Governor C. Rangarajan has advised the IMF managing director that India has moved over to Article VIII status in the IMF with effect from August 20, 1994, according to a release issued on August 19.

This is in line with the assurance given by the Finance Minister in his budget speech earlier this year that the country will move towards current account convertibility.

The major decisions announced include allowing non-resident Indians or overseas corporate bodies (OCBs), predominantly owned by the NRIs, to repatriate income on investments in a phased manner over a three-year period. However, these remittances would be allowed only after payment of tax in accordance with the provisions of the Income Tax Act.

Repatriation

Income on investments upto $1,000, accuring during 1994-95, and thereafter, can now be remitted freely.

For investment income exceeding $1,000 in a year the additional repatriation will be liberalised in three phases:

- During 1994-95, one-third of the annual income earned can be repatriated.

- During 1995-96, two-thirds of the annual income earned will be allowed to be repatriated.
- From 1996-97 onwards, the entire income earned will be allowed to be repatriated.

Since 1996-97 is the benchmark year for total income repatriation, the feeling is that the government might decide to go in for full convertibility on capital account as well in that year.

Among the other measures announced, the RBI has stated that the existing limits prescribed for remittances of foreign currency for purposes such as travel, studies, medical treatment, gifts and services, will now be only 'indicative'. Authorised dealers can now make available such funds without seeking RBI approval.

The RBI has also said that it would favourably consider any genuine demand for foreign exchange in excess of these indicative limits.

Currently, the RBI has limits for such purposes — such as $2,000 per year for a private trip abroad, allowing remittance up to $500 per family by way of gifts, a ceiling of $10,000 per transaction for payment of services.

The RBI has also decided to allow banks to repatriate interest accuring on Non-Resident and Non-Repatriable deposits (NRNR).

Repatriation will be allowed from October 1, 1994.

The principal amount under the NRNR scheme, however, will not be repatriable. Earlier, both the interest as well as the principal under the NRNR scheme were not repatriable.

The RBI has also decided to withdraw the Foreign Currency (Ordinary) Non-Repatriable Deposit Scheme (FCNOR) from August 20, 1994. No fresh deposits will be accepted under the scheme. However, the RBI has decided that interest according on existing FCNOR deposits, from the quarter beginning October 1, 1994, and up to the maturity of the deposits, can now be repatriated. Earlier, neither the principal amount nor the interest could be repatriated under this scheme.

With India now accepting the obligations of Article VIII, it cannot impose restrictions on payments and transfer for current international transactions or engage indiscriminatory currency arrangements or multiple currency practices without IMF approval.

On its side, the IMF will also exercise firm surveillance over India's exchange rate policy and oversee the elimination of exchange restrictions, which hamper the growth of world trade.

Obligations

The Reserve Bank of India in a press release states: IMF members accepting the obligations of Article VIII undertake to refrain from imposing restrictions on the making of payments of transfers for current international transactions or from engaging in discriminatory currency arrangements or multiple currency practices without IMF approval.

Two of the main purposes of the IMF, as stated in its Articles of Agreement, are to facilitate the expansion and balanced growth of international trade, and thereby to contribute to the promotion and maintenance of high levels of employment and real income, and to assist in the establishment of a multilateral system of payments in respect of current transactions between IMF members.

In seeking to achieve these objective, the IMF exercises firm surveillance over the exchange rate policies of its members, and oversees the elimination of exchange restrictions which hamper the growth of world trade.

By accepting the obligations of Article VIII India gives confidence to the international community that it will pursue sound economic policies that will obviate the need to use restrictions on the making of payments and transfers for current international transactions, and thereby contribute to amultilateral payments system free of restrictions.

Authorised dealers can now make foreign exchange available for purpose of travel, studies, medical treatment, gifts, services etc. up to the indicative limits without the approval of the RBI. The RBI will consider favourably bona fide requests for additional foreign exchange.

Under the currency limits, a person travelling abroad is eligible to get $350 per day for a stay more than 15 days. For any stay up to 15 days the person is entitled to $5,000 for the entire period. For chief executives, the limit is $500 per day with an entertainment allowance of $5,000 per trip. For others, it is $2,000 per trip.

Depending on the course applied for, a student is entitled to a limit of $30,000 for the whole course. In case of medical treatment, individuals get foreign exchange to the extent of the estimate given by the foreign hospital on an actual basis with the attendant being entitled to $150 per day to the extent of the stay of the patient.

India is the 80th member of the IMF to make the local current fully convertible on current account. The liberalisation is the latest so far in a graduated sequence of steps in the direction of complete convertibility of the rupee, on both current account and capital account.

It all started on July 1, 1991, when the value of the rupee declined by 8 per cent to 9 per cent. On July 3, 1991, it was further brought down by 10 to 11 per cent.

In end-July, 1991, a new trade policy was announced along with the announcement of a dual exchange rate system. The old system of import replenishment for exporters was changed and exporters were permitted to keep 40 per cent of their export revenue for exchanging in the free market or for making their own imports.

This proportion was raised to 60 per cent in 1992. Non-export inward remittances also were brought under the 60:40 scheme.

Unification of exchange rate was introduced in early 1993-94. From the on, the exchange rate of the rupee came to be determined by the market, and even the government was to buy forex at the market rate of exchange.

Full convertibility on current account technically means that all intended transactions in current account are wholly free from restrictions or anyone's discretion.

In the Indian case, it means that Indians are free to exchange rupees for dollars when they need foreign exchange for any of the following purposes; studies abroad; travel; medical treatment; gifts; insurance; hiring of consultants abroad and purpose of other services; maintenance of dependents residing abroad; and remittance of income from assets in India owned by Indians who have migrated. The last one should include interest, dividends, rent and profit.

Ceilings

Each one of these, except payment for the maintenance of dependents abroad, is formally permissible now. Insurance payments, of course, are permitted only in case of business related insurance. But each is subjected to a ceiling. An individual is entitled to $2,000 per year for travel. A man in business can get $300 per day for the period of stay. The maximum permissible for gifts in $500 (add other items).

If the ceilings were lifted, then Indians would have been free to spend as much on travel as they would have liked. Entertainment could have been included. Medical treatment abroad would have been easier, since the present ceiling is insufficient for meeting the minimum hospital expenses, which are quite high in most western countries, affluent persons would have had the opportunity to send their children or other relations for residence abroad, including residence for education.

But that could have also meant that they would have been free to transfer funds abroad for investment or for future expenditure, after having got foreign exchange under current account heads.

With the rupee becoming fully convertible with effect from August 20 as per the RBI announcement, the existing restrictions on foreign exchange allowances for travel, studies, medical treatment, gifts and services are now removed.

The foreign exchange quota for the neighbourhood travel scheme will now be $250 per person per year. Foreign exchange for studies abroad will henceforth be released by authorised dealers to any student who has secured admission in a foreign university/

educational institution/college.

The limit up to which gift remittance can be permitted by authorised dealers is now raised from $200 to $500 per family in a calendar year.

As per the announcement, authorised dealers will now be permitted to remit donations by residents up to $500 to charitable/cultural/educational/religious organisations abroad.

The limit up to which authorised dealers are permitted to allow remittances to overseas parties by way of payments for services rendered such as arbitration fee, legal expenses, correspondence course/examination/registration fees, membership subscription, export information, payment of honorarium, cost of tender documents, registration/renewal of patent/design/trade mark etc. is now raised from $5,000 to $10,000 per transaction.

Outflow

Bankers are of the opinion that there will be no large foreign exchange outflow as a result of the rupee being made convertible on current account.

Foreign bankers feel that the changes are mainly cosmetic in nature. Standard Chartered Bank's Chief Dealer, Mr. Janak Desai, said, "Current account convertibility will have no impact on the real flows. It will mainly provide the non-resident Indian with the psychological comfort that he can pull out his money. With the interest differential being so large, the NRI will not choose to pull his money out". The fact that the rupee was not likely to weaken would only add to NRI confidence, Mr. Desai said.

Mr. N.R. Sampat, NRI Division, State Bank of India, said, "The impact of the current account convertibility on forex reserves is likely to be marginal. The steps taken by the RBI will serve more as a psychological boost to the NRI that the country's reserves are strong".

According to a banker, "There will be no major outflows. Most of the NRNR deposits are from salaried NRIs in West Asia. Only a few of them may need the money from these deposits to supplement their income abroad. Even dividend repatriation will be spread out and have little impact on the reserves".

The new rules allow repatriation of interest but not principal on these deposits. Says a banker, "The country has around Rs. 5,000 crores to Rs. 6,000 crores in NRNR deposits. Nearly 90 per cent of this is from NRIs in West Asia. They are not permitted to invest in the stock exchange, business, real estate or even a house in these countries, and are not likely to need the money".

Bankers also feel that the present limit of $2,000 which is around Rs. 60,000 under the foreign travel scheme (FTS), is ample enough and it is unlikely that additional exchange will be availed of. With the rupee being undervalued, foreign exchange dealers feel the demand for foreign exchange to buy good abroad and sell them here has also gone down.

The decision to scrap the Foreign Currency (Ordinary) Non-Repatriable Deposit Scheme will also make little difference, bankers feel.

Welcomed

The full convertibility of the rupee on the current account is unlikely to result in a substantial outflow of foreign exchange in the medium term.

For example, though the RBI has allowed interest repatriation in the deposits scheme, this freedom is unlikely to send NRIs scrambling to remit the interest proceeds abroad.

As Mr. A.R. Barwe, General Manager at the State Bank of India, points out : "Depositors who invest under this scheme are primarily interested in maintaining rupee funds for meeting expenses in India. Moreover, if the rupee continues to remain stable and interest rates continue to remain attractive at 12 per cent, compared to the low interests rates of 4-5 per cent that they would earn per year on foreign currency deposits, there is no reason to fear an outflow of foreign exchange".

It may be recalled that the NRNR scheme had gained in popularity because the rupee was perceived to the stable. The NRNR scheme had also gained popularity by default — interest rates under the FCNR deposits scheme were overtaken by the corresponding London inter bank offered rate (LIBOR).

So unless depositors expect a sudden depreciation in the rupee, the move will not result in a sizeable outflow of interest income.

Again, the scrapping of the foreign currency (Ordinary) Non-Repatriable Deposit Scheme and the permission to repatriate interest accrued after the first quarter of October 1994 till the maturity of the deposit is unlikely to affect forex outflows.

Bankers say that the scheme never really took off because depositors did not want to freeze their accounts for three years.

The scheme was not open to deposits of less than three-year maturity. Further, though the scheme offered a rate of interest higher than the FCNR (this was initially fixed at one percentage point over the FCNR rate, later raised by two percentage points and thereafter freed), the RBI did not provide any exchange cover on these deposits, which added to the costs.

In other words, bankers feel that the decision to allow repatriation of interest on existing deposits will not affect forex outflows.

The decision to change the statutory limit on remittances for gifts, travel, medical facilities, services, to an indicative ceiling and the clause that the RBI would consider favourably any demand for forex above the stipulated amounts too will not result in large forex outflows.

As Mr. Barwe points out, though there are currently no restrictions on overseas medical and educational expenses, this has not resulted in any major outflows of foreign exchange. So there is no reason to assume that the informal ceiling will result in forex outflows. However, the 'indicative limit' signifies caution. What could have an impact on forex outflows is the decision to allow NRIs and overseas commercial bodies (OCBs) to remit income.

Logical Development

Finance Secretary Montek Singh Ahluwalia described the RBI's announcement as a "very good decision" as it would place India in the company of a large number of nations, including its neighbours, which have already achieved Article VIII status. "It is logical development which reflects our much-strengthened balance of payments position," he said.

Mr. Ahluwalia said that while the measures announced represented the "final step" towards achieving full convertibility on the current account, it was not an "insubstantial step" and that it would "add to the sense of confidence about India's economic reforms programme". He added that recent decisions were in pursuance to the Finance Minister's statement in his budget speech that the country would move towards current account convertibility.

The measures follow the RBI decision to phase out those foreign currency non-resident accounts in which the Government bore the exchange rate risk.

Thus, all the steps that the IMF's Senior Resident Representative in India. Mr. Charles V.A. Collyns, had listed as necessary for India to move to Article VIII status have been completed.

Mr. Collyns said he welcomed the measures and was not surprised that they had been taken. He said it was an important step taken by India and would boost international confidence in the strength of the Indian economy and currency.

"It will send very positive signals about India's integration with the global economy", Mr. Collyns added. The step was important not just for foreign investors, but also for Indian citizens, who would now have greater freedom in foreign exchange transactions.

Economists also agreed that the move to full current account convertibility was predictable. "We were almost there and now we have taken the final step", said Mr. S.L. Rao, Director General of the National Council for Applied Economic Research, echoing the general view.

Mr. Rao also dismissed apprehensions of any large outflows of foreign exchange as a result of these steps. "The effect on outflows and inflows should by and large balance out and there may even be a net positive impact on inflows", he observed, adding that Indians who had so far held foreign exchange abroad illegally to circumvent restrictions may now decide to bring the funds back to the country.

Prof. Abhijit Sen of Jawaharlal Nehru University, while agreeing that there was "no problem" with a system of indicative limits as opposed to absolute limits for travellors, students and others, felt some issues would have to be tackled with regard to repatriation of interest on NRI accounts.

He pointed out that the interest rate on these rupee schemes would either have to be brought down or the schemes phased out. The decision to allow NRIs repatriation of investment incomes was in a sense putting them on an equal footing with multinationals, who already have this facility, he noted.

Mr. Rao of NCAER felt the next steps of the Government should be to ease restrictions on Indian companies spending hard currency on travel and brand promotion activities, besides imports of bullion and consumer goods.

Dr. Shankar Acharya, Chief Economic Advisor, says "the presence of indicative limits should not make one feel that the full convertibility is not real".

The Reserve Bank has provided for indicative limits to avoid capital account convertibility being disguised as current account convertibility. Suppose, a person says he needs $1 million towards the education of his son, this claim is totally absurd.

"Or, for instance, another individual claims that his requirement for travel abroad is $5 million. Should that be accepted at its face value? So, the indicative limit should be viewed in the proper perspective.

"The RBI was very particular that the income on investment of NRIs or OCB predominantly owned by them should be repatriable in a phased manner over a period of 3 years". Dr. Acharya said.

Trade and industry have hailed the RBI's decision to make the rupee fully convertible on current account.

In the statement, the Federation of Indian Chambers of Commerce and Industry (FICCI) said the measures taken to ease the two-way movement of foreign exchange would not result in substantial outflow of foreign exchange in the short and medium term.

However, since 70 per cent of the foreign exchange inflow was volatile, attractive packages should be evolved to ensure that NRIs and overseas corporate bodies maintain foreign exchange in India on a permanent basis.

Cll President Subodh Bhargava said that with foreign exchange earnings at a high level, the announcement of full convertibility would boost the sentiments of the business community and foreign investors while reinforcing the government's determination to go ahead with liberalisation.

The measure would check inflation with the increase in demand for foreign exchange and the corresponding reduction in money supply, he added.

The President of the North Indian Chamber of Commerce and Industry (NICCI), Mr. L.K. Modi, said the move will send positive signals to foreign direct investors, FIIs and active players in the Indian financial and capital markets.

The President of the Chamber of Chartered Accountants (CCA), Mr. V.D. Aggarwal, said it will limit the direct flow of foreign exchange to the RBI, reducing its foreign exchange management problems.

The acting President of the Federation of Indian Export Organisations (FIEO). Mr. P.H. Mahtani, in a release, said the RBI decision to allow NRIs and OCBs predominantly owned by NRIs to repatriate income on their investments in a phased manner would attract investment from such OCBs and NRIs. FIEO plans to capitalise on this measure by publicising this aspect among NRIs, encouraging their investment in EOUs, and enabling a "quantum jump in exports".

ANNEXURE-I

TEXT OF RBI PRESS NOTE

CURRENT ACCOUNT CONVERTIBILITY

Pursuant to the Finance Minister's announcement in the Budget speech to move towards current account convertibility, the Reserve Bank of India has announced further measures to liberalise current account transactions which have been separately announced. Dr. C Rangarajan, governor of the Reserve Bank of India, has advised the managing director, International Monetary Fund, on Friday that with effect from August 20, 1994, India has moved over to Article VIII status in the International Monetary Fund.

Relaxations on Current Account Payments

The Reserve Bank of India has in the recent period announced certain relaxations on current account payments. The Bank on Friday announced certain further relaxations. These are as follows :

1. Indicative Limits on Current Account Payments

Reserve Bank has delegated powers to authorised dealers to allow remittances for various purpose like travel, studies, medical treatment, gifts, services etc. to the extent specified by it. The Bank has now clarified that these are indicative limits up to which authorised dealers can make available exchange facilities without the approval of the Reserve Bank. In the case of bona fide requests for additional exchange facilities the

Reserve Bank will favourably consider such requests.

2. Non-resident (Non-repatriable) Rupee Deposit Scheme (NRNR)

At present, under the Non-Resident (Non-Repatriable) Rupee Deposit Scheme (NRNR), both the principal and the interest are not repatriable. It has been decided that interest accuring on NRNR deposits from the quarter beginning October 1, 1994, will be eligible for repatriation. The principal amount under the scheme would continue to be non-repatriable.

3. Foreign Currency (Ordinary) Non-repatriable Deposit Scheme (FCNOR)

At present, under the Foreign Currency (Ordinary) Non-Repatriable Deposit Scheme (FCNOR), the principal as well as the interest earned are not repatriable with effect from August 20, 1994, no fresh deposits will be allowed to be accepted by banks under this scheme. It has been decided that interest accuring on existing FCNOR deposits from the quarter beginning October 1, 1994, will be eligible for repatriation upto the maturity date of the existing deposits.

4. Repatriation of Investment Income by Non-residents

Income on investment by non-resident persons of Indian nationality/origin (NRIs) or overseas corporate bodies (OCBs) predominantly owned by such persons would now be repatriable in a phased manner over a three-year period as indicated below:

(i) With immediate effect such income accuring in the financial year 1994/95 and onwards to the extent of $1,000 per annum will be remittable.

(ii) For income earned over and above $1,000 in a year the following additional remittance would be allowed:

(a) one-third of the annual income earned during the financial year 1995/96.

(b) two-thirds of the annual income earned during the financial year 1995/96.

(c) the entire income earned during the financial year 1996/97 and onwards.

Remittance of income as stated above would be allowed only after the payment of tax as per the provisions of the Income-Tax Act.

ARTICLE VIII

General Obligations of Members

Section 1. Introduction

In addition to the obligations assumed under other articles of this Agreement, each member undertakes the obligations set out in this Article.

Section 2. Avoidance of Restrictions on Current Payments

(a) Subject to the provisions of Article VI, Section 3(b) and Article XIV, Section 2, no member shall, without the approval of the Fund, impose restrictions on the making of payments and transfers for current international transactions.

(b) Exchange contracts which involve the currency of any member and which are contrary to the exchange control regulations of that member maintained or imposed consistently with this Agreement shall be unenforceable in the territories of any member. In addition, members may, by mutual accord, cooperate in measures for the purpose of making the exchange control regulations of either member more effective, provided that such measures and regulations are consistent with this Agreement.

Section 3. Avoidance of Discriminatory Currency Practices

No member shall engage in, or permit any of its fiscal agencies referred to in Article V, Section 1, to engage in any discriminatory currency arrangements or multiple currency practices, whether within or outside margins under Article IV or prescribed by or under Schedule C, except as authorised under the Agreement or approved by the Fund. If such arrangements and practices are enegaged in at the date when this Agreement enters into force, the member concerned shall consult with the Fund as to their progressive removal unless they are maintained or imposed under Article XIV, Section 2, in which case the provisions of Section 3 of that Article shall apply.

Section 4. Convertibility of Foreign-Held Balances

(a) Each member shall buy balances of its currency held by another member if the latter, in requesting the purpose, represents :

(i) that the balances to be bought have been recently acquired as a result of current transactions; or

(ii) that their conversion is needed for making payments for current transactions.

The buying member shall have the option to pay either in special drawing rights, subject to Article XIX, Section 4, or in the currency of the member making the request.

(b) The obligation in (a) above shall not apply when:

(i) the convertibility of the balances has been restricted consistently with Section 2 of this Article or Article VI, Section 3;

(ii) the balances have accumulated as a result of transactions effected before the removal by a member of restrictions maintained or imposed under Article XIV, Section 2;

(iii) the balances have been acquired contrary to the exchange regulations of the member which is asked to buy them;

(iv) the currency of the member requesting the purchase has been declared scarce under Article VII, Section 3(a); or

(v) the member requested to make the purchase is for any reason not entitled to buy currencies of other members from the Fund for its own currency.

Section 5. Furnishing of information

(a) The Fund may require members to furnish it with such information as it deems necessary for its activities, including, as the minimum necessary for the effective discharge of the Fund's duties, national data on the following matters :

(i) official holdings at home and abroad of (1) gold, (2) foreign exchange;

(ii) holdings at home and abroad by banking and financial agencies, other than official agencies, of (1) gold, (2) foreign exchange;

(iii) production of gold;

(iv) gold exports and imports according to countries of destination and origin;

(v) total exports and imports of merchandise, in terms of local currency values, according to countries of destination and origin;

(vi) international balance of payments, including (1) trade in goods and service, (2) gold transactions, (3) known capital transactions, and (4) other items;

(vii) international investment position, i.e., investments within the territories of the member owned abroad and investments abroad owned by persons in its territories so far as it is possible to furnish this information;

(viii) national income;

(ix) price indices, i.e., indices of commodity prices in wholesale and retail markets and of export and import prices;

(x) buying and selling rates for foreign currencies;

(xi) exchange controls, i.e., comprehensive statement of exchange controls in effect at the time of assuming membership in the Fund and details of subsequent exchanges as they occur and

(xii) where official clearing arrangements exist, details of amounts awaiting clearance in respect of commercial and financial transactions, and of the length of time during which such arrears have been outstanding.

(b) In requesting information the Fund shall take into consideration the varying ability of members to furnish the data requested. Members shall be under no obligation to furnish information in such detail that the affairs of individuals or corporations are disclosed. Members undertake, however, to furnish the desired information in as detailed and accurate a manner as is practicable and, so far as possible, to avoid mere estimates.

(c) The fund may arrange to obtain further information by agreement with members. It shall act as a centre for the collection and exchange of information on momentary and financial problems, thus facilitating the preparation of studies designed to assist members in developing policies which further the purposes of the Fund.

Section 6. Consultation Regarding Existing International Pacts

Where under this Agreement a member is authorised in the special or temporary circumstances specified in the Agreement to maintain or establish restrictions on exchange transactions, if there are other engagements between members entered into prior to this Agreement which conflict with the application of such restrictions,the parties to such engagements shall consult with one another with a view to making such mutually acceptable adjustments as may be necessary. The provisions of the Article shall be without prejudice to the operation of Article VII, Section 5.

Section 7. Obligation to Collaborate Regarding Policies on Reserve Assets

Each member undertakes to collaborate with the Fund and with other members in order to ensure that the policies of the member with respect to reserve assets shall be consistent with the objectives of promoting better international surveillance of international liquidity and making the special drawing right the principal reserve asset in the international monetary system.

ARTICLE XIV

Transitional Arrangements

Section 1. Notification

Each member shall notify the Fund whether it intends to avail itself of the transitional arrangements in Section 2 of this Article, or whether it is prepared to accept the obligations of Article VIII, Section 2, 3 and 4. A member availing itself of the transitional arrangements shall notify the Fund as soon thereafter as it is prepared to accept these obligations.

Section 2. Exchange Restrictions

A member that has notified the Fund that it intends to avail itself of transitional arrangements under the provision may, notwithstanding the provisions of any other articles of this Agreement, maintain and adapt to changing circumstances the restrictions on payments and transfers of current international transactions that were in effect on the date on which it became a member. Members shall, however, have continuous regard in their foreign exchange policies to the purposes of the Fund, and, as soon as conditions permit, they shall take all possible measures to develop such commercial and financial arrangements with other members as will facilitate international payments and the promotion of a stable system of exchange rates. In particular, members shall withdraw restrictions maintained under this Section as soon as they are satisfied that they will be able, in the absence of such restrictions, to settle their balance of payments in a manner which will not unduly encumber their access to the Fund's general resources.

Section 3. Action of the Fund Relating to Restrictions

The Fund shall make annual reports on the restrictions in force under Section 2 of this Article. Any member retaining any restrictions inconsistent with Article VIII, Section 2, 3 or 4 shall consult the Fund annually as to their further retention. The Fund may, if it deems such action necessary in exceptional circumstances, make representations to any member that conditions are favourable for the withdrawal of any particular restriction, or for the general abandonment of restrictions, inconsistent with the provisions of any other articles of this Agreement. The member shall be given a suitable time to reply to such representations. If the Fund finds that the member persists in maintaining restrictions which are inconsistent with the purposes of the Fund, the member shall be subject to Article XXVI, Section 2(a).

4

Business and Public Policy: Studies of Two High-Profit Industries

1. OPEN SKIES POLICY AND PRIVATE AIRLINES

India took another step forward on the fast lane to the open skies when the Lok Sabha passed a Bill repealing the Air Corporations Act of 1953, ending the monopoly of state-owned airlines. The Air Corporations (Transfer of Undertakings and Repeal Bill, 1994, which replaces an Ordinance promulgated by the President on January, 29, 1994, was passed by the Lok Sabha after a two-day debate on February 23, 1994.

Operation of a safe, efficient and adequate air transport service and the development of the air transport industry in a competitive environment are the twin hallmarks of the air transport policy announced by the Government. The basic elements of the policy, Civil Aviation Minister Gulam Nabi Azad said, were to end the monopoly of the air corporations in the scheduled air transport service and the conversion of the corporations into public limited companies. The policy seeks to provide a statutory framework for orderly development of airlines in a competitive environment.

On the open sky policy, Mr. Azad said, the Government was opening the Indian sky for operation on scheduled flights by domestic airlines only and not foreign carriers. The Government has no intention of making Indian skies free for all, he said, adding that hardly any country in the world had a totally open sky policy for scheduled international passenger services. As far as international services were concerned, it would be the Government's endeavour to obtain for the national carriers—Air India and Indian Airlines—commensurate rights of operation under the prevailing international practice of bilateral agreements with different countries, while giving them rights to operate air services in India. He dispelled the apprehensions of members that the government was privatising Air India and Indian Airlines, saying the government would continue to hold 51 per cent of the equity of both the airlines.

The Government notified the conversion of Indian Airlines and Air India as Indian Airlines Ltd. and Air India Ltd. as a follow-up of the Air Corporation (Transfer of

Undertakings and Repeal) Ordinance issued by the President. The repeal of the Air Corporation Act of 1953 came into force with effect from March 1, 1994.

The private airlines are now emerging from the shadow of Indian Airlines. Dubbed as "air taxi operations" and denied the opportunity to publish schedules, these airlines were choked for the past two years. Now with controls easing, there is a chance to get closer to the customer and offer services befitting a major industry. The five major private airlines—East West, Jet Airlines, Modiluft, Damania and Sahara — are vying for the glory.

The domestic air travel market, estimated to be 13 to 14 million passengers in 1994, is growing at about 10 per cent annually. This growth rate is likely to be sustained over the next five years, offering good scope for the domestic air travel industry to take off.

The Business traveller segment is the largest, contributing about 70 per cent of the air passenger traffic, according to airlines executives. (Annexure 1 gives traffic forecast from 1993-94 to 2009-2010.

Problems

The problem with Indian civil aviation is that air fares are among the lowest in the world, but they are very high compared to the average income of Indians. Domestic airlines pay $ 1.70 per US gallon of airlines turbine fuel (ATF), whereas international airlines fueling in India pay an average of 80 cents. So domestic airlines are paying two times more than international airlines for fuel. This does no good to the cash flow of domestic airlines.

Further, the margins for business are water, thin. The yield per mile is as low as 6 to 7 U.S. cents as against 11 to 12 cents worldwide. But the September 1993 hike in air fares came as a boon as several private airlines lost no time in matching the increases.

With the repeal of the Act, private airlines will now be able to compete with Indian Airlines. To get a bigger slice of the market, private airlines are vying with each other in offering personalised services, entertainment and onboard comforts, which make even short trips memorable for the passengers.

The private airlines have been operating mostly on trunk routes where even terminal capacity is highly utilised. Minimum service obligations are now being imposed on private airlines whereby those operating on trunk routes must deploy proportionate capacity in the far-flung area in the northern, western, eastern and southern regions. The law provides for the entry of new scheduled airlines within the discipline of scheduled operations. Once a minimum requirements regarding equipment, service, safety and trained crew are met and they opt for routes that are well spread, they will be confered scheduled status on application, according to a spokesman of the Civil Aviation Ministry.@ BODY LEFT = Guidelines

In the sweeping changes in the aviation sector, the government on March 1 converted Air India and Indian Airlines into public limited companies and also issued guidelines for air taxi operators to make them eligible to turn into scheduled airlines.

Under the Air Corporation Ordinance all assets, liabilities and functions of Air India and Indian Airlines have been vested in two public limited companies called Air India Ltd. and Indian Airlines Ltd. (Annexure - 2 gives facts on Air India and Indian Airlines).

For this purpose, the government has also constituted a new joint board for the two companies who will now have a joint chairman in Mr. K. Padamanabhiah, at present Secretary, Urban Development Ministry.

Under the new guidelines to enable the air taxi operators to become scheduled airlines, it has been made imperative on their part to have three aircraft registered in India, all with weights of more than 5,700 kg. each (Annexures Lists the guidelines and criteria).

According to the notification, only air taxi operators with not less than Rs. 15 crore subscribed equity capital, if operating aircraft of more than 40,000 kg weight, and Rs. 5 crore for operating aircraft of weights upto 40,000 kg would be eligible to apply for scheduled airlines status.

Other criteria fixed for eligibility include having three sets of flight and cabin crew per aircraft, an approved maintenance organisation for facilities to carry out maintenance of aircraft up to 500 hours or check 'B' for Boeing 737 aircraft, approved manuals for operations, and training and quality control maintenance cells for pre-flight medical examination of crew.

It has also been made mandatory for air taxi operators eligibility for scheduled airlines that they should have flight planning, reliability of analysis of aircraft components and systems, defect investigations, compliance of service bulletins and record of major components.

They would also have to have a security programme approved by the Bureau of Civil Aviation Security and trained security personnel at all operation stations.

The operators have also been asked to abide by any further conditions which the Directorate General of Civil Aviation (DGCA) may consider necessary for monitoring of scheduled air transport service and operation of safe and reliable service.

All the air taxi operators who might be interested in converting themselves into scheduled airlines have been asked by the government to obtain permission from the DGCA and comply with the provisions of Schedule 11 of the Aircraft Rules, 1937.

Routes

The Civil Aviation Ministry has also earmarked air routes in the country into categories with the first category being on trunk routes, the second category being routes connecting stations in the north eastern region, Jammu and Kashmir, Andaman and Nicobar and Lakshadweep Islands.

The routes put in category one are Bombay-Bangalore, Bombay-Calcutta, Bombay-Delhi, Bombay-Hyderabad, Bombay-Madras, Bombay-Trivandrum, Calcutta-Delhi, Calcutta-Bangalore, Calcutta-Madras, Delhi-Bangalore, Delhi-Hyderabad and Delhi-Madras.

Under the new guidelines, anyone who operates a scheduled transport services on one or more routes under categoy A is required to deploy in category two routes at least ten per cent of the capacity that the operates on category A.

Similarly, the air taxi operators would have to deploy 50 per cent of the capacity in category three of the capacity he deployes in category one. However, it makes clear that a service operated on category one as part of the international air service will not be reckoned for the above purpose.

The guidelines also make it clear that capacity deployed will be reckoned in available seat kilometers (ASKM).

It also implies that in multiple sector routes like Delhi-Calcutta-Guwahati-Imphal, the Delhi-Calcutta sector would be taken as a category one route, Calcutta-Guwahati and Guwhati-Imphal as category two routes.

For operating these categories services, the air taxi operators have been given the option of utilising their own aircraft or those of another's fleet on mutually agreed terms, with the approval of DGCA.

Ordinance

President Shanker Dayal Sharma on January 29, 1994, promulgated Ordinance to turn Indian Airlines and Air India into public limited companies, ending the state monopoly in the aviation sector.

The repeal of the Air Corporation Act, 1953, ended the monopoly of Indian Airlines and Air India and simultaneously gave legal sanction to the operation of private air taxis.

The Air Transport (Transfer and Repeal of Undertakings) Ordinance comes in place of a Bill with a similar title, which was introduced in Parliament some 18 months ago. The ordinance was enacted owing to lack of time available to Parliament during the winter session in 1993 to pass the Bill.

In 1990, the then V.P. Singh Government had allowed the operation of private air taxis in the country, but legal sanction eluded these "unscheduled airlines."

In fact, there has been a general clamour from private air taxi operators that the Air

Corporation Act, which gave only Indian Airlines and Air India the right to operate scheduled air services, be repealed.

With the promulgation of the ordinance, Indian Airlines and Air India have been placed at par with private airlines as far as domestic operations go, though only these two companies can fly to destinations abroad.

According to official sources, this is one of the major steps taken to denationalise the public sector. Though there have been demands from the private industry to de-monoplise the aviation industry, the employees of these air corporations have been against such a move.

The Air Corporations Repeal Bill was referred to the standing committee of Parliament attached to the Ministry of Civil Aviation and Tourism. In its report, the committee concurred with the Government that the Air Corporations Act needed to be repealed and Indian Airlines and Air India turned into a public limited companies.

With the repeal of the act, the age of "open skies" has dawned in the country. Private airlines, finally, have been conferred leal status.

Recently, the Government had allowed its personnel to fly on private airlines on domestic routes which meant a loss of several crores of rupees to the nationalised Indian Airlines.

Welcomed

Welcoming the repeal of the Air Corporation Act, the Managing Director of East West Airlines — the country's largest private airlines — Mr. Thakiyuddin A. Wahid, said the ordinance would provide stability of operations to private airlines in the country.

The private airlines now look forward to internal air routes being thrown open to them. There was no conflict of business interests in allowing private airlines to operate on international routes as the private carriers could be offered the routes not covered by Air India and Indian Airlines, he said.

After the repeal of the act, private airlines are suddenly waking up to the reality that the government has loosened their fetters. The accent is now on planning future strategies amid brimming confidence and hope.

Senior government officials and private airlines are confident the domestic aviation scenario is poised for a dramatic change in character. With the repeal of the Act, a number of new players are expected to enter the market, many of whom will be from big corporate houses, which have the financial muscle to endure in the high-cost aviation sector.

For the older players, with about two year's experience in the business, niche marketing' and 'expansion' are the key words. This would essentially involve targeting a particular market, increasing their fleet strength and making their presence felt in more sectors.

For example, Modiluft, according to its Chairman Mr. S.K. Modi, intends to increase its fleet strength from three to 14 by December, 1994, by taking aircraft on lease from Lufthansa.

East West Airlines is thinking of connecting tourist sports which have not been serviced adequately so far. Says Mr. Kaul, "For instance, Goa and Agra, despite being the most popular tourist spots, do not have a direct air link. Tourists have to touch Bombay for the purpose."

East West is also keen on international routes. Says Mr. Wahid, "Although at present international traffic rights out of India are handled by Air India once A-I Ltd. comes into being, there may be some relaxation. The government should permit private airlines to fly to countries that have an open sky policy—Sharjah, Bahrain and Male for instance."

Competition

The size of the airline is expected to play a major role in determining the success of the players. Of the 19 air taxi operators at present, only five have 'reasonable' fleet strength. The rest are operating with a fleet strength of one or two which government officials say is uneconomical in the airline business. While the small players are expected to be a hit, the bigger ones will have to grow bigger to be in business.

But in the short run, the size of the market may not permit all the players to make profits. Competition so far has been largely limited to the quality of service. But most of the players fear the worst—the presence of a large number of airlines is expected to lead to fierce price wars. Already the move by Sahara Airlines to reduce its fares on trunk routes by Rs. 500 has caused heartburn among the other airlines. But then, this is a natural fallout of a free market economy system. Only the fittest will survive.

The airlines feel the need for a regulatory agency to monitor unethical practices. "Competition could intensify, once DGCA frames the new guidelines," according to Mr. Wahid.

Adds Parvez Damania, Chairman Damania Airways, "The DGCA regulations are expected to cover a wide spectrum, including fares. The present price wars, which are an unhealthy sign, could be a thing of the past once the DGCA steps in. It could even frame a new tariff structure."

When air taxi operations were started in India, it was considered necessary for them to fly to destinations hitherto unconnected, such as the north-east. The experience over the past two years shows this has not happened. Instead, most private airlines have concentrated on the trunk routes.

Says a government official, "One major reason why IA suffers losses is because of its social obligations. It is made to necessarily connect destination such as Aurangabad or Imphal, for which there are hardly 10 passengers in a 120-seater aircraft. If it were not governed by any of these obligations, even IA could refuse to fly to such sectors, concentrate on just the trunk routes and make profits."

Officials do not rule out a scenario in which even the private airlines would be forced to fly uneconomical routes. The DGCA is expected to don the policeman's helmet to restrict traffic on many trunk routes and insist that private airlines operate on shorter and non-lucrative routes.

While expansion and niche marketing could help the private airlines, a major block on which many would stumble and fall is operation on uneconomic routes.

Another problem that will soon crop up is that of more players jostling for the already insufficient infrastructure. Government officials, however, feel it is foolish to create infrastructure before expanding.

Says Mr. Damania, "We will now get the same facilities as IA at Indian airports. Space constraints at airports are a major problem. At Bombay, for example, IA continues to occupy space at the old terminal, even though the new terminal is under-utilised. And the private airlines are forced to operate from a cramped end of the old terminal."

Hiring of pilots is also a contentious issue. According to sources, the Civil Aviation Ministry may examine the legality of pilots requiring a no-objection certificate (NOC) from the managements of IA, IA, Vayudoot and Pawan Hans before they can join a private airline.

The measure was introduced last year by the DGCA to check the exodus of pilots from IA to the private airlines. Last year alone, over 120 IA pilots quit to join private airlines, which offered them better salaries.

Report

Earlier, the Standing Parliamentary Committee on Transport and Tourism had criticised the Government's confused and indecisive policy on aviation and demanded a "clear-cut aviation policy without further delay" by defining the status of national and private air carriers.

In its second report on 'Governmental Policy on Private Air Taxi Operations,' which was tabled in Parliament by Committee Chairman Pramod Mahajan, the panel said neither had Indian Airlines been allowed to retain its monopoly status nor was it thrown open to competition.

The committee also asked the centre to define the role and status of the government and the DGCA and the national and private air carriers. "The private taxi operators are neither allowed to grow freely nor are they asked to shut immediately," the report said.

The committee has noted that section 18 of the Air Corporation Act (ACA) 1953 confers monopoly right of operation of scheduled air-transport services on AI and IA and their associates, whereas a suo-moto statement made by the minister in April 1990 gives the impression that it permits unrestricted operations of air taxi operators.

As a result, a number of private companies came forward to share the aviation industry. Though in legal terms these air-taxi operators are operating non-scheduled flights, for all practical purposes they are operating as regular private airlines.

The second report deals with the government's policy on private air taxi operation and matters connected therewith.

Stating that private air taxi operators were constantly complaining about step-motherly treatment, from the denial of permission to the publishing of time-tables, space problems and daily overdose of guidelines, the committee said the ACA should be repealed in the current session of Parliament.

"Such a confused and indecisive policy will prove to be disastrous for the entire aviation industry, and therefore, the Act should be repealed in the monsoon session of Parliament" the report said.

Recommendations

The committee also recommended the chalking out of a clear-cut aviation policy without further delay, defining the role and status of the government and the Director General of Civil aviation, national and private air carriers and enacting new law, if necessary.

The report took serious note of the fact that even partial privatisation of airlines would create problems for implementing the reservation policy for SC/ST and other backwards, as under the present laws this policy was not applicable to the private sector.

Therefore, it asked the government to take the initiative in formulating a policy and, if necessary, enacting a law by which the reservation policy would remain unaffected even after the privatisation, partially or fully.

With the profit generated on trunk routes, the report pointed out that IA continued with its operation in the loss-making routes (areas like Bihar and UP) and very loss-making routes (north eastern states) thereby, discharging its social obligation towards the nation.

Although the present share of air taxi operators in the country was only 20 per cent of the total air traffic, but as their operation was mainly restricted to the trunk routes, their actual share of passenger traffic on these routes was between 45 per cent and 56 per cent.

The committee, therefore, was of the opinion that the government should enact a law or evolve a regulatory system to check this trend of operation by the private air taxi operators on the profit-making trunk routes.

In view of the problem plaguing the aviation industry, the report recommended that a committee, consisting of representatives of Indian Airlines, private air taxi operators and members of Parliament, be set up by the government and be asked to go into the various aspects of the problem in the aviation sector and submit its report soon.

Passenger Traffic

Anyone aiming for the sky could fall flat on the ground, and none more so than the airline companies in India. For there are more empty seats in aircraft today than there were a few years ago. Year after year, projections of passenger traffic growth have been belied, but airlines continue creating more capacity in the hope that more passengers will need to be accommodated.

During 1993-94, total daily domestic traffic was projected to be around 30,000 passengers. But official sources reveal that both Indian Airlines and the air taxis carried only an average of 27,000 passengers per day.

There are various estimates of traffic growth for the next five years, ranging from seven per cent to 12 per cent. Some private airlines, such as East West, are bullish about future prospects. Says Mr. Kapil Kaul of East West, "We are looking at a market that is expected to reach the 40 million mark by the end of the decade."

But experience shows the market reached saturation point after recording an average 10 per cent growth between 1982 and 1988. In fact the market has recorded a negative growth in the last four to five years, except during 1991-92. The average growth in passengers per day between 1990 to 1993 has been a dismal 1.5 per cent, according to a Confederation of Indian Industry background paper.

According to another estimate, the present domestic carrier fleet has 90 aircraft. In 1994-95, traffic is expected to grow by eight per cent to 32,400 passengers per day. This would require only 75 aircraft.

In a market that has remained stagnant so far, the air taxis have cut into Indian Airlines' share. During 1992, IA's share of the domestic traffic was 95 per cent and that of the air taxis, five per cent. But in 1993, till December, its share had dipped to 7.5 per cent while that of the air taxis had risen to 25 per cent.

After the repeal of the Air Corporations Act, IA appears set to regain it lost market. The process has already begun with the national carrier improving its service in an effort to refurbish its image. The number of passengers carried by IA has already started increasing—from 0.575 million in September 1993 to 0.730 million in December.

The competition to grab passengers is certainly hotting up. But will history repeat itself with the repeal of the Act? Civil aviation secretary S. Kanungo has already presented the worst-case scenario before the Pramod Mahajan Committee: "The traffic is not growing as it should. The capacity has increased considerably. The entire industry may become sick, including private airlines. Our objective should be to see that in our desire to liberalise, we do not repeat the same mistake we did prior to 1953. There were 10 private operators then and the entire industry became sick because of internecine problems."

If the market does not grow enough to make room for all the players, a price war could ensue, which, in a capital-intensive industry like aviation, could lead to the collapse of the entire industry.

"Now that a number of people have come into the air taxi business... there is indication of some of them getting hurt, not to speak of the damage already done to the public sector airline. Some element of purposeful regulation may become necessary," Mr. Kanungo told the Committee.

Fares

The Air Taxi Operators' Committee has decided on a uniform fare pricing strategy ending the undercutting of fares that had started among them. All the air taxis would operate on a uniform fare structure from March 31.

The decision was taken after the entry of Sahara India into the association, which earlier had East West Airlines, Jet Airways, Damania Airways and Modiluft as its members. The association is now planning to open its membership to other smaller non-jet air taxi operators.

Addressing the press on the consequences of the repeal of the Air Corporations Act, the ATOs demanded that the 15 per cent Inland Air Tariff (IATT) being levied on them be abolished.

Complaining about the display in A T E prices, Modiluft Director S.K. Modi said they were being made to pay double the price of the fuel and compared to foreign airlines.

Suggestions

The PHD Chamber of Commerce and Industry has suggested a 10-point strategy for the development and growth of the nascent private airline industry.

In a note submitted to Tourism and Civil Aviation Minister Ghulam Navi Azad, Chamber's Tourism, Civil Aviation Transport and Communication Committee Chairman Vidhyanidi Dalmia has envisaged a new autonomous, self-reliant, profit-making entity, committed to provision of services on an efficient and commercial basis.

He said airports should attempt to promote their services in order to earn more revenue. Rather than providing services as a grudging favour, airports should attempt to obtain more business for themselves.

The Chamber has stated that ground handling services such as ramps, coaches, tractors and trolleys be provided by Indian Airline at various airports for the use of private airlines. This would bring additional revenue to IA and ensure optimum utilisation of assets. It would also avoid unnecessary expenditure on and duplication of such assets and problems associated with storage of equipment at airports, particularly the smaller ones. Air India is already extending similar facilities to foreign carriers.

All domestic carriers, including IA, pay for aviation turbine fuel at rates more than double international rates. Reduction in the rates of duties on ATF, both Central and State, would lead to lower operational costs. This, is turn, would lead to lower fares and travel costs.

Mr. Dalmia said the Inland Air Travel Tax (IATT), at 15 per cent, was excessive. This tax led to higher fares for the domestic traveller and was tax on domestic tourism. Removal/significant reduction in the tax would lead to market expansion and encourage domestic tourism. Air travel was no longer a luxury and the tax should no longer be viewed as a socialistic measure designed to tax the affluent sections of the population.

Interline agreements should be signed by IA with the private carriers. For this purpose, the Government should encourage IA to participate in the setting up of a domestic clearing house to introduce interline ticketing. This would be a pro-consumer measure and provide great assistance to the travelling public. Ultimately, the aim should be permitted to provide common services and flight information systems among all carriers.

A thorough review of IA cancellation rules is overdue. The lead by IA in this regard would provide the ground work for a full review by all airlines. It was necessary to eliminate outdated regulations and unnecessary charges in this regard.

The private carriers should be allowed to undertake international charter, flights, NRIs should be percharter flights. NRIs should be permitted to travel on international charter flights with the condition that payment be made in convertible foreign exchange.

Fares should not be regulated or mandated in any way. Regulation would eliminate competion and act to the detriment of the travelling public. Carriers should be allowed the freedom to set fares according to the rules of the market place.

Air India

Indian Airlines and Air India will come out with public issues in one year's time after enlarging their capital base, consequent to the ordinance repealing the Air Corporations Act.

As a first step, the present capital from the Government of India in the two corporations is being converted into share capital. The Government would retain a majority share in IA and AI, while the public would be offered the rest. The size of the issue and the share to be retained by the government were yet to be worked out.

A Civil Aviation Ministry official said employees of the two companies would get preference in the share allotment.

A section of employees has expressed fears that the government planned to disinvest in IA and AI. But they should not have any worries on this score as the controlling interest would rest with the government and the public issue would only be to mop up additional capital. The government's capital in AI and IA stands at Rs. 153.84 crore and Rs. 105 crore respectively.

The official said while the capital had remained more or less the same over the past decade, the turnover had increased ten-fold.

A reassessment of capital from the government would have to be made before deciding on capital restructuring.

The official said new norms would be set for air taxis desirous of becoming scheduled airlines. The norms would concern size of fleet, destinations and other parameters like ground facilities, safety features and crew. The guidelines would be formulated by the DGCA.

The air taxis would have to make a fresh application to be converted into airlines and would be evaluated against the new guidelines. The official said the economic provisions of the Aircraft Act of 1934 would be applied to the private airlines and to the new public companies of IA and AI on matters concerning fleet size, safety features and aircraft maintenance.

East West Airlines

The two-year-old East West Airlines is the forerunner among air taxi operators. From a solitary Boeing 737 aircraft serving three stations with a passenger capacity of 11,250 a month, operations have now extended to a fleet strength of 11 aircraft—8 Boeing 737-200s and 3 Fokkers. The airlines undertakes 68 flights every day to 28 destinations all over India. It plans to expand further. The expansion plans include induction of 10 more aircraft by the end of the current year. It has also plans to come out with a Rs. 100-crore public issue to meet the expansion costs. As an extension, it has already started carrying cargo under East West Cargo. East West has an interline agreement with foreign airlines to act as alink carrier. The company also plans to go global and operate on international routes, particularly West Asia and South-east Asia. It has a tie-up with Aerlingus, Ireland's national carrier, for maintenance and other associated technical requirements.

Damania Airways

Among the private air taxis in the Indian skies, Damania Airways Ltd. has tried to project itself as a 'Swissair' among Indian air-taxis. Targetted at the up-market service-oriented passenger, Damania's marketing line talks about international service in India and says 'except the world of us.' The company is part of the Damania group, whose other company is Agritech Hatcheries. Damania is currently operating with three Boeing 737-200 aircraft, leased from Air Portugal (TAP) and one 12-seater Beechcraft. The latter has been leased to meet the DGCA's requirement of flying to sectors less than 900 km. The Beechcraft operates exclusively on the Bombay-Pune-Bombay sector. Damania's routes are slightly unconventional being the only private operator not flying to Delhi but operating on the Bombay-Calcutta sector. The air-taxi has a tie-up heavy maintenance and supply of spares with Singapore Aerospace. It is planning to increase its fleet to 10 aircraft.

Jet Airways

Jet Airways, owned by Mr. Naresh Goyal, a non-resident Indian, has started flights to and from Bombay linking Ahmedabad, Goa, Cochin, Calicut, Mangalore, Bangalore, Hyderabad, Madras, Coimbatore and Delhi. The airlines has taken four new aircraft—Boeing 737-300-on lease from Ansett Worldwide Aviations, Australia. Ansett will also train its crew, both flight as well as maintenance. The company has plans to acquire four more aircraft in 1994 and another eight by 1995. The company has a very good marketing set-up. Jet Airways is associated with Jet Air, which is the GSA for 12 international airlines and has been in the business since 1974.

Modiluft

Modiluft is the product of a technical partnership between the German carrier Lufthansa and MG Express, a company in the Modi Group, headed by Mr. S.K. Modi. Under the deal, Modiluft will get engineering know-how and maintenance support, repaires and components from the German national carrier.

The company obviously intends making full use of its Lufthansa tie-up and as an extension, has signed an inter-line agreement to ensure regular passenger flow to ModiLuft. This would help passengers to organise their air tickets by ModiLuft to any part of the world, for inbound and outbond flights.

The company has already got its marketing set-up well organised. Modiluft, which operates 737-200s, has three planes now, but plans to increases its fleet to 14 by the year end. According to company sources. ModiLuft will fly a blend of trunk routes, linking Delhi with Bombay, Calcutta and Bangalore and short-haul flights to other business and tourist destinations.

Sahara Airlines

Sahara Airlines, which has at present Boeing 737s, is planning to expand in a big way. Unlike other airlines, the company plans to buy aircraft, instead of wet leasing them. The Lucknow-based airline is buying two more smaller aircraft from the U.S. The company is planning to diversify its services from four metros and is starting services to Guwahati in the North Eastern Sector.

The company is planning to tie up with Delta Airlines of the United States. Company sources said that under the tie up with Delta, passengers coming from abroad by Delta will be flown to their destinations by Sahara Airlines.

TABLE 4.1

Traffic Forecast (Passengers Per Day)

1993-94	*30,000 Growth @ 5%*	*8%*	*10%*	*12%*
1993-94	31,500	32,400	33,000	33,600
1999-2000	40,203	47,606	53,147	59,215
2004-2005	51,310	69,949	85,594	1,04,356
2009-2010	65,486	1,02,778	1,37,349	1,83,912

TABLE 4.2

AI and IA Facts

	AIR INDIA		
1.	Revenue	:	1992-93 Rs. 2,583 crore; April-Dec. 1993 Rs. 2,000 crore
2.	Equity	:	Rs. 79.47 crore
3.	Reserve and Surplus	:	Rs. 1,000 crore
4.	Net worth	:	Rs. 1,074.36 crore
5.	Passenger load factor	:	1992-93 64.9 pc; April-Dec 1993 60.9 pc.
6.	Loans	:	$ 700 million
7.	Employees per aircrafts	:	700
8.	Net Profit	:	1992-93 Rs. 333 crore
9.	Number of Employees	:	1,75,000
10.	Number of Aircraft	:	23
	INDIAN AIRLINES		
1.	Revenue	:	1991-92 Rs. 1,487 crore 1992-93 Rs. 1,578 crore
2.	Equity	:	Rs. 55 crore
3.	Net worth	:	Rs. 344 crore
4.	Passenger load factor	:	1991-92 73.4 per cent 1992-93 73.6 per cent
5.	Fixed Assets (Net)	:	Rs. 2,324 crore
6.	Employees per craft	:	420
7.	Loss	:	1991-92 Rs. 198 crore 1993-93 Rs. 195 crore
8.	No. of employees	:	22,279
9.	Number of Aircraft	:	55

GUIDELINES FOR AIR TAXI OPERATORS

Following is the text of the Government press note issued on March 1, 1994.

Government have notified March 1, 1994 as the appointed day for restructuring of Air India and Indian Airlines and repeal of the Air Corporations Act, 1953, in pursuance of the Air Corporations (Transfer of Undertakings and Repeal) Ordinance, 1994.

Accordingly, assets, liabilities and functions of Air India and Indian Airlines have been vested in two public limited companies, namely, Air India Ltd. and Indian Airlines Ltd. respectively. Government have also constituted the Boards of Directors of the two public limited companies.

While Air India, Indian Airlines and Vayudoot will continue to provide scheduled air transport services, air taxi operators and others fulfilling the prescribed criteria, can also apply for permission to operate such air services within the country. No one can operate any scheduled air transport service except with permission specifically granted for the purpose.

Government have issued guidelines and eligibility criteria, on the basis of which applications for permission to operate scheduled air services within the country can be considered by the Director General of Civil Aviation to accord permission. The guidelines are detailed subsequently.

Keeping in view the need for orderly development and exercise of self-discipline, members of the air transport industry have agreed to adopt a code of conduct under which:

(i) No operator will employ any pilot or aircraft maintenance engineer already in the employment of another operator, without obtaining a "No Objection Certificate" from that employer.

(ii) The operators will participate in the development of facilities for training of flight crew and aircraft maintenance personnel. Towards this end, they will make contribution to national institutions, like Indira Gandhi Rashtriya Uran Akademy, on the basis of mutually agreed norms.

(iii) The operators' will set up a forum for mutual consultation to promote fair practices in the industry and prevent adoption of means that are unethical or otherwise injurious to common good.

Minimum Requirements to be Met by an Operator of Scheduled Air Transport Service

1. A fleet of minimum three aircraft registered in India. All-up-weight of aircraft more than 5,700 kgs. each.
2. Not less than Rs. 15 crores subscribed equity capital in respect of operators having aircraft of all-up-weight exceeding 40,000 kgs. and not less than Rs. 5 crores for operators having aircraft of all-up-weight not exceeding 40,000

kgs.

3. Not less than three sets of flight crew and cabin crew per aircraft.
4. An approved maintenance organisation and facilities to carry out maintenance of a aircraft upto 500 hours inspection or Check 'B' for Boeing 737 aircraft.
5. Approved manuals for operations, training and equality control cum-maintenance.
6. Cells for pre-flight medical examination of crew, flight planning and despatch, realiability analysis of aircraft components systems, defect investigations, compliance of service bulletins and modifications and records of major components.
7. Security programme approved by Bureau Civil Aviation Security and trained security personnel at all operating stations.
8. Those operating scheduled air transport service on any route specified in the annex, under Category-I, will be required to provide a minimum of scheduled service in Category-II and Category-III sectors as indicated in the annex. For rendering the prescribed minimum service on routes in Categories-II and III, an operator may have option to provide the service either by aircraft in his fleet or in another operator's fleet on mutually agreed terms. In the latter case, the arrangement should have prior approval of DGCA.
9. Operators shall abide by any further conditions which DGCA may consider necessary for monitoring of scheduled a transport service and operation of safe and reliable services.
10. Operators who desire to obtain permission to operate scheduled air transport service may apply to DGCA complying with the provisions of Schedule XI of the aircraft Rules, 1937, and the above requirements.

Provision of Service in Different Categories of Routes Annex

Category-I

Routes connecting directly

Bombay	—	Bangalore
Bombay	—	Calcutta
Bombay	—	Delhi
Bombay	—	Hyderabad
Bombay	—	Madras
Bombay	—	Trivandrum
Calcutta	—	Delhi
Calcutta	—	Bangalore
Calcutta	—	Madras
Delhi	—	Bangalore

Delhi — Hyderabad

Delhi — Madras

Category-II

Routes connecting stations in North-Eastern region, Jammu and Kashmir, Andaman and Nicobar and Lakshadweep.

Category-III

Routes other than those in Category-I and Category-II.

Any one who operates scheduled air transport service on one or more the routes under Category-I, shall be required to period such service in Categories-II and III as indicated below:

The operator will deploy on routes in Category-II at least 10 per cent of the capacity he deploys on routes in Category-I and of the capacity thus required to be deployed on services or segments thereof operated exclusively within the North-Eastern region, Jammu and Kashmir, Andaman and Nicobar and Lakshadweep.

The operator will deployed on routes in Category-III, at least 50 per cent of the capacity he deployes on routes in Category-I.

Note 1: A service operated on a Category-I routes as a part of international air service will not be reckoned for the above purpose.

Note 2: Capacity deployed will be reckoned in Available Seat Kilometres (ASKM).

Note 3: On multiple sector routes like Delhi-Calcutta-Guwahati-Imphal, the capacity provided on Delhi-Calcutta sector will count towards Category-I, that provided on Calcutta Guwahati sector will count towards Category-II and the capacity on Guwahati-Imphal sector will count towards service exclusively within Category-II.

New Delhi Phalguna 10, 1915/March 1, 1994

Ministry of Civil Aviation (Director General of Civil Aviation).

2. GARMENT EXPORT INDUSTRY

In the recent past, textiles have emerged as the single largest group of export products, accounting for 28 per cent, of the total exports. And in the textiles sector, garments account for 15 per cent of India's entire exports, second only to gems and jewellery.

The apparel industry has the highest growth rate among all the industries — 36.4 per cent. No less significant is the employment it provides — 2.5 million jobs in some 50,000 small and tiny-scale garment industrial units, according to recent estimates. These units are scattered all over the country, but there are large clusters in and around

Delhi with an output of 3000 million pieces per annum. The garment industry's turnover is a staggering Rs. 20,000 crore, which is remarkable considering it had its birth only in the 1970s.

The garment industry, including hosiery units, is largely export- oriented with 18,000 of the 50,000 units accounting for the bulk of the exports. The industry is competing in the world market against several countries, notably Korea, Taiwan, China, Hong Kong and Pakistan. Although garments are subject to import quota restrictions under the Multi Fibre Agreement (MFA) in a large number of countries in Europe and North America, the industry's potential is very great. In India's case, the potential has been only marginally exploited, with its share in world apparel being only two per cent.

1993 witnessed the crossing of yet another milestone. Exports of readymade garments upto November 1993 amounted to $ 3195 million (Rs. 9807 crore) — a jump of more than 20 per cent in value terms, compared to the performance during the same period of 1992.

The expansion of world markets, the liberalised and progressive policies of the Government, aggressive export promotion strategies adopted by the Apparel Export Promotion Council (AEPC) and the inherent initiative and drive of the garment exporters have all contributed to this spectacular export performance.

However, India's share in world garment trade is only 2 per cent. The world textiles and clothing trade is predicted to grow by around 2.8 per cent annually upto the year 2002 in volume terms. India would be able to take the lion's share if it countinued to grow at rates higher than the overall world trade growth rate.

One of the weakest links in the Indian garment industry today is processing. South Korea, for example, does wonders with the same Indian fabric with its superior printing, dyeing and processing technology.

However, it is encouraging to note that joint ventures between some Indian processing units and firms of international repute are on the anvil. The Apparel Export Promotion Council (AEPC) has also been trying to attract joint ventures in this sector with the help of UNIDO and the Government of India under the Integrated Investment Development Programme.

Industry

India's garment industry is sustained mainly by cottage industries located around textile centres. There are over 50,000 units spread all over the country with an average of 15 to 20 machines under a single roof. The main reason for the growth of this industry is its labour-orientation. The abundant availability of unskilled and semi-skilled labour in India has worked to its advantage.

Rising labour costs, have brought South Korea's share in global exports down from 10 per cent in 1987 to 7 per cent in 1990 and Taiwan's from 6 per cent to 3 per cent. The share of other countries like Hong Kong and Japan is also shifting towards India, Bangladesh and China.

Indian exports mainly consist of fashion garments and casual articles at the bottom end of the market. Nearly 70 per cent of Indian exports consist of five types of garments — ladies blouses, dresses and skirts and mens shirts, trousers and shorts. The bulk of the world clothing trade consists of daily use shirts, overalls and suits at the upper end of the market, in which India's share is very low. Most of the units in this sector are small-scale industries (SSI), which operate with obsolete machinery. The SSI limit of Rs. 75 lakh for this industry prohibits the setting up of large capacities within the garments industry and modernisation of the existing set-up. Even a small country like Bangladesh has 60 units, each having more than 500 machines under one roof, whereas in India there are only about a dozen such units.

The biggest advantage of the Indian readymade garments industry is that all the raw material required is available locally. India is a major cotton producing country. It also manufactures all types of man-made fibres like polyester, viscose, nylon and acrylic. Except China, no other Asian country has this advantage. The share of cotton fabric-based garments in the export basket is 64 per cent, while that of synthetic-based garments in 34 per cent. But on the other side, the price of synthetic textiles in India is very high. Although these are allowed to be imported for export purposes, the procedures are cumbersome. Non-availability of quality fabrics is one of the major hurdles which Indian industry faces today.

The readymade garments business being labour-oriented, it suits the small, centralised ownership type of management. Capital requirements too are low, which also suits Indian conditions. The passing on of skills from rather to son helps in generating skilled manpower without investing in training institutes. But the drawback of this factor is that it can be helpful only so far as Indian industry caters to the bottom end of the garments market. To target the higher end of the scale, a professional approach to marketing, distribution and fashion designing is required.

The Government has supported the development of this industry for a long time and it is included in the list of thrust sectors. Higher floor prices of $ 5.9 per piece fixed by the Government has also helped generate more sales, as the number of pieces to be exported are limited due to quota restrictions.

Abolition of the Multi Fibre Agreement could provide a boost to exports, as quotas are being utilised almost 100 per cent. Also, quota countries import about 70 per cent of the total exports. Exports to non-quota countries have increased from Rs. 288 crore in 1986 to Rs. 3,300 crore in 1992.

What is necessary is a complete overhaul in the product range which at present remains skewed. Exports of childrens garments and sports wear, which comprise the bulk of the international cloth trade, is relatively very low at present. This reflects the lack of availability of quality, knitted fabrics, resulting in a poor production base in wool and acrylic.

Indian exporters could attempt to develop indigenous brands in the international markets to maximise export earnings. The average garment exported from India undergoes a lot of changes in the form of sophisticated accessories and brands before it hits the retail market. This results in a price realisation atleast 40 per cent lower than the final consumer price.

The government has liberalised imports of many items, but those required for the garment industry are still under control or face heavy import duties. For example, a shirt which fetches four dollars could very well fetch another dollar if proper trimmings worth barely 20 cents were imported and used.

Fairs

Trade fairs in recent years have started to play a major role in boosting exports and are the right platforms for promoting and creating awareness about Indian garments. Various organisations are involved in promoting Indian garments.

The Indian Trade Promotion Organisation (ITPO) organises exclusive garment fashion accessories fairs. ITPO organised the 13th India and Fashion Accessories Fair in Osaka, Japan in 1992. AEPC too organises many trade fairs throughout the world. In India, AEPC holds garment fairs twice a year in New Delhi — a winter fair in January and a summer one in August.

Policy Measures

The government has realised the importance of the industry to the national economy and taken suitable policy measures from time to time. The most important of these initiatives is the regulation of quotas among the exporting units. The latest of this policy measure was only lately announced by the Government for a period of three years, 1994-96. To encourage wider capital base for modernisation, the investment limit for readymade garments units in the small-scale sector has been raised from 25 lakh to Rs. three crore. A liberal export-import policy already allows free access to essential inputs in order to meet the requirements of the ever-changing fashion industry Manpower development is another area the government has contributed to for the development of the industry, setting up the National Institute of Fashion Technology (NIFT). International agencies, like UNDP and the EEC, have assisted NIFT in serving the Indian garment industry.

The Garment Export Entitlement (quota) Distribution Policy announced periodically principally aims at maximising export earnings. The quota policy announced last September is no exception though this year its formulation was influenced by the recommendations of the Task Force appointed by the Textile Ministry. The findings of this Task force itself were no less shaped by the views of the garment industry, according to the government. Firstly, the number of categories for entitlement has been reduced to three. The first come first served (FCFS) category has been, in effect, abolished in that exporters in this category will only be allotted surrendered quotas. The FCFS category for new exporters has been sharply decreased. At one time, 80 per cent of the quota allotment comprised FCFS.

Quota Policy

Large exporters account for 60 per cent of the Past Performance Entitlement (PPE) and under the new policy this is the level that has been maintained for them, with 10 per cent added for high value entitlement. This is a big gain for a dozen major exporters who make the bulk of export garments. This is one aspect of the new policy that has come in for sharp criticism from the industry. The PPE is seen by exporters as a privilege specially conferred on a few and amounts to segmentation which is unfortunate. The new policy is also seen not to take into consideration non-quota entitlements which also increase exports. A large number of exporters, therefore, favour that at least 10 per cent of the annual levels be allotted for the FCFS system so as to help small exporters and keep the quota prices within reasonable limits.

Among the quotas abolished is the two per cent entitlement which is now available for the public sector. The non-quota entitlement (NQE) has been reduced from 18 per cent. But the two per cent allocation being made for handloom garments has been retained keeping in view the economic and social necessities. Quotas under NQE are distributed based on the exporters in the markets other than MFA restraints. A major consideration for changes in the policy has been the necessity to realise maximum unit value for quota items, simplification of procedures and greater transparency in the allotment of quotas. A twin objective is sought to be balanced of liberalisation of some restrictive provisions and tightening, at the same time, of the monitoring of quota utilisation and prevention of quota frauds.

While the quota entitlement policy will be periodically changed to suit the requirements of the industry, there are critical areas awaiting policy decisions. Around 80 per cent of exports are still accounted for by countries which restrain exports to them. There has to be a meaningful shirt to new markets, particularly outside the quota regime. World trade in textiles and clothing will undergo changes with the integration of the textile sector with the General Agreement on Tariffs and Trade (GATT) as envisaged in the Uruguay Round. Consequently, there will be no quotas and exporting countries will have to compete. The Indian industry too will have to face competition.

Exports

Not many sectors can claim the envious position attained by the garment export industry. The industry has already exceeded the export target for 1992-93 and is getting geared up to improve its performance in 1993-94.

In the first six months of 1993-94, 410 million pieces, valued at $ 1638 million were exported — up by the 18 per cent in terms of volume and 21 per cent in value terms — over the corresponding half of the previous year. Normally, the second half (October-

March) is considered the best for the garment trade. Thus, actual exports should easily surpass the revised target of $ 3510 million (previous target $ 3250 million). For the near future at least, with global consumer preference having tilted in favour of cotton, the outlook seems bright. By the end of 2000 A.D., readymade garment exports are expected to fetch India $ 10,000 million.

A strong base in cotton combined with low labour costs is the fundamental reason why garment exports are booming today. From a mere $ 2060 million in 1989-90, exports have jumped to $2512 million in 1991-92. In 1992-93, as against a target of $ 2707 million, actual exports totalled $ 3052 million, registering a growth rate of 22 per cent over the previous year. Throughout the entire decade of the 1980s, the surge in garment exports was impressive. Since 1983-84, aggregate exports have invariably crossed targets, receiving a slight setback only in 1991-92 (attributed to the recession in the major economies of Western Europe and the US).

Growth

At a growth rate averaging 20 to 25 per cent in the past two decades the readymade garments sector remains the fastest growing segment of the textile industry. In 1991-92, it accounted for almost half the aggregate textile exports. In the overall export basket, the trend has been equally buoyant. In 1980-81, garment exports formed 8.4 per cent of India's exports and by 1985-86, the percentage share rose to 10 per cent and in 1991-92, it rose further to 15 per cent. With very little import content, garment exports rank high in value addition and are perhaps the largest of the country's manufactured exports.

What is impressive about this performance is that most of the contribution has been from the small and medium scale units which have an investment in the range of about Rs. 25 — Rs. 50 lakh. They have succeeded in going global in spite of international trade barriers and quantitative restrictions, fully utilising the quotas allotted to them. An analysis of the market profile reveals that a bulk of the exports are to quota countries — US and EEC. The major non-quota countries are UAE, Japan, Switzerland, former Soviet Union, Sweden, Australia and Hungary. Besides this, the other restricted countries are Norway, Finland and east European countries.

Trends

In 1992-93, EEC countries accounted for 44 per cent of exports followed by the US 28 per cent, non-quota countries 23 per cent and other restricted countries five per cent. The percentage share in the previous year was EEC 41, the US 26, non-quota countries 27 and other restricted countries five. However in terms of value, the highest per unit price realisation was from the US $ 5.3 (up from $ 4.7) and EEC $ 4.3 (previous year 3.5). Per unit value from other restricted countries declined from $ 3.8 to $ 3.5 while the realisation from non-quota countries remained constant at $ 2.8.

In terms of products exported, the bulk of exports is concentrated in a few items like shifts, blouses, T-shirts, pullovers and other knitted items. The main fibre used is cotton followed by synthetic and very little in woollen. In 1992-93, the fibre-composition of export revealed that cotton constituted 74 per cent, synthetics 25 per cent and woollens only 1.6 per cent. During, 1991-92 the percentage share of the fibres was cotton — 70, synthetics — 30 and woollen — 0.4. In terms of value added there is a sharp differential between the per unit price of woollen garments and others. As against $ 8.2 for a woollen garment, a cotton item fetches $ 3.3.

Design

Design and quality are significant determinants of unit value in the garments industry and more so in exports. Growth in this industry has taken place mainly through increase in the quantity of exports, with little diversification of the product mix. There is hardly any design element in Indian garment exports. About 85 per cent of exports are 'basic' garments in the $ 10 to $ 30 range which have a steady demand in foreign markets. As regards quality, there has been considerable improvement in recent years, particularly in the making-up stage, and export rejects are about 10 per cent for the majority of exporters. A few facts about the Indian garment industry would help explain the present structure of exports and the neglect of quality and fashion aspects in it.

Unorganised Production

The haphazard growth of the industry has resulted in a highly skewed production structure, with a preponderance of small individual units doing job works, medium-sized factory-based manufacturers with some semblance of organisation, a small but significant (in terms of market share) group of manufacturer- exporters and finally large export houses or merchant exporters, who source their merchandise from the smaller manufacturers, availing of the export entitlement benefits themselves.

As a result, the production process is broken up over a largely unorganised subcontracting system. The smaller units carry out specific functions and invest in light machinery, thus distributing capital costs. Payment on piece-rate basis ensures low labour costs for the entrepreneur, who also has the advantage of hiring labour according to need. The other side of this is that the exporter cannot afford to diversify the product base into newer types of garments and has to stick to a fairly standard mix of garments which will even out differences in time, labour, amount and type of fabric (which affect cost of production) and which he could rely upon the small manufacturers to deliver with ease.

The scattered production structure gives the exporters very little leverage for quality control; each unit may produce articles of the required specification, but when their output is pooled together to make up one bulk order, there may be slight variations in size or kind of finish provided.

Skill Variation

India, unlike China, Japan and the western countries, lacks integrated production units. Processing the fabrics (dyeing and printing), designing, cutting, stitching, finishing and packaging are done with varying levels of skill and a lack of quality consciousness at any of these stages affects the final output.

Exporters sourcing their orders from various parts of the country complain of considerable regional differences as well. South India has shown promising potential for higher value exports. Manufacturing units in Madras and Bangalore have better technology assembly line production and a female-dominated, skilled workforce that facilitates meeting international standards.

Raw Material Base

India has a traditional advantage in cotton yarn and naturally, the bulk of its exports are cotton leisure wear. But India does not use the high quality long staple cotton which gives better strength of colour and reduces colour variation. Another problem is that 70 to 80 per cent of the fabrics are from powerlooms. While this turns out cheaper it also means lower quality of fabrics and therefore of the garment, so it commands lower prices in the world markets. Fashion garments require special fabrics which are costly to produce or have to be imported.

Technology and Marketing

Indian exporters are not strong on marketing techniques, a professional attitude towards business is lacking and real time merchandising is not possible given the scattered production structure and uncertain nature of transport and shipping facilities.

Technology for fabric processing and machines for standardised cutting and stitching in India are way behind those of its competitors. Reservation of the readymade garments sector has kept out the big manufacturers, and the small units engaged in production have no incentive to reinvest their earnings for technology upgradation or to train their workers in the latest methods of making-up garments. Under these conditions it is easier to produce and export unstructured readymades than style-specific fashionwear. It also explains why Indian exports lag behind in quality.

Polarisation

The assured demand in the home market, with emphasis on more variety at reasonable prices, has led to a manufacturing sector which has so far scant regard for quality. Standard sizes, colour fastness and strength of fabric, thread and components like buttons and zips are often overlooked to cut costs.

The export market, in contrast, is largely a buyer's market. Here even a minor difference in cost or quality can turn the buyer towards an exporter who gives him higher value for money.

Fortunately, the two markets are segmented. Design plays a more important role in the home market, where it is easier to cater to the individualistic choices of the upper income groups as custom-made garments can be produced at low cost and slow moving fashion trends make it profitable to produce high priced fashion garments in larger quantities. The fluctuating fashion trends abroad, seasionality element in foreign demand for garments and lack of indigenous infrastructure for design have made export of fashion garments a risk proposition for Indian exporters. At present, these form only 15 per cent of the total.

Boosting fashion exports for the upper segment is commendable, because that is where the real profits lie. But doing this at the risk of neglecting exports of basic garments, for which India's production structure is ideally suited, is clearly impractical, feel the majority of exporters. It is best left to the select few who have ventured into fashion exports with some success. Instead, enhanced quality and diversification of the product mix within the basic garments category would be more rewarding. Availing the 100 per cent EOU facility for fabric processing and making-up garments is one way. Technological upgradation and promoting buyer-awareness for Indian-garments abroad are areas where the government can help. Reduction of customs duty on capital goods to facilitate import of sophisticated machinery for garment manufacture, innovations in the quota policy like 10 per cent reservation for high value entitlements, etc. may encourage exporters to strive for quality improvement and higher unit value realisation.

Financing

Readymade garment exports touched Rs. 8500 crore in 1992, making it the largest single item of India's exports. Export volumes have been growing at the rate of about 20 per cent per annum and with no sign of any levelling off a demand overseas, there seem to be few limits to growth in this sector. Finance, which used to be a constraint till recently, has now ceased to be so, thanks to liberal bank finance being extended to exporters at concessional rates of interest.

During the past one or two years, a number of other facilities have also been made available to exporters. These include grant of finance in dollar terms, both at the pre as well as post-shipment stage, at rates comparable to interest rates abroad, grant of pre-shipment credit without insiting on prior production of the letter of credit/firm order, extension of running account facility for packing credit, permission to retain a portion of export earnings in an exchange earners' foreign currency account, re-discounting of export bills abroad, etc.

According to most garment exporters, the finance is no longer the problem it once was. However, as competition from traditional rivals, China, South Korea and Taiwan hots up, the only way India can possibly improve upon its competitive edge is by ensuring that its products are better than those produced by its competitors. In such a situation, removal of bottlenecks in the system that currently go toward increasing the cost of exports is imperative for improving the overall competitiveness of the industry.

Today, two of the major bottlenecks that hamper the garment export industry in India are directly related to certain characteristics peculiar to the industry. Unlike other industries, there are a large number of sub-suppliers, each engaged in job work. Thus there are dyers, printers, fabricators, cutters and so on.

Since concessional credit is extended by banks on the strength of the relative export order/letter of credit, it is usually the exporter who receives the L/C or firm order who gets the benefit of a lower interest rate. This, despite the fact that the actual manufacture is done by the other agencies.

Regulations

According to current regulations, banks may provide pre-shipment credit to both the manufacturer-exporter as well as the merchant-exporter. The only proviso is that the banker must be sure that supplies made by the indirect exporter go towards execution of the export order and no pre-shipment credit is provided simultaneously to the holder of the letter of credit/export order. However the benefit of concessional credit is not passed on further down the line, to the fabricators or dyers. Not only are bankers hesitant to extend credit to these categories of workers who are mostly in the unorganised sector, but the rulers at present provide only for appointment of credit between merchant-exporters and manufacturer-exporters, leaving out the other participants in the manufacturing process. This obstacle could perhaps be overcome in inland L/Cs are allowed to be operated if favour of these participants on the strength of the original L/C, enabling banks to provide cheap credit.

Again, the bulk of readymade garment exports is subject to quota restrictions. Almost 75 per cent of the total exports from the country goes to quota countries. But for the exporter, the operation of the quota system invariably raises his cost of production. Under the quota system as operated by the Apparel Export Promotion Council all exporters under the 'first come, first served' category are required to make an earnest money deposit of 5 per cent of the fob value with the Council. Similar deposits are also required to be made at the time of seeking extension of the validity period of quotas obtained under the past performance entitlement or the manufacturer-exporters' entitlement. Though exporters may submit bank guarantees in lieu of earnest money deposit, banks invariably insist on margin money for the issue of guarantees, resulting in funds being blocked.

As most garment exporters are small-scale units, immobilisation of even a portion of funds inevitably raises their cost with adverse consequences on the final price of the product. This results in the blocking of their funds, particularly since release of funds is often delayed. Streamlining of the system to ensure early release of guarantees/earnest money deposit is, therefore, essential.

5

Business Environment in Japan: Basic Industries Policies

I

STEEL AND MOTOR CAR INDUSTRIES

The first two case studies concern Japanese industries which are currently international leaders in the products they manufacture—steel and motor cars.[1] The studies document the government policies which helped these industries to develop, through both crisis and expansion. It also demonstrates how, once the ability to compete internationally was achieved, the government's role receded sharply. Particularly interesting is the ability of MITI to apply a precise, light touch to a problem. MITI's policy initiatives generally recognise the varying economic requirements for success in different businesses. Interesting, too, are the conflicts among the ministries and between a particular ministry and the industry. Most conflicts are resolved through an orderly process and are eventually translated into effective action. A few problems—like MITI's attempt to consolidate the motor car industry—remain unsolved.

The Steel Industry

The Japanese steel industry is the world's third largest in tonnage output behind the USSR and the United States. It is, however, the world's most efficient. Several major studies, public and private, over the last few years have indicated that the Japanese are significantly lower cost producers of the normal range of basic carbon steel products than any other major producer. Even the American Iron and Steel Institute has acknowledged that the Japanese have a 15 per cent productivity advantage over U.S. producers.

Steel is traditionally the *sine qua non* of industrial development and military strength. Accordingly, governments have always kept a close watch over their steel industries. Some countries, including many in Europe and the Third World, have fully nationalised their steel industries while others, like the United States, have limited the government role to a careful monitoring of the industry's pricing.

The Japanese government has played a supportive role in its steel industry and has derived a great deal of influence from its actions. Steel in Japan is not government owned, and competition is considerable among major producers. But the results have been very much in the public interest — low cost steel inputs to other manufacturing industries, a major source of foreign exchange, and reasonable viable steelmaking companies.

Japan's policy toward the industry over the last thirty years illustrates the characteristic flexibility and attention to competitive business economics of its industrial policy in general. In the late 1940s, the government identified steel as crucial to Japanese reindustrialisation and took immediate measures to restore prewar production capability. Beginning in the late 1950s and 1960s, steel received special priority as a key feeder industry to shipbuilding, motor cars, domestic appliances, and other capital-intensive industries. By the early 1970s, Japan's steel industry had achieved world dominance and could be considered self-sustaining. Government assistance to the industry therefore virtually disappeared. Today, despite its continued preeminence worldwide, the industry is understood to be entering its declining phase, and MITI is discouraging domestic investment, promoting rationalisation in the industry, and supporting steel investment abroad.

Throughout this evolutionary process, three basic forms of assistance have been at the heart of Japanese policy: financing to build new plants, assistance in procurement of scarce raw materials necessary for growth, and assistance with cash flow during recessions.

Capacity Expansion

Financing. Steel is an extremely capital-intensive industry, with an assets-to-sales ratio exceeding 1.5 to 1. Over time, as the optimum scale of steel plants and of individual mills has risen, the cost of building new greenfield plants has increased enormously. As discussed in Chapter II, U.S. steel companies have not been able to justify the construction of new greenfield plants on a return-on-investment basis, and instead have tended to add capacity and make modernisation investments in a less efficient, roundout fashion. The Japanese pursued a very different course. In a climate of rapid domestic demand growth, companies incurred extremely high debt-to-equity ratios and made the investments needed to build the new greenfield plants.

Immediately after the war the Reconstruction Finance Bank, a government financial institution, provided most of the capital for rehabilitating the industry. The government subsidised the steel price level to help the relatively inefficient industry begin to rebuild its markets. In the early 1950s, MITI developed the first rationalisation plan for the industry: industry growth was to be promoted through both tax incentives and financing assistance.

The tax measures applicable to the steel industry were proposed by a study group within the Ministry of Finance after examination of the tax systems of other nations. Five tax and duty exemptions were enacted in 1951-52:

(1) Import duty exemption on designated steel-making equipment (60 percent of such equipment was imported at the time);
(2) Fifty percent increase in depreciation base allowed on designated equipment;
(3) Tax exemption for reserves meant to cover price changes in inventories and securities;
(4) Tax exemption for revaluation of assets, which effectively increased the depreciation base; and
(5) Tax exemption for additional bad debt reserves.

These measures increased the funds available for reinvestment and, in particular, for investment in optimum scale facilities embodying "state-of-the-art" technology. Between 1951 and 1955, about one quarter of all capital investment originated internally, primarily through these tax exemptions.

The greater part of investment capital—roughly 65 percent—was financed by debt, primarily through government financial institutions, although supplemented by private financial institutions. Loans from the Japan Development Bank and the Long Term Credit Bank (both government owned) and the Industrial Bank of Japan (government influenced) accounted for roughly half of the $95 million in debt incurred by the steel industries during the period. The government encouraged commercial banks to finance steel expansion, and the Ministry of Finance permitted $11 million of foreign exchange loans to the industry.

The first rationalisation plan (1951-1954) doubled Japanese crude steel production from 4.8 to 9.5 million tons. Equally note-worthy was the nature of the government's involvement in this process. MITI avoided the role of direct central planner and concentrated instead on mobilising financial resources and creating financial incentives for growth. Government banks and private financial institutions were persuaded to provide funds to the industry, but final judgments on specific borrowers and amounts were left to the banks, particularly among the commercial banks. The tax measures also helped direct investment appropriately without overt government dictation. The reserve and special depreciation measures favoured growing firms at the expense of stagnant firms, and steered investment toward designated types of equipment.

Between 1955 and 1960 a second rationalisation plan, embodying similar measures, produced another doubling of capacity. This pattern continued throughout the 1960s. Japan's capital/output ratio in steel production (stock of physical capital per ton of steel produced) consistently remained the highest in the world and nearly twice that of the United States during the latter part of the 1960s. In addition, because of the willingness to build greenfield plants, capital could be used more efficiently. Greenfield plants constructed after 1952 produced over 80 percent of Japanese carbon steel production compared to less than 5 percent in the United States.

Throughout the 1960s the role of direct government financing declined, although the government informally encouraged and, in some cases, insured private bank loans to the industry. Since the banks are important stockholders in the companies, they had incentives to continue to lend money. Between 1966 and 1972, the assets of the five largest producers grew at a formidable annual rate of 23 percent, representing a huge amount of capital expenditure. During this critical period, when crude steel production grew from 41 million tons to 100 million tons, the industry sustained a debt-to-equity ratio of almost 12 to 1. By this time, the government did not need to provide much of the funding directly, but it did guarantee much of the lending and in some cases subsidised low interest rates.

Coordination. In addition to assisting in the financing of capacity expansions, the government played a coordinating role in approval of expansion plans. Both government and steelmakers had long recognised that a joint determination of the rate of capacity additions was in both their interests. The impact of steel expansion on the economy, the massive financial requirements, and the difficulties of imbalance in steel demand and supply dictated that the government should influence the rate of growth of capacity. Steelmakers, in turn, were generally willing to cooperate among themselves and with MITI because of the cash flow crises and price instability that follow over expansion.

The capacity expansion approval process has changed somewhat over time, but it operates roughly as follows: Representatives of the privately owned steel producing firms gather under the umbrella of the Japan Iron and Steel Federation to present and discuss tentative investment plans for the coming year. (Often these representatives, usually managing directors, are MITI alumni.) The producers' plans are evaluated in relation to the demand outlook for the industry and the existing pattern of market shares. After these meetings and informal discussions among these managers and the officials of the Iron and Steel Section of MITI's Heavy Industries Bureau, the presidents of the steel companies try to reach a consensus on the rate and timing of the major investments of individual producers. MITI participates *ex officio* in these meetings. The frequency of consensus meetings varies with the complexity of the problem; in times of crisis, meetings are continuous.

After consensus has been reached, MITI issues a report recommending a course of action to the industry. In recent years this report has been prepared by the Iron and Steel Subcommittee of MITI's Industrial Structure Council, a policy advisory group which reports at the vice-ministerial level. The council's membership includes officials from several ministries including Finance, prominent businessmen, and leading academics.

This process should not be viewed in terms of the Western dichotomy between public and private forces. The government neither plans nor dictates the rate of capacity expansion. The Industrial Structure Council does not unilaterally accept or reject the industry's consensus, but rather evaluates it in view of Japan's wider economic objectives. It has been, said that no application from a major firm for a capacity increment has ever been flatly rejected, although some have been delayed. This of course is the mechanism of the consensus process: the expanding firm is persuaded either to delay its application or to accept a delayed approval. When this persuasion fails, consensus is frustrated.

The government can draw on both official and unofficial sources of authority to facilitate consensus. MITI''s control over imported raw materials is one crucial policy instrument. Through foreign exchange import quotas, MITI directly controlled the importation and allocation among producers of both ore and coal until 1965, and still retains control over the import of coking coal. Since Japan currently imports 98 percent of its iron ore requirements and 90 percent of its coal needs, this tool gives MITI reasonably effective control over the rate of production, and hence the rate of expansion. Foreign exchange control also permits the Bank of Japan to limit steel producers' foreign borrowing, which has been a source of finance for the Japanese steel industry.

The Bank of Japan and the Ministry of Finance bring another perspective to the discussions regarding steel expansion. While MITI focuses on the relative competitiveness and growth of the Japanese steel industry, the financial authorities share a broader concern with macro economic effects and international payments balances. Hence in 1970 the Bank denied requests for increased foreign borrowings in order to avoid undermining its domestic deflationary policy and depressing the rate of increase in dollar reserves. This forced the delay of capacity additions in the early 1970s.

The steel industry's good relationship with the bureaucracy, and with the broader economic policymaking community in and out of government, has made these negotiations generally successful. Harmony between MITI and the industry, however, is not universal. A case in point is sumitomo's recalcitrance in the middle 1960s.

Sumitomo is perhaps Japan's most aggressive steelmaker. Since the middle 1950s, the company has achieved between results in profitability, modernity of facilities, export sales, and market share than any of its competitors in the industry. In 1965 Sumitomo challenged the industry consensus recommendation that steelmakers should delay all new investments in rolling facilities except those which replaced existing capacity. It went ahead with a new installation which, while technically a replacement, substantially improved productivity; at the same time, Sumitomo stepped up production while the majority of producers were trying to keep prices stable by moderating production levels. Fuji Steel vigorously protested against Sumitomo's action and comparable aggressive behavior on the part of smaller steelmakers, and argued that only special legislation governing steel investment could resolve the industry's fundamental problem of overcapacity.

Response with MITI was mixed. Many, including the outgoing vice-minister, defended the traditional system of industrial consensus reached under MITI's watchful eye—an arrangement which Sumitomo felt put the fast-growing, efficient steelmakers who were responsible for Japan's international success at a disadvantage. It may be inferred that Sumitomo's view was echoed by the Fair Trade Commission, as it reiterated its disapproval of existing production cartels as anti-competitive. At the other extreme, a study committee of the Industrial Structure Council used this occasion to argue that the problems of capacity regulation and price stability could best be solved by a thorough consolidation of the steel industry.

The upshot of these confrontations was continuation of the status quo. Sumitomo continued to build its new facilities and produce aggressively. MITI disciplined the company by limiting its allocation of imported coking coal to what it considered appropriate levels. Before Sumitomo really felt the effect of this action, however, demand for steel recovered sharply, and by 1967 Sumitomo's additional capacity was needed to meet domestic requirements.

The Sumitomo incident clearly indicates the limitations of the consensus system. But the majority of industry or government leaders would not have tolerated a more radical form of control. The consensus system struck an acceptable balance between autonomy and control, though this might have been more difficult had demand not recovered.

More recently, as steel has come to be regarded as less important in Japan's future, MITI has begun to discourage major investments at home, and to call for further industry rationalisation. As early as 1974, MITI was reluctant to support continued general expansion in the industry in Japan, despite the then current steel boom. Since then, a long-term recession and worldwide overcapacity in steel have confirmed them in this view. Japan's remaining small local open-hearth furnace producers have been designated as a troubled industry and are being encouraged to come up with a long-term plan to reduce capacity. MITI has, however, favoured foreign investment by Japanese firms in overseas steel mills, particularly in developing countries, as a way of maintaining Japanese dominance in steel while promoting the growth of the Japanese steelmaking machinery and whole plant export industries. MITI has encouraged Japanese participation in steel projects in Qatar, Iraq, and Saudi Arabia, among others.

In general, then, MITI helped industry growth very directly in the beginning, and more indirectly and informally during the 1960s and early 1970s. Its actions stemmed from a belief that having the largest, most efficient steel industry in the world would be a valuable national asset for many years to come, benefitting many other Japanese industries using steel. Means were found to spread the risk inherent in the commitment of vast financial resources to the industry while still providing a good return on equity for investors in the steel companies.

Raw Material Acquisition

Scale plants alone cannot guarantee a competitive steel industry; low-cost, high-quality raw materials are also essential. Because Japan produces only about 10 percent of its total coking coal needs and almost none of its iron ore needs, ensuring a steady supply of good quality raw materials at a reasonable cost has been a major preoccupation of government policy. Long-term contracts arranged by the steel industry account for roughly four-fifths of the resources consumed in steelmaking itself. The Japanese government has provided a good deal of financial help. Government institutions such as the Export-Import Bank and the Overseas Economic Cooperation Fund directly finance imports. These institutions provide the assurance of long-term financing which is necessary in order to enter into supply agreements with overseas mining operations, many of whose total output and hence total investment is targeted for Japan. In addition to providing a long-term source of funds, the government designates iron ore and coal as priority import categories and ensures that foreign exchange is allocated to purchase them.

The government has also assisted steelmakers in undertaking direct overseas resource development investment. The Ministry of Finance once designated special sources in its annual budget in accordance with a standing policy to favor such overseas investment. During the 1950s and 1960s, when Japan's currently productive resource development projects were undertaken, capital exports of scarce foreign exchange were authorised first for ore, coal, and petroleum exploration and mining ventures. Resource development accounted for 30 percent of total cumulative Japanese foreign investment in 1970.

Just as important as the formal availability of loan funds for development has been priority the government has given this type of investment and the resulting diverse forms of support. On several occasions MITI's alacrity in directing funds to a Japanese development coordinator, usually a large trading company, has proved critical to the project's success. Similarly, the government can ensure that funds are available for the export of Japanese equipment and technology that usually attends the overseas development project. MITI and the steel companies have dispatched teams of exploration experts to investigate possible coal development sites in Canada and Australia and to advise the developer. The Japan Overseas Development Corporation, a public corporation and a counterpart to the Japan Petroleum Development Corporation, assists in the organisation and financing of development projects abroad. The government has unequivocally demonstrated its commitment to develop foreign sources of ore and coal supply.

A third, more minor form of government financial assistance has been tax incentives and insurance against development losses. A contingency reserve for possible losses and thorough development loss insurance facilities are available to overseas ventures.

The government is also supporting basic geological exploration in prospective supply areas. In addition, public funds have established a resource development college to provide professional training in exploration and mining. However, the state has not directly invested in resource development on a significant scale nor does it direct the efforts of manufacturers and trading companies in exploration or mining.

While government's role in assisting capacity addition in the steel industry has declined in recent years, its interest in raw materials acquisition has increased. In the past, although Japanese companies and the government would agree to enter into long-term purchasing contracts for Australian and Brazilian iron ore and U.S., Canadian, and Australian coal, actual Japanese investment in these developments was minimal. Since the 1973 energy and raw material shortages demonstrated that availability (not just the cost) of supply was an issue, Japanese companies, with government assistance, have invested in new mining projects. The increasing strength of the yen and the existence of dollar surpluses have also spurred overseas investment.

In general, the government has not itself invested in these projects or directly provided the funds for investment, but rather has helped to convene consortia and, through MITI's and the Ministry of Finance's involvement in discussions and negotiations, has influenced the direction taken. Government has also contributed to the success of development projects by relaxing antitrust regulations to allow cartels to invest and import raw materials; in some cases, the government has guaranteed financing.

Cartels

A final kind of government assistance to the steel industry has been the formation of recession cartels and export restraint cartels. Steel production is capital-intensive both in the form of fixed and working capital. Reductions in steel production, leading to under-utilisation of capacity, can be extremely damaging, and the cyclical nature of the worldwide steel production has often caused severe cash flow problems for producers. Most American companies, for instance, show great swings in profitability and usually only have funds to invest during boom periods. It requires a few years to build new capacity, which then may come into use at the time of the next recession, thus exacerbating cash flow problems. As a result, producers are often tempted to cut prices in order to maintain capacity utilisation; this can compound the industry's problems and distort its long-term growth potential.

This problem first appeared in Japan during the mild recession of 1957, when the country's economic growth faltered in the midst of the steel industry's expansion, creating overcapacity. Because Japan's steelmakers operate with exceptionally high fixed financial and labour costs, and because capacity additions were accelerating, a severe cash flow crisis resulted from substantial under-utilisation. Prices dropped as producers tried to restore normal levels of capacity utilisation. As the crisis deepened, individual firms began to cut prices drastically.

Self-motivated collusion among firms to restrict production and stabilise prices would have violated the anti-monopoly act. In this impasse, MITI led informal consultations with industry management and developed a public sales system to ameliorate the problem. Under this arrangement, steel producers agreed upon and reported their scheduled monthly production levels to MITI along with price schedules. Prices were made public, and the industry's entire monthly output was to be sold at the announced prices. Thus, without unilaterally setting production limits and price levels, MITI was able to bring producers to an enforceable consensus.

Since the late 1950s, similar means have been used during major recessions to promote an orderly cutback in production and to manage pricing. In normal economic conditions, however, there is no price fixing or price control, and Japanese steel prices have steadily fallen as the industry's productivity and raw material supply have improved.

MITI has also coordinated voluntary export restraint cartels. The Export-Import

Transaction Law of 1952 allows exporters to "enter into an agreement with respect to price, quantity, grade, design, and other items in the export business of a designated category of goods to be exported to a specified destination by reporting to MITI," and gives MITI the authority to alter or suspend the agreement if it cannot function effectively or if it fails to serve legitimate purposes. Such export restraint cartels were organised in the late 1960s in response to pressure from the U.S. government to limit exports of Japanese steel products to the United States.

Specialty Steels

The most significant government cartel intervention in the industry came in response to the specialty steels crisis brought about by the recession of 1964-65. Specialty steel production—stainless, tool, etc.—grew rapidly from 1960 to 1965, but capacity grew even faster. By 1965, significant overinvestment had occurred. The major source of overinvestment was the entry of additional carbon steel producers into the stainless, tool, and structural alloy fields.

In February 1964 the Japanese government initiated a deflationary monetary policy. As economic growth began to slow down, machinery and motor car producers reduced their steel orders. Specialty steel producers cut prices sharply to maintain market share and plant operating levels, but specialty steel production actually declined from 1964 to 1965.

The industry and MITI responded quickly. MITI suggested guidelines for voluntary production cutbacks as early as April 1964. Demand fell faster than production, however, and by the end of 1964 production cuts of 10 to 15 percent from previous-year levels were necessary. A formal production cartel was organised by MITI in January 1965 for structural alloy steel. In March of the same year a more stringent measure—a price cartel—followed as prices continued to deteriorate. March 1965 also marked the financial collapse of Sanyo Specialty Steel, the largest bankruptcy of the postwar period. In December, MITI organised a production cartel for stainless and bearing steel. The economy recovered in 1966, and by September all cartels were abolished.

During the crisis, MITI took the initiative to push for a reorganisation of the industry. The Specialty Steel Policy Subcommittee of the ministry's powerful Industry Structure Deliberation Council recommended a program for reform. In November 1965 the subcommittee issued a report calling for cooperative efforts between MITI and the industry in three areas: vertical rationalisation of production among carbon steel and specialty producers, specialisation within steelmaking groups of particular products, and formal mergers of competing or complementary producers. Some significant changes were made over the next five years.

The government also acted to rescue individual firms from bankruptcy. Two major producers, Sanyo and Nippon Specialty, slid toward bankruptcy in 1965. Under the Corporate Rehabilitation Act, the government sponsored the reorganisation and refinancing of these two firms. MITI, the Ministry of Finance, the Bank of Japan, and the commercial banks all played important roles. In the case of Nippon Specialty Steel, the rehabilitation plan was drawn up in December 1966 by the major creditors and shareholders under the supervision of the Ministry of Finance. In short, the method of rehabilitation was to reduce by large amounts the unsecured debt and paid-in capital without compensation to creditors and shareholders. Under the guidance of the Ministry of Finance, new shares were issued to creditors holding the cancelled debt instruments, mortgaged debt was frozen, and new management was installed. New debt was arranged through the intervention of the Bank of Japan.

In the commodity steel industry, such extensive government intervention has not been needed. Since the early 1970s, government has been working to rationalise existing capacity in commodity steel by enforcing agreements to close the least efficient furnaces during recessions as new ones came onstream and, more recently, by strongly encouraging the rationalisation of the small weak competitors. These actions, like those in specialty steels, have come in response to industry crisis and at the request of the companies involved rather than as an imposition from government.

Summary

As discussed, Japan's success in steel can be largely attributed to aggressive investment strategies which allowed the country to build the world's lowest cost steel industry.

The value of government support to the industry cannot be measured in terms of cash expenditures. By the judicious application of support in the areas where it could be most effective, government has done a great deal for the industry. Selective measures—help through the insurance of debt for building greenfield plants, assistance in procuring raw materials and forming anti-recession cartels—have provided support without extinguishing competition or stifling initiative in individual companies. Even capacity expansion cooperation has been carried out in such a way as to allow substantial continued internal competition and even greater market share than occurred in the United States. The actual flow of funds from government to the industry represented by loans, grants, and tax allowances has been minimal, at least since the late 1950s. Per ton of steel, such assistance has been substantially less than that supplied by many European governments (often to subsidise the losses of uncompetitive plants).

II

THE MOTOR CAR INDUSTRY

The Japanese motor car industry, with two of the world's four largest companies in terms of output, is now second only to the United States in total production, and is the largest exporter of automobiles in the world. The top three foreign cars sold in the United States are Japanese, and this success has come in a comparatively short period of time. In 1965 Japan exported only 100,000 cars, primarily to other Asian countries, and even in 1970 fewer than 700,000 cars were exported. By 1978 exports had risen to more than 3 million units.

The Japanese car manufacturers have remained strong despite the revaluations of the yen and the rapid rise in relative Japanese labour costs over the past decade. In fact, the true potential of the industry has not yet been realised, primarily because of formal and informal import restrictions on Japanese-produced cars, particularly in Europe.

The success of Japan's major car firms—Toyota, Nissan, and Honda—stems mainly from their accomplishments in product design and production process. They have focused on a relatively limited range of chassis and engine types. They have achieved significantly higher levels of product reliability through greater discipline in tolerances and extensive pre-production testing. They designed and built high volume automated facilities which, when operating near capacity, are low cost, and they have gained high volume through the growth of their domestic market and a major effort in marketing abroad.

As in other industries, the lethargy of American and European competitors contributed to Japan's success in the sales of motor cars. Except for Volkswagen, non of the European car manufacturers was willing to parallel Japan's heavy investment in marketing, distribution, and service for the large U.S. market; Detroit was slow to develop a true subcompact alternative car to those being imported, and Volkswagen lagged in replacing "the Beetle." Thus Japanese producers were able to capture a large part of the rapidly growing U.S. small car market.

Finally, the large home market was an important asset to the Japanese car industry, providing rapid initial growth and a proving ground for domestic producers. European producers have recently begun cooperative efforts that have consolidated their own market base and made it possible to amortise investment in research and development and automation over greater volume. Had they taken such steps earlier, they might have posed a more effective deterrent to Japanese producers.

Postwar Reconstruction

The Japanese government's role in the motor car industry began in the 1930s, when for military and foreign exchange reasons the government passed a law that forced the market leaders, General Motors and Ford, out of Japan. After failing to encourage Zaibatsu to enter the industry, the government provided incentives for Toyota and Nissan to do so.

In the immediate postwar period, the car industry was in disarray. Toyota, the largest producer, had to be saved from bankruptcy in 1949 by the Bank of Japan. The Bank opposed development of the industry, but MITI was in favour. The Korean War resolved the issue by creating an export market for Japanese-produced motor cars. Thus in 1952 MITI developed a policy to protect and help fund development of the industry and to help it acquire needed technology.

The government played a significant role in the industry in the 1950s and 1960s. Government intervention in the car industry was characterised by three major policy goals: discouragement of foreign capital in the Japanese industry and protection against car imports, attempts to bring about rationalisation of production, and assistance with overseas marketing and distribution expenditure. Recently the Japanese government has played only a minor role to assist in arranging voluntary European export cutbacks and in the industry's research and development program to develop an electrically powered car.

Protection. The government devised a comprehensive and imposing set of protection measures which discouraged foreign investment in the car industry. These laws specified that no repatriation of earnings or capital would be guaranteed from foreign investment in marketing facilities. Repatriation would be guaranteed for investment in production facilities only if it "contributes to the development of the domestic industry."

MITI's purpose was to discourage import marketing investments while leaving the door open for selected joint ventures with foreign producers who had superior car parts technology. Admission of large American and European motor car assemblers was ruled out. Two instruments—quota and tariff—were used to protect the industry. Quotas were applied throughout the mid-1960s, and prohibitively high tariffs through the mid-1970s. The imposition of import quotas and tariffs created for Japanese producers a market opportunity which they were not technologically prepared to exploit. Domestic producers turned out only 4,317 passenger cars in 1951, and these were uncompetitive in price and quality with Western imports. Parts technology and production methods were undeveloped, and most manufacturers agreed with MITI on the necessity of importing foreign technology.

MITI controlled all foreign licensing agreements. To make technology agreements more attractive to the licensor it guaranteed the remittance of royalties from Japan. The policy stipulated, however, that continued remittance would be guaranteed only if 90 percent of the licensed parts were produced in Japan within five years. MITI had struck a compromise. Obtaining operational foreign technology required substantial imports of foreign "value-added" in the form of parts and sub-assemblies. By making remittance conditional on the transfer of parts manufacture to Japan, however, MITI served notice that knock-down imports would be permitted only for a limited period. Domestic manufacturers were thus given additional incentive to develop manufacturing capability for their licensors' parts.

A year after this policy was adopted, six domestic manufacturers had negotiated agreements for knock-down assembly of foreign cars in Japan under license. Of the six, Nissan was the only one then producing passenger cars; Hino, Mitsubishi, and Isuzu were traditional truck manufacturers. MITI approved the applications of these four, while rejecting those of the two others—Fuji Auto (no relation to Fuji Heavy Industries now producing cars) and Nichiei. MITI considered those firms too financially weak to survive, and it did not want a fragmented industry. Nissan and Isuzu cooperated with Austin (U.K.) and Rootes (U.K.) respectively, while Hino cooperated with Renault and Mitsubishi with Willys (U.S.). Toyota and Prince, two of the three major passenger car producers of the period, used domestic know-how exclusively. The four licensees rapidly developed their own technology, with the result that the assembly of European cars in Japan did not last very long. The Isuzu-Rootes agreement was the longest, running until 1964, but producing less than one million dollars in royalties over twelve years.

Industry Rationalisation. In the past two decades, the government has used a variety of financial assistance programmes to aid the car industry. The Japan Development Bank extended reconstruction loans to car producers from 1951 to 1955, financing roughly 9 percent of their total investment. Special accelerated depreciation rates were extended to car producers, permitting rates of up to 50 percent depreciation in the first year. Finally, during the 1950s, direct subsidies amounting to roughly one million dollars were awarded to the Automobile Technology Association, representing manufacturers. After this initial financial assistance, the major investment role played by the government (primarily MITI) was to encourage rationalisation, both of the parts industry and of the motor car industry itself.

The car industry has from its inception been highly competitive internally. As a result, MITI has often met opposition from producers when it advocated mergers and associations within the industry. Particularly in the 1960s and 1970s, the limits of MITI's control can be seen clearly.

MITI's attempts at industry rationalisation have been most effective in the parts industry, where they had the cooperation of the major car producers; MITI has been last effective among the producers themselves, where competitive rivalries and the unwillingness of inefficient producers to go out of the business have frustrated the ministry's plans.

The Car Parts Industry. The structure of the motor car producing sector in the Japanese economy resembles a series of pyramids, with the products flowing from the bottom to the top. At the top are the vehicle producers—Toyota, Nissan, etc.—which manufacture engines and design and assemble vehicles. Each assembler is supplied by an affiliated group of primary parts manufacturers. These firms, roughly 300 in number, usually sell exclusively to one assembler.[2] The bottom layer comprises the small parts subcontractors who supply, both exclusively and nonexclusively, the primary parts firms. There are several thousand small subcontractors, many of whom are affiliated through ownership, technology agreements, or simply captive arrangements with primary parts manufacturers or the assemblers themselves.

This system gave the assembler a stable yet elastic source of supply, as demand fluctuations were absorbed by the marginal subcontractor. Labour costs at the subcontract level were usually lower than in the large firm. However, as design improvements required more advanced parts technologies, the system proved to have some serious drawbacks. The chief problem was the large number and small size of the primary parts manufacturers and subcontractors. A low production scale precluded economies of scale and modern production technologies, and the firms were financially weak. Both MITI and the major car producers recognised that the production efficiency and technological progress of the industry would be inhibited if this structure remained.

MITI had taken a serious policy interest in the parts industry since the early 1950s. In 1952 MITI directed budget monies originally allocated to the car assemblers' development to immediate subsidies for specific parts producers. Over the next few years, it recommended that the Japan Development Bank extend long-term credit to large, viable parts suppliers of the four major car producers. At least ten parts manufacturers participated.

In 1956 MITI used a major piece of new legislation to implement a more thorough financial assistance and rationalisation programme in the parts industry. An Auto Parts Committee including MITI Heavy Industry Bureau officials, presidents of various parts manufacturers trade associations, and senior officers of the Automobile Industry Association, representing the car manufacturers was formed to coordinate the programme. This *ad hoc* committee was responsible for taking the initiative to develop operational programs acceptable to all its constituents and formally proposing them to MITI. The car parts programme was planned in five-year intervals and formally lasted until 1971.

The committee worked between 1956 and 1966 to modernise facilities and concentrate production among fewer producers in forty-five of ninety-five parts categories. Mergers, although encouraged, were not explicitly directed. Using criteria heavily influenced by MITI, the committee approved borrowing for large, specialised exporting firms. Within the constraints of the affiliated system, MITI wanted to develop a small group of large, specialised parts firms capable of competing with American suppliers. At one time MITI reportedly suggested that the number of primary parts manufacturers could be reduced to forty-five. (There presently remain over 300.)

The ten-year programme from 1956-66 was reasonably successful. Nearly $50 million in low-interest long-term loans were extended by the Japan Development Bank and the Small Business Finance Corporation over the period. Market share concentration occurred and costs were reduced. Price reductions over this period were critically important to Japan's subsequent export penetration of the U.S. market. Annual percentage price reduction from 1960 to 1965 averaged roughly 30 percent.

Despite gains in industry concentration and efficiency, however, the primary parts manufacturers in 1966 remained largely one- or two-product companies. (The criteria used for the advancement of loans had in fact encouraged specialisation.) In addition, Japanese parts manufacturers were smaller than their American counterparts. MITI thought that larger, horizontally integrated parts manufacturers would improve Japan's competitive position and would reduce the need for domestic firms to seek foreign technology through joint equity ventures. Consequently, the rationalisation program which MITI approved for the third five-year period (1966-71) emphasised horizontal combination, even across affiliated group lines. The government offered financial assistance either to mergers or to jointly established research efforts by parts producers. MITI hoped to create large "unit system" sub-assembly producers, but the programme was not successful. Despite annual production growth rates of 25 to 40 percent during this period, which made low-cost, long-term lending sources extremely attractive to these capital-constrained single product companies, borrowings were not heavy and governmental programme budgets were not fully utilised.

Nor was the horizontal consolidation phase of the programme successful. A number of subcontractors merged into primary parts manufacturers. For example, two large Nissan affiliates in the lighting equipment area merged, and a three-way clutch venture including Toyota and Nissan affiliates was considered. But there was little impact on the primary parts manufacturers who were the real targets of the programme. The major reason for the relative failure of MITI's efforts was that the car producers themselves, especially Nissan, were reorganising their affiliates during this period. This inevitably caused some tensions. The vertical nature of the affiliate system did not easily accommodate the horizontal, total market orientation of the government's programme.

Overall, the consolidation and modernisation of parts suppliers during the 1950s and 1960s was essential to the emergence of a world competitive industry. It is clear that government played a crucial role in this effort, although its wishes did not always prevail. By the early 1970s the industry had attained competitiveness, and MITI moved to a "hands-off" policy vis-a-vis the parts industry.

Consolidation Efforts. MITI's attempts to rationalise the manufacture of motor cars failed, although they did exert some influence on producers. The history of this interaction gives a good picture of the tensions within Japanese industrial policy formulation.

During the 1950s and 1960s, MITI attempted to consolidate the industry into fewer and larger "groups" of car producers. Although MITI introduced various consolidation plans, the government and the manufacturers never achieved consensus. A number of business combinations (in the form of mergers and cooperative production arrangements) did occur after 1965. These were largely self-motivated, however, and usually consummated by the producers without direct ministry influence. The consolidations were clearly not responses to MITI's several "grouping" plans enunciated during the decade.

To understand MITI's ambitions requires an appreciation of the circumstances of the motor industry. From the introduction of foreign technology in 1952 until 1960, the number of conventional passenger car producers had remained stable, with Nissan and Toyota the dominant firms. In 1960 three more firms Mitsubishi, Fuji, and Toyota entered the passenger car business. The combined car market share of Toyota and Nissan dropped from three-quarters to less than one half between 1960 and 1962. Rapid market entry was, of course, to be expected as passenger car demand soared. During 1961, for example, while Toyota and Nissan together lost 11 percent of their market share, their combined sales revenue grew by 38 percent.

MITI viewed this increase in the number of producers with anxiety. In 1953 the ministry had rejected two of six applications for the import of foreign technology. Two years later, MITI suggested that all car producers should develop a prototype People's Car, and then permit MITI to select one design and subsidise its production by the single preferred manufacturer. The hope was that a single popular car which could dominate the market would be developed. The car manufacturers quietly but strongly objected to the single company subsidy concept, and the plan never reached the Diet. This was perhaps the manufacturers' first major resistance to MITI policy.

MITI's interest in the structure of the industry reflected it concern not only for the efficiency of domestic production but also for international competitiveness. Because liberalisation of passenger car import quotas was clearly inevitable, Japanese cars quickly had to become competitive in Japanese markets. Resisting imports was also important for developing the export opportunity. Japanese producers has to preempt all domest, market growth in order to gain sufficient production scale and experience to compete in American and, it was hoped, European markets. Either slow domestic growth, excessive product fragmentation, or premature import liberalisation could keep the country's motor car producers from reaching competitive parity. MITI viewed this possibility with great concern, and made a series of efforts to consolidate the industry.

Proposed Reorganisation of the Industry. At a 1961 meeting of the Industry Structure Advisory Council, MITI proposed that passenger car producers be organised into groups based on the car's basic design type. Three groups—regular passenger cars, minicars, and specialty cars (including sportscars)—were defined. A firm's entire production would be limited to one group, and minimum volumes would have to be met within three years. The objective was to force a concentration of product line and eventually eliminate small producers.

Toyota and Nissan—neither of whom produced minicars—reportedly did not voice strong opposition to the plan, which would have reduced competition in conventional passenger cars. Toyo Kogyo, Mitsubishi, Daihatsu, and Fuji, on the other hand, all produced both conventional and minicars, and together had roughly 30 percent of the total car market by 1962. These producers reacted with hostility to MITI's proposal, and after a series of unsuccessful discussions, it was dropped.

MITI, it should be noted, did not try to force consolidation upon reluctant car manufacturers. Industry attitude and the limitations of MITI's direct power kept it from ordering formal combinations of producers.

Development Law for Specific Industries. In 1962 MITI was concerned with structure in several major industries, including motor cars, petrochemicals, and tires. It sought a comprehensive legislative charter to undertake, in cooperation with industry, major programmes for producer specialisation, establishing appropriate investment levels and promoting mergers and groupings. Toward this end, MITI drafted the Development Law for Specific Industries. The law conferred major financial advantages on the motor car industry and on other industries, if they chose to participate. The programmes themselves would be jointly conceived by the manufacturers, the commercial banks, and MITI.

The wide scope of this ambitious proposal attracted attention from many elements of government. The leadership of the ruling Liberal Democratic Party strongly favoured enactment. The Fair Trade Commission (FTC) and the car producers themselves generally opposed the legislation. The FTC complained that the law would extend the government's intimacy with industry beyond desirable limits, while the motor car manufacturers did not want to put their autonomy at risk. More importantly, even the secondary producers did not yet feel any financial necessity to seek consolidation. While the industry was exceptionally competitive, it was uniformly profitable during the early 1960s for major producers, all of whom earned a sufficient return on their investment to finance the required growth. Five secondary producers—Toyo Kogyo, Mitsubishi, Fuji, Daihatsu, and Honda—gained or maintained their market share between 1963 and 1965 while following relatively conservative financial policies.

Other Measures. The draft law failed because of the opposition of producers in the motor car and other designated industries. The government, however, did not give up its effort to make mergers financially attractive should the occasion arise. Motor car manufacturers qualified for the existing government Investment and Loan Programme, while the Japan Development Bank would help to finance any bona fide formal merger or cooperative production affiliation. In addition, the two ministries devised and secured approval of a special tax deductible allowance which rewarded mergers. It reduced tax liability for a limited period in proportion to the increase in a firm's capital through a merger.

MITI did not limit its techniques of persuasion to the financial area. The ministry was discriminating in its approval of foreign technology introduction by domestic producers. In 1968, for instance, Toyo Kogyo, the third-ranking car producer and a staunch opponent of consolidation, was denied permission to import radiator technology from Renault. Only later, in conjunction with the approval of an application from Nissan to import essential the same technology, was Toyo's request granted.

By the middle 1960s, MITI's concern with structure was acute. Two facts were clear by 1965. First, the fragmentation of market share was pronounced: eight firms each held at least 5 percent of total vehicle production. Only Toyota and Nissan were internationally viable. Second, the prospect for continued protection from foreign competition was limited. In October 1965, quantitative restrictions on passenger car imports were removed. During the preceding year, Japan had become a member of the Organisation for Economic Cooperation and Development (OECD) and had given a commitment to liberalise restrictions on foreign capital investment. To defuse the inevitable liberalisation of investment in the motor car industry became MITI's dominant objective for the remainder of the 1960s. Quite apart from the fact that consolidation would strengthen the domestic industry competitively against American capital, merger and affiliation of Japanese producers were the only effective ways to deny foreign manufacturers domestic partners.

A marginal, independent domestic car producer would be the naturally desirable partner for foreign companies trying to enter the Japanese market.

Nissan/Prince Merger. The first major consolidation in the industry occurred in 1966 with the merger of Nissan and Prince. Although financial needs prompted the merger, MITI seized the opportunity when it arose and took steps to encourage it. The merger was consummated in May 1966. The negotiations principally involved the two companies and their banks, although the chief executive of the Japan Development Bank also entered the discussions and promised financial assistance to the merger.

The merger served many interests. MITI accomplished its strategic aim—the merger of a secondary producer with one of the two dominant companies. Nissan, which had struggled with inadequate passenger car capacity, acquired Prince's modern and under-utilised plant. Prince's technical staff was highly regarded, and its dealer network gave Nissan improved distribution coverage. Prince, of course, was financially extricated, and the bankruptcy of one of the country's major firms was avoided.

The Japan Development Bank extended roughly $15 million in credit to the merged company. This was the Bank's first loan to the motor car industry since MITI announced the new criteria for loans three year earlier. Only one other government-sponsored loan was made subsequently, when Hino became affiliated with Toyota later in 1966.

Producer Affiliations. The Nissan-Prince merger apparently stimulated other manufacturers to pursue consolidation. Within two years of the merger, six separate car producer affiliation arrangements were negotiated, though only two were consummated. These six were not formal merger proposals but rather "groupings", limited bilateral arrangements by which minority shares were exchange, overlapping production was rationalised, parts were standardised, and dealerships were shared. The six negotiations are summarised below :

Year	*Companies*	*Outcome*
1966	Toyota-Hino	Success
1966	Fuji-Isuzu	Failure
1967	Toyota-Daihatsu	Success
1967	Mitsubishi-Fuji-Isuzu	Failure
1967	Mitsubishi-Isuzu	Failure
1968	Nissan-Isuzu	Failure

The only successes involve Toyota. In both cases, the product lines were complementary: Hino's trucks and Daihatsu's minicars with Toyota's conventional passenger cars. Both affiliations were arranged by Mitsui Bank, which was the primary creditor for all three firms. At the request of the manufacturers, MITI did not intervene in the discussions.

MITI's effort to bring Nissan and Isuzu together was one of several attempts in the late 1960s to consolidate the industry around Toyota and Nissan. Merger efforts focused on grouping secondary producers around the two dominant ones, but MITI failed to push through these mergers. An effort to merge Nissan and Toyo Kogyo met with similar resistance. Eventually, Nissan and Fuji did merge, but MITI did not play a significant role.

At the end of the decade, it was clear that MITI's attempts to consolidate the industry had failed. Neither the three-group nor the two-group concept had materialised. MITI's legislative programmes for consolidation had not been enacted, and its financial incentives for affiliation had drawn limited response. The effect of this failure can be seen in the accelerated flow of foreign capital into the industry after the liberalisation of restrictions which occurred in the early 1970s. Isuzu and General motors joined forces, as did Chrysler and Mitsubishi. Toyo Kogyo and Ford also formed many agreements. On the other hand, it is the indigenous and wholly Japanese producers which continue to dominate the Japanese market. Nissan, Toyota, and Honda have been the most successful companies, and Toyo Kogyo, despite its unsuccessful wankel engine gamble, remains in fourth place.

Export Assistance. A further way in which the Japanese government has aided the automobile industry is through export assistance, including some financial support and direct functional assistance. Such aid was directed toward the development of overseas marketing and distribution capacity for Japanese car producers.

Financial Support. In 1949, six motor car manufacturers established an Export Promotion Association to perform basic overseas market research. The Ministry of Commerce and Industry subsidised the research and the preparation of catalogues written in English perhaps Japan's first car export marketing step.

Long-term export credit offered by the Export-Import Bank of Japan dates from 1950. The Bank historically emphasised heavy equipment industries with large export financing requirements, including cars, ships, and locomotives. Its lending was typically supplemented by commercial bank credit, with terms advantageous to the borrower. Since the early 1970s, however, preferential export borrowing terms have been disappearing.

The first tax assistance came in the form of an export income deduction provision in 1953. This system, which provided a maximum deduction of 8 percent of net export income, was initiated by MITI and approved by the Ministry of Finance. Less than 150,000 passenger cars were exported under this tax exemption, and the Japanese discontinued the practice in 1964 in compliance with GATT regulations.

In the same year, a series of more indirect financial incentives was established, including measures that permitted exporting firms to establish tax-free reserves for overseas marketing development and investment. Most notable among these income reserves was that for "overseas market cultivation," which allowed a firm to shield 0.5 percent of its export sales from tax. In addition, an accelerated depreciation schedule tied to export performance was instituted. A manufacturer who increased his export business relative to competitors or to the previous year's performance qualified for special accelerated schedules on export-related capital investment. For the rapidly growing firm these reserve and depreciation measures become a permanent and not insignificant source of funds. Suspension of these special provisions was announced in 1972.

Functional Assistance. Since the early postwar years, the Japanese government has made an effort to improve the quality of the country's exports, requiring that exports of specific products be inspected either by government or by industry association authorities. In addition, since the export Insurance Law of 1950, government has provided Japanese exporters with default insurance. Through the Heavy Machinery Export Council, manufacturers played an important role in developing the insurance programme, insisting on lower premiums and extended coverage. In 1965 Japan's official export promotion agency—Japan External Trade Rehabilitation Organisation—established the Chicago Automobile Parts Center to promote Japanese car exports to help solve the logistical problems of the overseas car part business, and to undertake market research. MITI partially subsidised the Auto Parts Center.

Like other forms of government assistance to the industry, however, overseas investment and export assistance declined in the early 1970s and is now virtually nonexistent.

III

ALUMINUM AND SHIPBUILDING INDUSTRIES

Next comes a discussion of two industries in decline—aluminum and shipbuilding.

Industries in serious trouble are not new to Japan. Japan's biggest manufacturing employer, the textile industry, has been in decline for twenty years. It has uncompetitively high wages, too many small and inefficient producers, and no advantage in raw material costs or market access against its Asian competitors. Today the industry employs 300,000 fewer people than in 1965, and the loss has been concentrated in a few regions. Still, the rapid growth of the economy during the late 1960s and early 1970s has absorbed these workers, and serious political repercussions have been avoided. Japan's major capital-intensive industries—steel, aluminum, synthetic textile fibers—have undergone serious recessions in the past, but these were cyclical in nature. Recession cartels and countercyclical monetary and fiscal policy always brought recovery.

In the late 1970s, however, a number of major industries are basically uncompetitive internationally and unlikely ever to recover fully. They include aluminum smelting, chemical fertilisers, ferroalloys, plywood, sugar refining, and synthetic textile fibers, among others. The source of their structural problems varies. Some have uncompetitive energy costs, while others have too high priced raw materials. Some have been poorly managed, while others are simply natural casualties of the industrialisation of the Third

World. The solution to the serious problems posed by these declining industries has not yet been found. The Structurally Depressed Industries Law enacted in May 1978 was drafted by MITI and passed by the Diet, but consensus has not yet developed to enable it to be used effectively. Major producers have been unwilling either to merge or to trim permanently their operations, and the national political leadership has already, in one notable shipbuilding case, shown itself unwilling to allow an uncompetitive firm to become bankrupt.

The law designates several industries—aluminum smelting and shipbuilding among them—as structurally depressed, and it sets forth criteria to cover others. To be eligible for reconstruction measures, an industry must have severe overcapacity, more than one-half of the firms must be in serious financial difficulty, and two-thirds of the firms must sign a petition seeking designation as a depressed industry. Once designed, the responsible ministry may develop a stabilisation plan for the industry wherein the ministry forecasts supply and demand, measures excess capacity, and identifies plants to be closed or cut back. Where scrapping capacity brings real financial stress, the law authorises a loan guarantee trust fund to encourage private banks to extend further credit to their ailing debtors. Most of this loan guarantee fund is subscribed by the Japan Development Bank and other public banks. To mitigate the employment effects of a reduction in physical capacity, two additional laws were passed in 1978. The first of these provides for an extension of unemployment benefits by ninety days and retraining allowances both for retained and dismissed employees. The second provides a variety of financial relief measures to small and medium-size firms in the depressed regions.

The law is typically Japanese in its intended operation. MITI is obliged to consult with those inside the industry, and labour unions are given an advisory voice. The law empowers MITI to restrict new investment in the industry. The FTC is able to review the stabilisation plan to ensure that it is not anti-competitive. Finally, the companies in trouble and MITI have to agree on a workable plan. Despite its good lineage, to date the law has been applied neither to aluminum nor to shipbuilding—two of the most protracted problem industries.

Aluminum

Japan has never been a world competitive producer of aluminum. The industry has grown at the same rate as the economy, but the volume of imports of aluminum was two or three times as great as exports in the period 1970 to 1976. Since 1974 the industry has been in especially difficult shape. Electricity is a key cost element in the smelting of aluminum. (About 15,000 kilowatt hours are required to refine one ton.) Since the oil shock in 1973, electricity prices for Japanese aluminum smelters have been about twice those in Europe and about four to five times those in North America. Japan's price for electricity is about 8 to 9 yen per kwh as against 1 to 2 yen in Canada. As a result, Japanese domestic aluminum costs in early 1978 were 320,000 yen per ton (of which one-third is electricity) compared with an import price of about 280,000 yen per ton (c.i.f. price).

In 1977, domestic capacity in the industry was about 1.1 million tons, with production at 650,000 tons; over 500,000 tons were imported. In that year, operating losses in the industry amounted to about 20 billion yen. Results in 1978 were even worse. Two major public policy issues face the industry: How much capacity reduction should occur, and should it be scrapping or mothballing? What should be the rate of allowable imports?

The producers disagree among themselves on these issues, but the firms in the industry would prefer short-term reversible measures, such as a production cartel, rather than permanent capacity reduction. They want a very limited scrapping of capacity (no more than 25 percent), and they claim that Japan cannot afford to let imports supply too large a share of consumption for economic security reasons. Finally, the industry wants to maintain corporate autonomy with no mergers or groupings.

MITI, on the other hand, wants at least a one-third reduction of capacity, with a higher proportion of scrapping than mothballing of facilities. One idea current in MITI today is to combine the current fourteen plants and seven producers into two large groups, with important operating and investment decisions made at the group level. MITI also would like to rely more on imports, which are far lower in cost; it claims that Japanese overseas aluminum projects such as Sumitomo (Indonesia), Nippon Light Metal (Canada), and Mitsui (Brazil) will add about 25 percent to Japanese-owned capacity and will guarantee sources of supply.

MITI and the industry also disagree on the question of rate of import flow. Currently, the volume of imports is about four times that of exports; imports account for about one-third of the total market. Imports come in two ways: via trading companies, which average low price imports with high price-affiliated domestic product to sell to all users, and via independent importers, who do not average and sell low priced imports directly to large users.

One producer wants the government to set up a public company to buy all aluminum, both imported and domestically produced, and sell to users. This step would allow the state to enforce a limit on imports by permitting only captive flows to enter. The producers also want an electricity rate subsidy so that they can supply competitively priced aluminum to the home market.

MITI regards protectionism via a state trading company as politically unacceptable inside and outside Japan; in any event it would not solve the industry's cost problems. The electricity subsidy is ruled out as being too costly, given the differential between Japanese rates and the rates of Canada, Norway, and other producing countries. MITI proposed instead the use of a tariff quota device whereby duty would be cut on a specified import volume but the user price would stay the same. The difference would go to a restructuring loan fund for the industry. MITI has estimated that about 3 billion yen could be available from this fund in the first year.

Thus MITI and the industry are at an impasse. A committee consisting of independent mediators is searching for appropriate means of rationalising the industry, but so far has not succeeded. Although the law has been in effect for a year, still no solution is in sight. MITI is essentially market-conscious and is looking for a permanent structure solution, resisting protection and agreeing to subsidise only when there is some rationalisation. The companies do not want to surrender their autonomy, or to regroup or cut a significant amount of capacity permanently. The stronger companies seem willing to wait for a survival-of-the fittest solution, and many of the companies in the industry are part of larger multi-business companies which can absorb financial losses for a while, enabling them to resist pressures.

Shipbuilding

The shipbuilding industry provides an example of an industry that has gone through all three phases of development in Japan. In the 1950s and early 1960s, shipbuilding was a priority industry that received substantial government assistance in its attempt to gain international competitive dominance. In the late 1960s and early 1970s, the industry became a world leader, and government involvement in the industry waned. Now, in the late 1970s, the industry is declining with the rise of new developing country competitors (hastened by the collapse of the tanker market over the past few years.

The history of the industry reflects the full cycle of Japanese industrial policy. Shipbuilding was covered in the initial machinery reconstruction acts passed in 1956, and companies received considerable aid in modernising capital equipment. The government gave shipbuilding priority because of the need for a strong shipping industry in an island nation like Japan and because steel and labour are the major costs of ship construction in the 1950s Japan had an abundance of low cost labour, and steel was an investment priority.

Shipbuilding developed through Zaibatsu around sister trading companies and shipping companies. Some of the steel mills also formed their own shipbuilding companies. Thus the industry included a significant number of large powerful companies. Because of the steel and labour advantages, a number of smaller companies also grew up during the 1960s; these companies tended to specialise around particular types of ships.

During the initial phase of industry development, the Ministry of Transport (which has no jurisdiction over the industry) and the Ministry of Finance used various means to assist the introduction of new technology and also to encourage rationalisation. The government formed an industry development association to share techniques and to assist in overseas marketing. A key factor in the development of export markets in this period was the use of sugar import measures (described in Chapter VI) to allow Japanese shipbuilders to supply ships for export below their costs: shipbuilders received a compensating subsidy in the form of lucrative profits from the licensed import of raw sugar.

In 1959 an advisory council on shipbuilding and shipping was established. It authorised interest rate subsidies on loans to the shipbuilding industry for approved mergers, an interest rate subsidy to shipping companies in Japan to buy Japanese ships, and a series of favourable tax measures. The Japan Development Bank (JDB) was instrumental in providing loans to the industry, and a number of the quasi-public and private bank were also encouraged to participate. In the early stages about 70 percent of all industry financing was from the JDB. In some cases the interest rate subsidy went as far as a deferral of repayment up to fifteen years.

The government provided significant tax benefits to the industry. It allowed reserves for price fluctuations to be tax free, a large special depreciation account, establishment of export and investment losses reserves to avoid taxes, and tax and other financial incentives for investment in overseas market development. In one company studied, about 5 billion yen per year—one third of its tax burden—was subsidised through these tax measures alone during the mid 1960s.

While low interest and deferred loans for consolidation, price subsidies through the sugar license, and tax subsidies aided the industry's development, perhaps the most significant assistance to shipbuilding came from customer financing provided at very favorable terms through the Japanese Export-Import Bank. During the 1960s, about 70-80 percent of all loans made by the Bank were in the shipbuilding industry, and the terms of some of these loans provided a considerable subsidy to the manufacturers. Both the easy availability of financing and the competitive rates were of great assistance as Japan expanded its world market share.

By the late 1960s, Japan was the world's lowest cost producer of ships. The provision of low cost steel from Japan's efficient steel industry, the relatively cheap price of Japanese labour (pre-yen revaluations), and the large scale of Japanese shipyards allowed by the rapid growth of the industry during its development phases—all contributed to Japan's dominance in world shipbuilding. In the early and mid-1970s, Japan launched over 50 percent of all the world's ships, and shipbuilding companies were highly profitable.

During the maturity phase (late 1960s, early 1970s), government assistance to the industry all but disappeared. The government reduced tax subsidies, eliminated export price subsidies, virtually ended the JDB loans by refusing to allow deferrals on payments, and reduced export-import financing considerably. During the early 1970s, for example, one company which had received a 32 percent reduction in taxes during the growth phase (mid-1960s) received only a 9 percent tax reduction (entirely from depreciation); it did not receive any JDB loans.

The Japanese industry entered its declining phase after the 1973-74 tanker boom. In 1975 Japan launched 17 million gross tons of ships; in 1978 its launchings had fallen to 6.3 million tons. The collapse of the tanker market was the major cause of this decline, but Japan's market share also dropped (from 49.7 percent in 1975 to 34.7 percent in 1978) as lower wage countries like Korea, Spain, Brazil, and Taiwan increased their share. There was a rise in Japan's share of the market in 1979, but it is still significantly below mid-1970s levels. Currently, about 150,000 people are employed in shipbuilding in japan, of which about half are considered redundant. As a result of the market collapse, twenty-eight small and medium-sized shipbuilders went into bankruptcy between March 1977 and March 1978. Most of the large companies have withstood the serious situation so far because they are associated with major Zaibatsu or steel companies and can absorb losses.

The Ministry of Transport established an advisory commission for the shipbuilding industry which in 1976 recommended significant cutbacks in the industry's capacity in order to achieve a supply demand balance by 1985. The ministry has proposed that the seven major companies reduce capacity by about 40 percent, and the government wants small companies to close down. A plan to boost demand by retiring government ships ahead of schedule and expanding Japanese exports of ships to developing countries as a form of economic assistance has also been put forward. Finally, the government wants to refocus some industry capacity on liquid natural gas tankers, floating factories, and other, more sophisticated types of ships.

The Structurally Depressed Industries Law has given the Ministry of Transport tools to realise these objectives. However, the firms in the industry cannot agree among themselves or with the government on a plan to bring about this rationalisation. Large and small firms have disagreed about who should bear the burden of capacity reductions. Finally, the industry does not want to scrap capacity permanently, and is calling for greater temporary financial assistance from the government. In January, interest rate subsidies to the shipping companies were restored, and there are some signs that the government will provide some temporary subsidies even without the completion of a rationalisation plan: the employment and bankruptcy developments in shipbuilding have increased political pressures to rescue the industry.

The Sasebo case illustrates these pressures[3] Sasebo Heavy Industries is the eighth largest shipbuilder in Japan. Its major stockholders are Nippon Steel and Nippon Kokan, Japan's two largest steel companies, and its major bank is Dai Ichi Kanqyo. It is a major employer in the city of Sasebo, so its announcement in early 1978 of financial difficulty and its intention to seek voluntary early retirement by one thousand employees produced concern. Concern later became crisis when the major stockholders decided not to guarantee future loans, and the banks refused additional funds without guarantees. Confidence in the company's management was low and could not be restored. The major ministries involved—Finance and Transport—and the Bank of Japan chose not to arrange a rescue, and were prepared to see the company declare bankruptcy. The consensus of the regular policymaking apparatus was that the company should be allowed to fail.

This became politically unacceptable, however, when the work force and the Sasebo community petitioned members of the Diet, including the Prime Minister, to intervene. The Prime Minister requested the two ministries to find a solution. It was not forthcoming. Then the Prime Minister *ordered* that a solution be found. Eventually the banks, major stockholders, and ministries put together a package which the banks grudgingly accepted. It included some government financial relief, a hastily arranged American ship repair business to bolster demand, a syndicated bank loan from eighteen different banks, and a modest new capital infusion from the major shareholders. All of this was premised on a carefully negotiated change of management.

The Sasebo case is interesting primarily as a demonstration that politics can (and occasionally will) thwart the regular policy consensus process. The policymaking community had reached a clear consensus Sasebo should be permitted to fail—but the nation's highest elected officials (members of the Diet) could not resist expedient measures, and they overrode standard procedures. The ministries were aggrieved at this outcome because it clearly complicated the solution of the broader shipbuilding problem. Shipbuilders' resistance to the "rational" schemes of the public policy community has grown.

The resolution of the shipbuilding crisis is still unclear. Some of the major companies have been able to shift their capacity to other businesses, such as heavy industrial machinery and plant exports. The underlying obstacle to consensus is less whether the problem will go away and more how should the cutbacks be distributed among the producers. The producers are a heterogeneous lot—small versus large, diversified versus specialised—and they have very different reactions to any proposed solution. Recently a company was formed to purchase excess stocks. Loans totalling 90 billion yen have been obtained—90 percent from private financial institutions, 5 percent from shipbuilding companies, and 5 percent from government. The government has played the role of catalyst in this venture.

Summary

The plight of the aluminum and shipbuilding industries in the late 1970s in Japan is instructive. Traditionally Japan has demonstrated an ability to face major issues squarely. The Structurally Depressed Industries Law, by attempting to cushion the social problems at the same time that it accelerates the restructuring of industry, is in this tradition. So far the law has not been successfully implemented owing to disagreements among the parties which must reach consensus. In addition, political concerns have intervened. The challenge to develop a long-term sound public policy is great.

IV

INDUSTRIAL MACHINERY AND INFORMATION ELECTRONICS INDUSTRY

The last two case studies to be examined focus on sectors which are growing rapidly and are of increasing importance to Japan's future international competitive position: industrial machinery and information electronics. These studies show how industrial policy in Japan is applied to businesses where there is significant technology change and where Western companies are still competitively formidable. Both these industries are undergoing changes in their competitive structure, and the challenge to industrial policy has been to anticipate and to lead events in the marketplace.

In industrial machinery, the areas of intense competition and high growth have shifted away from single machine manufacture toward developing computer-controlled production systems and supplying whole plants, particularly for the rapid growth export market. Accordingly, government policy has focused less on industrial concentration and more on systems research and development and export financing.

In the information electronics sector, which includes data processing, telecommunications, and other applications of semi-conductor technology, competition among the major international companies and economies is intensive, and the Japanese government has made an enormous commitment to advancing the Japanese position. A complex pattern of government-sponsored cooperation in both research and development and equipment leasing has for at least a decade accompanied the intense competition among Japanese companies in designing, manufacturing, and marketing their own systems. Government has sought the advantages of both large, central research efforts at a national level and unrestrained competition for market share of a large and growing domestic market among the companies. While the government and the industry often disagree and the results of some programmes have been disappointing, it is clear that Japan's global position has advanced materially and that the government financing and coordination have been crucial to this progress.

Industrial Machinery

The Japanese have long regarded the machinery industry as critically important to their country's development. A knowledge-intensive industry employing highly skilled labour, it has a high growth potential and is shielded from competition from developing countries. Japan currently accounts for less than 11 percent of all OECD industrial machinery exports—behind Germany, the United States, and the United Kingdom, and only slightly ahead of France. This industry is destined for aggressive development in the future. Industrial policy for this industry has evolved in response to changes in the competitive position of machinery businesses throughout the world, and the aim of the industrial policy is for Japan to progress toward leadership in the industry.

The Changing Competitive Position

In 1950s and 1960s, the machinery industry consisted of two basic types of businesses. The first was the production of mechanical components such as gears, bearings, valves, heat exchangers, springs, etc. Production of mechanical components usually consists of pressing, machining, and some type of finishing operation. Competitive success depends primarily on large-scale production and long runs of standard products together with a sufficient volume of production to be able to dedicate production lines for special products. Marketing and engineering, while important, tend to be less significant, and large volume production enables an easier amortisation of costs.

The second basic type of business was machine assembly, in which mechanical components and structural metals and castings are assembled into paper machines, steel rolling mills, metalworking machine tools, etc. Since machine redesigns have an enormous effect on sales, research and development is crucial in this type of business. It has traditionally required coupling prime mover technology and metallurgical engineering to produce faster, more accurate, more powerful machines. The scale o production is less important to competitive success, although in some cases, large scale may enable a producer to gain advantage by manufacturing components within his own organisation.

Two broad industry trends have had a significant impact on industrial machinery businesses in the 1970s. The first is the development of so-called "systems businesses," or the sale of whole plants. Various machines are assembled with construction materials into whole plants and are sold and installed as a package by one producer (though he may subcontract parts of it).

One reason for the growth of systems businesses has been the increasing importance of developing countries as markets for machines. As industrialisation proceeds in OPEC and Comecon and advanced developing countries, non-OECD countries have come to account for roughly one half of all OECD machinery purchases. These countries are less able to design their own plants, whether for ethylene production or food processing, and prefer to buy them ready-made. The ability to sell, for example, a dairy separator may therefore hinge on the ability to offer the whole plant in which it will operate.

The growth of systems businesses has also been accelerated by progress in process control. Coordinated systems now allow the computer-centralised (or microprocessor-distributed) control of a whole factory, increasing the effectiveness of industrial machines. Maximum efficiency in the overall process is achieved by designing an entire plant for a given application rather than by assembling well-designed individual machines.

The development of the whole plant sale businesses has increased the significance of applications engineering in the overall cost structure of the industry. Because purchases are bigger, the importance of long-term buyer financing and insurance of seller's risk has also increased.

The other major development in the machinery industry in the 1970s has been the introduction of new technologies to be integrated into machinery design, particularly miniature electronics, lasers, and ultrasonics. Intelligent control in machines, the use of laser cutting and printing, and ultrasonic testing are examples. As a result, machinery makers have had to undertake massive research and development in unfamiliar fields in order to remain competitive in the industry.

Japan's Place in the World Industry

Japan was far behind major European and U.S. companies in production and design capability in the 1950s and early 1960s partly because of war damage, but by the mid-1970s had virtually closed the gap. As its producers have become more successful, the Japanese government has shifted its policy from massive aid and very close direction to a looser form of assistance and cooperation. The types of aid offered have also changed along with the needs of the industry, as it evolved from one which imported technology to one on the cutting edge of new developments.

Japanese government policy has recognised the complexity of the machinery industry, which is made up of both small and large companies with very different cost structures. Because of this heterogeneity, Japanese policy toward industrial machinery has consisted of almost one hundred programmes over the past twenty-five years. We will mention only a few important ones.

Active policy in the industry began in 1956 with the Extraordinary Measures Law for the Rehabilitation of the Machinery Industry, aimed at rationalising the industry's production and creating initial demand for its products.[4] The law focused on basic components and some simple machinery. Twenty-one industry areas were eventually designated under the law, including bearings, springs, gears, simple presses, castings, and machine tools.

Between 1956 and 1960, the Japan Development Bank provided funds for modernisation of equipment; MITI authorised rationalisation cartels for purchasing parts and importing materials; standards were set for the industry, and guidelines were established for production technology improvement. During this period the government provided almost four hundred loans totalling about 10 billion yen. Roughly 25 percent went to the machine tools industry, 13 percent to car parts, and the rest to various component makers of tools and gears. The main goal at this stage was to impose basic standards on an industry made up of thousands of small producers. To the extent that these standards could not be met by weaker companies and they left the industry, the industry as a whole was rationalised. In general, however, rationalisation measures were carried out primarily within individual firms.

In 1961 the Extraordinary Measures Law was extended and aimed at further rationalisation, this time through merger and joint investment rather than within one company. The government made available Japan Development Bank loans and preferential tax rates to encourage joint investments and mergers, and the Small Business Finance Corporation (established in the late 1950s) began to make loans to firms in the industry to assist rationalisation. Between 1961 and 1965, the JDB made loans totalling over 34 billion yen on more than 644 projects, primarily in the car parts, machine tools, and bearings industries.

Throughout this period, there was a twofold policy approach appropriate to the machinery industry. In areas like car parts and bearings, where large-scale production and long runs are essential to achieve low cost, mergers were encouraged. In other areas, like the making of special springs, gears, or castings, or certain parts of the machine tool industry, where scale of production is less important, modernisation was encouraged within the small companies. Industry associations were formed to facilitate the flow of information, and rationalisation cartels were authorised, but the emphasis was on financing (through the Small Business Finance Corporation) to modernise equipment.

By the mid-1960s, these measures had succeeded in rationalising the simple machine industry. When the law was extended again, emphasis shifted to making the companies internationally competitive. Major overseas enterprises were carefully examined as to size, capacity, and level of technology. In order to improve the structure of the Japanese industry, a cartel was formed to allocate product categories among companies and group enterprises and to establish joint ventures. In some businesses, like chemical machinery, individual producers were encouraged to cooperate in the development of new products; in other businesses, like machine tools, certain enterprises were encouraged to drop certain products. In other cases, such as printing machinery, joint ventures and mergers were sponsored. The JDB provided over 30 billion yen during the period 1965-69 for this purpose.

In general, the industrial policy of the late 1950s was aimed at improving individual company efficiency; in the early 1960s, basic mergers to consolidate the industry were encouraged; and in the late 1960s, emphasis shifted to the encouragement of greater specialisation.

Protection and Stimulation of the Home Market

Throughout the 1950s and early 1960s, only machinery which could not made in Japan was allowed to be imported. This guaranteed a market for Japanese producers and encouraged foreign producers to license their technology or to form joint ventures in Japan, since outright exports to Japan were impossible.

In addition, a series of loan programmes helped domestic machinery suppliers become more competitive in the home market (Table 5.1). In addition to these loan programmes, a series of special depreciation laws were enacted both to promote mechanisation and to encourage the purchase of Japanese-made machinery. (A recent survey by the Japanese taxation agency reports that between 1963 and 1976 the government forfeited over 174 billion yen of tax revenue in these special depreciation programmes). Finally, in 1961, the government instituted a credit insurance system designed to protect the suppliers of machinery against defaults by customers, particularly small enterprises.

These programmes served two purposes: they encouraged the modernisation of all Japanese industry, and at the same time they aided the Japanese machinery industry.

Export Promotion

The Japanese developed a variety of highly incentive means to encourage exports of machinery, including the formation of associations, export price subsidies of various sorts, both short and long-term export financing, and tax incentives.

The Japan Machinery Exporters Association was established in 1953 with a subsidy from the government to provide advice on technology together with information and promotional services to assist Japanese exports. The association is exempt from the anti-monopoly laws and can help the industry to implement orderly marketing agreements, to put price floors under exports, and to negotiate with MITI on export matters. With six hundred members, it can coordinate the formation of groups of companies to handle large overseas plant export orders. It is also in a position to coordinate financing arrangements and to provide government contacts in foreign countries.

TABLE 5.1

Loan Programme Examples

Between 1964 and 1969, a programme existed to allow Japanese producers to compete against foreign companies with installment low interest sales.[a] The Industrial Bank of Japan and the Long Term Credit Bank provided funds to enable the domestic industry to offer similar credit conditions to domestic users of machinery. The funds came from the Treasury. Loans were provided in the area of machine tools, plastic moulding machinery, printing machinery, etc. Loans of more than 25 billion yen were made during this period.

In 1974 the Japan Development Bank lent roughly 3 billion yen to manufacturers of packaging machinery, allowing them to establish a joint venture leasing company specialising in packaging machinery.

A series of measures during the 1960s and 1970s to assist leasing of labor-saving, safe new machinery (including packaging machinery, metal working machine tools, conveying equipment, etc.) was provided by the Long Term Credit Bank, Industrial Bank of Japan, and Nippon Credit from Treasury financing.

Japan Development Bank made loans in the 1960s to enable manufacturing companies to introduce new machinery in a comprehensive way so that the whole production process could be modernised.

[a]This is a method of selling which provides long-term low interest credit to the buyer. The ownership of the equipment is transferred at the time of sale to leasing companies.

In the early 1950s, a "linking" system enabled Japanese exporters of machinery to price competitively on international markets. The government controlled the import of raw sugar, but in order to provide a subsidy to machinery exporters, the control of raw sugar imports was handed over to the Machinery Exporters Association. The association sold the sugar at the international price, and the profit they obtained was used to compensate machinery exporters who had incurred losses in building export sales by pricing at international or even lower levels. This "linking" system was extremely important in shipbuilding as well.

Partly in order to improve its position in international trade negotiations, Japan has sinced reduced direct export grants to a minimal level. The only major grant programme still operative is the assistance given to the export associations by the bicycle racing fund, which totals about 3 to 4 billion yen per year. Loans, on the other hand, remain a major factor in export promotion. The Japan Export-Import Bank is much like those in other countries in its operations, and an ever-increasing proportion of its funds has gone to the machinery industry. Both supplier and buyer credits are extended according to rules laid down by the OECD.

In all of these loan programmes, MITI has review rights which give them influence over individual companies. Any transaction by the Export-Import Bank not settled within six months must be submitted to MITI for approval. Thus while MITI does not actively screen each transaction, it has a means of review whenever it is necessary. In Japan, the controls on foreign transactions have not been dismantled, just relaxed. Similarly, reviews are made of the credit worthiness of all manufacturers and exporters. This evaluation was especially important in the 1950s and 1960s, when capital was short and the export advance bills given by the bank were crucial to overall company financing. This made exports very popular, especially with smaller machinery companies.

Tax incentives have also played an important role in export production. The government has used a variety of different measures over the years, as shown in Table 5.2.

These measures played a very significant role in the 1960s, but have become less significant in the 1970s. Although several are still technically in effect, only the technology export income deduction is significant today. In 1976 these measures in total added about 32 billion yen to the cash flow of companies of which almost 20 billion came from the technology provision in the machinery industry. This accounted for about 5 percent of taxes actually paid in the industry. In addition to these measures, the government has two export insurance programmes—one covering all industries and another compensating for losses caused by inadequate consultation on overseas machinery projects.

Policy in the 1970s and 1980s

By 1970 the process of industry rationalisation had essentially been completed. World-scale component producers coexisted in Japan with a number of efficient producers of machines. The Japanese industry enjoyed a predominance in its home market and had made inroads into world markets for some products, particularly simple machine tools and textile machinery.

In the early 1970s, government policy turned away from rationalisation, home market protection and stimulation, and export assistance measures, and toward research and development assistance to companies for whole plant sales abroad. The goals are to move Japan into the forefront of machinery technology, to build world market share by attacking the new growth markets in developing countries, and to build upon strong Japanese process industries to emphasise whole plant sales.

These efforts to guide industry development have achieved considerable success. Japan has only a small export share in ordinary machine tools, compared to Germany and the United States, but a high share in numerically controlled machine tools. Over 50 per cent of Japan's machinery exports went to non-OECD countries in 1974-76, compared to 40 percent for the United States and 30 percent for Germany. Finally, Japan's most rapid export growth has been in steel mills, chemical plants, and other "whole plant" sales.

TABLE 5.2

Export Promoting Tax Measures

Years	*Measure*
1953-1964	Export income deduction *Export income was directly shielded from taxation.*
1953-1959	Export loss reserve system *A reserve against the possibility of cancelled export contracts was non-taxable.*
1953-1959	Special depreciation for overseas offices of trading companies *All depreciable assets in a new office overseas were subject to a 50 percent write-off the first year.*
1959 to present	Technology export income deduction *Companies are allowed to deduct a portion of royalties paid from abroad from their taxable income. The objective is to stimulate saleable technology development.*
1964 to 1972	Overseas market development reserve *A small portion of the revenue from current exports can be put into reserves from taxable income. Like all Japanese reserves, this must later be returned to the income stream. This provision still applies for small businesses.*
1964 to present	Overseas investment loss reserve *A small percentage of current foreign investment expenditure each year can be put into reserve to insure against investment losses. This reserve fund is non-taxable.*
1964-1972	Export accelerated depreciation *Accelerated depreciation was allowed on capital investment where the output was to be exported. The degree of acceleration depended on the proportion of plant and equipment devoted to export.*
1968-1978	Export special depreciation *An overlay acceleration on the previous provision.*
Early 1960s to present	Free trade zone investment loss reserve *Variation on the overseas investment loss reserve extended for free trade zones.*

Research and Development. The primary thrust of Japanese industry policy in machinery is currently in research and development. The policy includes grants, loans, and tax subsidies.

A number of grant programmes currently operate to benefit industrial machinery businesses. MITI's Agency for Industrial Science and Technology (AIST) administers the government's conventional research and development grants. This programme gives matching grants to specific research and development projects proposed by individual companies. On average, about 4 billion yen was provided annually to the industrial machinery sector during 1973-76 and 3 billion during 1977 and 1978. These appropriations have been primarily directed to the area of machine and whole plant integration.

A second source of research and development grants is the national Large-Scale Research project, which combines resources from the government and companies to fund development in areas of nationally critical technologies. In the industrial machinery area, a seven-year programme to develop in ultra-high performance laser-applied complex control system (a highly automated machine tool system) will receive 12 billion yen in government assistance plus individual contributions from companies.

A third source of research and development funding is the Bicycle Rehabilitation Association (JBRA). In 1976 the JBRA awarded almost 5 billion yen for research and development in the machinery area. An additional 150 million yen is awarded from a minicar racing fund. MITI undoubtedly influences, although it does not officially control, these allocations.

Another minor source of government funding is the subsidy for research and development by small businesses. This is administered in matching funds programmes primarily through the Subsidies for Important Technologies budget. About 450 million yen was allocated to industrial machinery through this channel in 1976.

Finally, the AIST maintains permanent research laboratories whose work principally benefits the industrial machinery area. These laboratories include the Mechanical Engineering Laboratory in Tokyo and the Industrial Research Institutes in Osaka (materials) and Nagoya (forming processes). About 6 billion yen in financing for these laboratories was provided by AIST in 1976.

In total, between 8 and 10 billion yen per year is spent in direct grants for research and development in the industrial machinery industries in Japan. In addition, there is a complex series of loan programmes to stimulate research and development. Over the years this lending, primarily carried on by the Japan Development Bank, has grown steadily and is now well over 30 billion yen per year, of which about 8 to 9 billion on average goes to industrial machinery companies. These project-related loans are essentially a means of providing low cost funds to manufacturers and buyers in areas such as the development of heavy machinery, commercialisation of new technologies in industry, development of prototypes for commercial production, and commercialisation of new technology for small enterprises. For example, the JDB will finance users' purchase of prototype machinery, manufacturers' purchases of equipment to be used in making new types of machines, and the actual development of new types of machines.

The final series of measures the government uses to aid technology development involves tax incentives for research and development. Twenty-five percent of all new spending on research and development can be taken by a company as a direct credit; these credits were worth about 12 billion yen to the machinery industry in 1976. In addition, the government allows special depreciation on equipment. Although the impact of this provision is hard to measure, we estimate its annual value at roughly 5 billion yen.

From 1968 until 1975, a special depreciation programme existed for machinery embodying commercial application of new technologies. Regional property taxes as well as corporate income taxes were shielded by this programme, which assisted both users of new machinery and manufacturers. Overall, about 78 billion yen of equipment was covered in this programme during its existence.

Finally, tax credits are allowed on the dues for establishing cooperative research associations among companies. Over twenty-five of these associations have been created, and the funds paid into them can be subtracted from the individual company's income as depreciation. Over the past few years, grants and loans have accounted for 10 to 15 percent of all research and development spending in the machinery industry. Tax credits related to research and development have averaged about 3 percent of the industry's total tax paid.

Whole Plant Sales. A second major thrust of current industrial policy in machinery is to aid whole plant sales. Many of Japan's institutions work effectively together to promote whole plant sales. MITI has published a 400-page book on whole plant selling and has informally assisted the formation of groups of companies to study particular market opportunities. The industry association and trading companies also play an important role in coordination. The informal connections among MITI, the banks, the industry associations, and the companies, along with the legislation which enables cartels to be formed, allow a flexible model of interaction very helpful in making the complex arrangements needed for whole plant sales.

Financing is crucial to the purchase of a large plant, particularly in developing countries, which now account for about half of the market for machinery. Fully 60 percent of Export-Import Bank loans are now directed to plant export; these loans are often supplemented by financing arranged through large banks (to which the government has close ties). The most significant form of financing assistance, however, is government-to-government credit (in yen), often indirectly tied to machinery sales.

Large national project sold to the governments of other countries can be financed by mechanisms which fall under the broad heading of economic aid, and thus (in contrast to Export-Import Bank loans) are not regulated by the OECD. In Japan, the agency responsible is the Overseas Economic Cooperation Fund, a public policy company funded via the FILP and under the direction of the Ministry of Finance, the Ministry of Foreign Affairs, and the Economic Planning Agency. Yen credits are a highly desirable form of financing from the borrower's point of view: very low interest is charged (3 percent and less); amounts can exceed the value of the narrowly defined project; and longer repayment terms than those of Export-Import or private financing can be provided.

It is often difficult to discover an explicit link between a government-to-government or even a central bank-to-central bank financing package and a particular large machinery or plant order. Yet clearly such connections are there. Though the Japanese feel that the French are the masters at this type of activity, they themselves have devised a number of inventive financing measures, helped by the strength of the yen and japan's large dollar balances. Apart from sales arranged between governments, the trading companies play the most significant role in arranging financing, making three cornered deals, and putting together packages for a sale as well as doing promotion and research, etc. The government may review prices or give guidance on selection of a particular subcontractor, but most of the work is done by the manufacturers and trading companies involved.

Summary

Although Japan is currently behind some other OECD countries in the export of industrial machinery, the priority being placed on this industry will clearly make Japan an increasingly formidable competitor. The groundwork being laid by government research and development, whole plant export coordination, and financing programmes will no doubt assist the industry greatly over the coming decade. Though these programmes have existed for a number of years, their results will be most pronounced in the near future. These measures reinforce the extremely good cooperation among Japanese companies, which allows a prompt and well coordinated response to market opportunities. Western companies in this industry would be well advised to keep a close watch on current and potential Japanese competitors.

Information Electronics

Computers and semiconductors are the heart of information electronics. The Japanese government is committed to developing an internationally strong position in computers, and has given the industry significant support. The task of overcoming American leadership is a large one. U.S. companies have over one-third of the Japanese market, dominate their own large domestic market, and are keenly fighting the Japanese challenge. Japan's overall trade balance in computers, including peripherals and attachments, is distinctly negative. In 1977 the value of imports was three times as great as the value of exports, but exports were growing considerably faster. The two leading Japanese producers—Fujitsu and Hitachi—together have had a smaller share of the Japanese market over the last five years than IBM in the value of computers sold or leased. Japanese producers have advanced quickly, but so have manufacturers in other countries.

Most of the Japanese industry is concentrated in six companies—Fujitsu, Hitachi, Nippon Electric, Toshiba, Mitsubishi Electric, and Oki. They all produce computers, peripherals, and semiconductors, and most of them produce telecommunications equipment as well. Jurisdiction over this sector lies primarily with MITI, although the Ministry of Post and Telecommunications has some responsibility for the development of the telecommunications industry.

Computers

The government's assistance to computers can be reviewed under three categories: technology development, leasing and financing, and market protection.

Technology Development. The government provides funds for approximately one quarter of all computer-related research and development in Japan, while three quarters is funded by the manufacturers of computers and private laboratories. Total computer research and development in Japan in 1976 was 116.5 billion yen. Government grants to companies and associations were 18.9 billion yen. (Major undertakings like the Very Large Scale Integration [VLSI] circuit development project typically involve matching funds from business and government to ensure a worthwhile effort.) Another 5.8 billion yen of public funds was spent in university and government laboratories. In addition to direct government spending, two tax mechanisms—the research and development tax credit and accelerated depreciation of research and development facilities—offer significant assistance to the industry. One estimate puts tax saved by the computer manufacturers at 3.4 billion yen per year, roughly 5 percent of total expenditure on research and development in the industry.

The government has also offered special help to the software sector. In 1967 the Japan Information Processing Development Center was established as a joint venture of government, the major manufacturers, and the software houses to develop general purpose end user application software. The government invested one billion yen in equity and between 1970 and 1977 contributed 8 billion yen in research and development funds. Not surprisingly, Japan Development Bank is the largest lender. Special tax benefits have been made available to the software industry as well.

The principal rationale for government research and development assistance is the small scale of Japanese producers relative to the American leaders—despite the concentration of all major computer and semiconductor activity within a few Japanese firms. Up to the mid-1970s, research and development funded by Fujitsu, Hitachi, and Nippon Electric combined was less than half of IBM's total expenditure on research and development, while the combined semiconductor research and development expenditure of these Japanese companies is less than Texas Instruments' total.

As with other Japanese industries, MITI has tried to use government funds to rationalise the industry's research and development effort. MITI has also tried unsuccessfully to rationalise the industry itself through mergers. The companies have preferred to remain independent, and a system has emerged in which there is cooperation in the funding of new technology projects, rationalisation, and concurrent specialisation in peripherals, but continued fierce competition in existing products and in the production and marketing of new products.

The first cooperative research and development project was in 1962, when MITI formed an association of Fujitsu, Nippon, and Oki to develop a new computer. After IBM introduced the 360 model in 1964, MITI conceived a more ambitious large-scale computer project and budgeted for 10 billion yen of government funding. In designing this project, MITI matched the five participating companies and tasks very carefully. Fujitsu, Hitachi, and Nippon were asked to build the memory and central processing unit and to develop the operating system software. Toshiba and Oki were asked to build time-sharing peripheral equipment. (Mitsubishi, the sixth competitor, did not join the project.) Later, MITI organised a peripheral equipment production cartel which enabled the six producers (each of whom had low production scale because of substantial product line overlap) to pool and specialise some equipment. The products handled through the cartel included standard peripherals whose design had stabilised and where further innovation was remote. Seven types of punched card and paper tape equipment were cartelised in 1969. Line printers and magnetic drums were added a year later.

In the early 1970s, MITI tried to organise the industry into three groups (Fujitsu/ Hitachi, Nippon/Toshiba), and Mitsubishi/Oki), again to force a specialisation of development efforts and, it was hoped, a long-term competitive segmentation of the business. Then the target was the IBM 370 series, and a government-sponsored joint development programme was conceived. By 1975, however, the targets of this programme were obsolete, and an extraordinary joint effort—the VLSI semiconductor project—was substituted. The four-year project involves all major Japanese producers and two government electronics research laboratories in diverse roles; it is budgeted at 72 billion yen. Roughly 40 percent is government-funded. The technical targets are highly ambitious, aimed at developing the "state-of-the-art" technology in both logic and memory circuits. Completion is scheduled for 1980-86. The project's key members are shown in Figure 5.1.

While Japanese producers have cooperated in these development efforts and benefited enormously, they continue to compete independently on existing products and new systems. MITI has tried to consolidate their computer operations but has failed, and must now rely on the market mechanism to restructure the industry. The business moves extremely fast, and it is not clear whether MITI's policy initiatives of the 1970s to reduce the number of competitors were appropriate. On the one hand, computers will turn out to have been an expensive adventure for some Japanese producers, as for some large American and European companies. On the other hand, it is difficult to predict which company will succeed and in what sector in this rapidly changing business.

Leasing and Financing. Apart from support for research and development, the government's major contribution to the industry has been in giving financial assistance to purchasers of computers—a crucial element in computer marketing.

In the early 1960s, it became clear that by leasing rather than selling computers, IBM was using its financial position to take advantage of its Japanese competitors, who could not compete in the leasing arrangements, though MITI proposed a joint venture of government and computer manufacturers; this joint company would lease only Japanese made computers. Neither the manufacturers nor the Ministry of Finance would accept government equity participation, and the compromise reached in 1961 was a joint venture, with the equity shared among the seven manufacturers then active, financed heavily by the Japan Development Bank. This venture was called the Japan Electronic Computer Corporation (JECC).

FIGURE 5.1
Very Large-Scale Integration Project

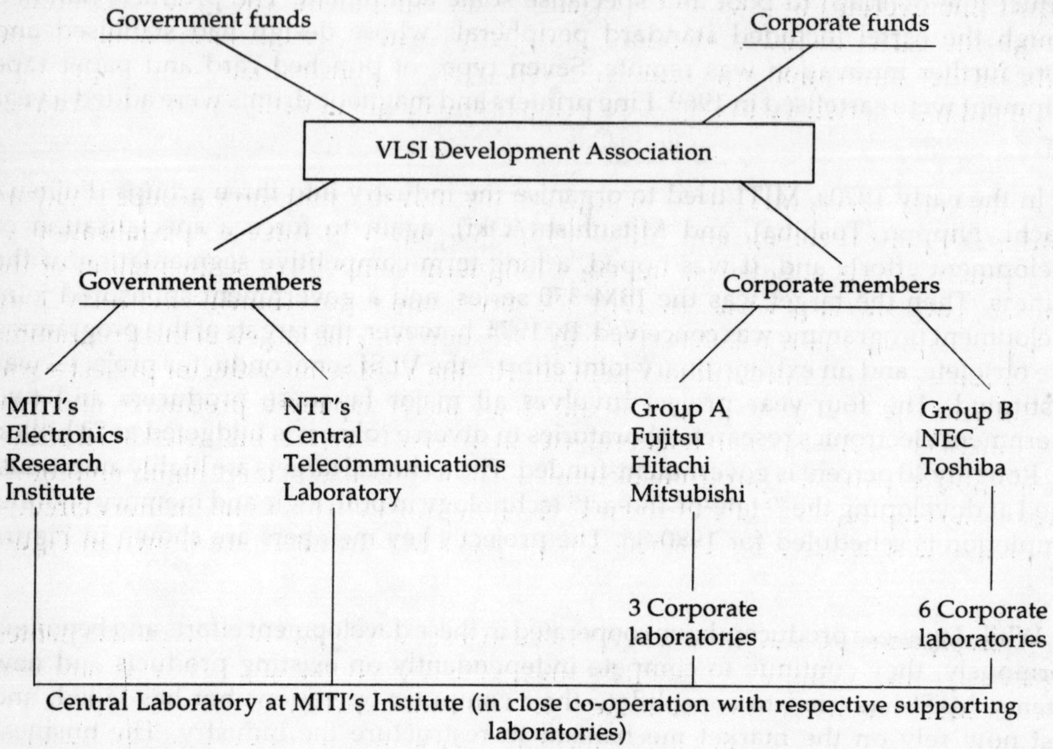

JECC purchases computers from the manufacturers and then leases them to customers. At the end of 1978, the gross value of JECC's rented assets was over 400 billion yen. Over one third is financed by the JDB at interest rates roughly one percent below the market rate, while city banks finance most of the rest. JECC has been generally successful, particularly in financing the explosive market growth which took place in the 1960s. In recent years, the two major manufacturers—Hitachi and Fujitsu—have increasingly leased directly to customers as far as their cash flow permitted. The reason for this is the competitive nature of the market. Large users want a better price than is permitted by JECC's fixed price policy. If the large manufacturers do not try to accommodate these large users by dealing with them directly, the transaction would in all probability go to a foreign supplier.

When a new computer model appears, customers trade in the existing leased equipment, and the manufacturer must repurchase at JECC book value. As technology moved swiftly in the 1960s, the resale value of the equipment sank well below book value, which created a new financial problem for the manufacturers. MITI and the Ministry of Finance developed a tax reserve in which initially 10 percent, then 20 percent, of the original selling price to JECC could be reserved from taxable income against future estimated trade-in losses. After five years, the reserve had to be put back into the company's income stream. The cash flow effect of this provision research a peak in 1972, when 10.3 billion yen in taxation was saved by the industry. Since then, budget pressure has forced a cutback in the provision. In 1977, 3 billion yen was saved.

To help clear the market of obsolete machines and make way for the new models, and to promote the use of computers among small businesses, the government has encouraged the Chambers of Commerce to repurchase traded-in leased machines from JECC. Resale price is set at 60 percent of the original book value; half is paid by government and one quarter each by the user and by the original manufacturer, who then charges it against his trade-in tax reserve. Total government subsidy in 1976 was 40 million yen.

Other devices to preserve the manufacturers' cash flow and develop the market have also been used. Special accelerated depreciation is extended to some computer production facilities. Special depreciation was also established in 1970 for the purchase of larger computers, which enabled buyers to write off 20 per cent of initial book value in the first year in addition to normal depreciation. This provision aims to make the ownership of a computer more attractive than the leasing of foreign computer in Japan. Computers were also afforded preferential treatment in property taxation. Industry pays a standard local tax of 1.4 per cent of taxable real assets every year; the taxable value of the computer can be reduced by 20 per cent. There are miscellaneous other tax benefits including a tax credit for training expenses for data processing engineers. The sums involved are far smaller than those committed to technology development and JECC.

Market Protection. The government has used both direct and indirect forms of market protection. Tariffs assessed against computers and semiconductors have always been high relative to Japan's other products. Quantitative restrictions on both components and computer systems were the last to be lifted in the mid-1970s. Until recently, MITI actively discouraged Japanese companies from buying foreign computers as long as a domestic offering met the specification. At present, however, the private sector computer market in Japan is essentially open. Western companies can import or manufacture what product they wish. Informal protection continues in the public sector market, which includes all of civilian government and military expenditure as well as a large portion of the university and research institute market. Consequently, while domestic producers have between 50 and 60 per cent of the total Japanese market in value, they have over 90 per cent of the public sector portion. The only exceptions to this informal rule arise when the Japanese supplier cannot meet the specifications or when a Japanese supplier subcontracts a key part of the system to a superior foreign supplier in order to outperform other domestic bidders. MITI does not like this practice, but it does occasionally happen.

In the semiconductor area, government purchases are confined to domestic producers, and, for different reasons, much of the private market is closed to foreign suppliers.

Japanese computer and telecommunications equipment producers are both the major users and major suppliers of integrated circuits. Consequently, only where Western technology is unique or the cost is dramatically less are chips imported. The lengthy period of market protection posed a dilemma for MITI. The prohibition of any foreign investment into Japan, in either new ventures or existing domestic producers, preserved the industry's domestic character. As a consequence of this protection, producers were to some extent more dependent on MITI because of its influence on the market and the financial incentives it could provide. On the other hand, protection delayed any shakeout among the six producers, and there was not enough competitive pressure to make producers bend to MITI's consolidation schemes.

Telecommunications

There are four major telecommunications equipment suppliers in Japan—Nippon Electric, Fujitsu, Oki, and Hitachi (the Big Four). MITI and the Ministry of Post and Telecommunications delegate most policy authority to Nippon Telephone and Telegraph Corporation (NTT), a public corporation charged with maintaining a domestic telecommunications network. The Ministry of Post and Telecommunications controls NTT and authorises its budget; the directors of NTT are appointed by the Prime Minister with Diet approval. In addition to controlling the telephone and telegraph systems, NTT monopolises all common carrier network transmission in Japan, including data, and offers data processing time-sharing services in competition with private companies. NTT also licenses all communications, including private microwave and citizen-band radios.

Japanese industrial policy in telecommunications has concentrated on supporting research and development and helping the industry to build an export capability by allowing high prices to be charged on domestic sales. Telecommunications research and development and system engineering is generally performed by NTT laboratories, much as Bell laboratories serves American Telephone and Telegraph Company in the United States. NTT makes all decisions on technical specifications, and engineers of the Big Four manufacturers are invited to develop new equipment jointly after basic research is completed by NTT's own engineers. Therefore all research and development expenses incurred by manufacturers are mostly application and production related. Since new equipment is jointly developed by NTT and its designated manufacturers. NTT assigns actual production and supply to each manufacturers, depending on availability of technical capacity and actual performance of the company on past assignments.

NTT's research and development programme has evolved as competitive needs have changed. In the 1960s, development of each component was assigned to a manufacturers (e.g., the switch frame to Nippon Electric and high speed transmissions to Hitachi). In order to develop overall telecommunication/computer technology, however, all four manufacturers are now involved in jointly developing future technical specifications with NTT. Opportunities are given equally to manufacturers to learn everything, from the switching system components to materials technology.

In addition to assistance for research and development, NTT also helps its suppliers in financing exports. The relationship between NTT and its major suppliers—Fujitsu, Hitachi, and Oki—has helped these manufacturers to finance the growth of their businesses. First, prices are not bid but negotiated on a generous cost-plus basis (somewhat less generous in recent years because of NTT's operating losses). Profit margins are widely alleged to be higher on NTT business than on export sales, though figures are not publicly available. Second, the exclusion of foreign equipment stabilises process and production volumes. Third, NTT advances a portion of the purchases price to the manufacturers, in effect providing interest free funds. As a result of these factors, combined with NTT's financing of the research and development, the manufacturers can be very flexible in pricing exports. In this respect, Japanese producers enjoy an advantage over some major international competitors such as ITT and Ericsson.

Japanese companies got off to a late start in telecommunications exports, in large part because of their undistinguished technology. However, the boom in the OPEC and developing Asian markets in the middle and late 1970s, combined with lower growth at home, brought them into export markets. Exports—only 8 per cent of sales in the early 1970s—are now 18-20 per cent. Because of the higher investment required in the new generation of digital equipment, NTT is encouraging firms to export more in order to spread the revenue base. The direct forms of assistance which have been indicated, combined with liberal financing from Japanese banks, have contributed significantly to this goal.

Telecommunications policy is closely related to that of computers, which brings the Ministry of Post and Telecommunications into close contact with MITI. Coordination of policy between them is difficult. MITI has pressed for a faster and more meaningful liberalisation of imports in telecommunications equipment than MOPT has conceded. Disagreements arise over research directions and over data communications policy. The two ministries are being brought into more contact by the convergence of data processing and data communications technologies, and policy coordination will continue to be difficult.

Summary

As with the nuclear reactor and aircraft industries, the computer and telecommunications industries have been the subject of government interest throughout the world. The U.S. Defense Department research and development funding and purchases were essential to the development of the miniature electronics industry in the United States, and governments have played a key role in the development of the computer and telecommunications industries in a number of European countries. Japan continues to make a large commitment to information electronics. It is too early to tell whether these policies will be successful. The Japanese still have not achieved technological parity, and the strong, aggressive U.S. leaders are unlikely to follow the mistakes of their counterparts in steel and consumer electronics.

REFERENCES

1. The discussion in this chapter draws significantly on earlier published Boston Consulting group case studies in *Japan: The Government—Business Relationship* (Washington D.C.: U.S. Department of commerce, 1972).
2. It should be noted, however, that several large independent parts manufactures have now emerged.
3. This discussion draws heavily on an unpublished paper by Kent E. Caldor of Harvard University entitled "The Emerging Politics of Aid for the Uncompetitive: The Case of Sasebo Heavy Industries."
4. Before 1956, the Reconversion Finance Bank and the Japan Development Bank had helped to rebuild some of the large machinery manufacturers from before the war in order to supply the needs of UN forces in the Korean conflict. This aid, however, was not part of any industrial plan.

6

Business Environment in China: Reforms of the 1980s

A. THE CHANGING ENVIRONMENT FOR SCIENCE AND TECHNOLOGY POLICY

The Ideology of Science and Technology and the Problem of Structural Change

From the late 1970s onwards, Chinese culture was permeated with an emphasis on the significance of science and technology. Science and technology were regarded as the "magic" ingredient that could automatically transform and modernise the Chinese economy and society. As in many other countries, science and technology may be imbued with strong ritualistic elements with ideological power. The image of science could be conjured up as an appealing approach to mobilising mass support, promise being that science, progress, and modernisation would all be brought by the new times (Schwartzman, 1991). Further, the commitment of the Party leadership to science and technology helped to legitimise the progressiveness of its "leading role."

As analysed in Chapter 2, Section B, much of the rhetoric of the Deng Xiaoping regime tied in with the May Fourth Movement's celebration of science and technology as the key to solving all China's problems. Disillusionment with the prevailing ideology—Maoism and Cultural Revolutionary radicalism — once more created an ideological vacuum that the leadership and intellectuals again sought to fill with a utopian idolisation of science and technology (Simon and Goldman, 1989:9).

Thomas Fingar (1979:2) suspects that leading scientists probably contributed to the euphoria by over-stating prospects for rapid progress in discussions with newly attentive political leaders. He further maintains that wanting to believe these promises, and because it was expedient to do so, senior officials selected the politically risky strategy of promising immediate benefits while basing their own legitimacy on their ability to deliver. Since the promises were unrealistic—the efficient application of science and technology for achieving modernising goals is a time-consuming and complicated process—continued emphasis on science-based benefits entailed high risk for both the leadership and the scientific community.

Deng's modernisation programme thus confronted a dual political problem: a problem of theory and rhetoric and secondly, a problem of creating appropriate institutions which could be seen to be effective vehicles for modernisation.

In the early 1980s, there were signs of a retreat from the previous emphasis on "politics in command" over all aspects of social and political life and a growing recognition of areas of autonomy from political controls and state intervention. Chinese leaders became aware that scientific and technological advance is not likely to flourish in tightly controlled economic and political settings, and that progress in science and technology requires a major transformation of the economic and political environment. The new reform programmes demanded heavy reliance on the expertise of professionals and this necessitated a weakening of the Party's grip over both state and society. The new development strategy of mixed planning-market economy also implied the relaxation of state control over production units.

Given the increasing complexity of economic and technological systems, the crux—and the difficulty—of successful and comprehensive reform in China not only lay in bringing together several elements of market regulation or the glorification of science and technology, but a parallel rationalisation of the state apparatus and the creation of proper institutions which could generate innovative activities thus promoting development.

A series of attempts were made in the 1980s to reduce gradually the Party's role in both the state apparatus and in research and industrial sectors. *While retaining its politico-ideological function, the Communist party divested itself of its technico-economic function and transferred the latter to the government and the planning agencies.* Consequently, the establishment of "think-tanks" within the government signified its increasing importance in decision-making, especially in carrying out technico-economic reform. The re-establishment of various economic and planning commissions in the late 1970s and their subsequent expansion in the 1980s (Dittmer, 1990: 412) due to the alliance formed between liberal economists and political leaders further complicated the structure of the Chinese state.

The decentralisation of industrial management and the introduction of market mechanisms also led to the emergence of new actors such as local government, industrial enterprises, and entrepreneurs involved in China's science and technology policy. At the same time, the evolution of political and economic structures offered new channels for various bureaucracies and research establishments to exert influence, thereby creating policy tensions and fragmenting the process of decision-making.

One of the legacies of China's pre-1980 S&T policy was the concentration of investment in military R&D and the bureaucratic links established between the defense and heavy industrial sectors. The core of the scientific community residing at the Chinese Academy of Sciences, though frustrated by various political upheavals, recovered its strength in the late 1970s and began collaborating with eminent overseas scientists for pressing research in advanced fields. Both groups' vested interests were threatened in the 1980s as a result of the government's reform policies, transferring defense technologies to the civilian sector and pressing for more applied research to benefit the development of the national economy. They thus allied themselves with Party leaders, initiating high-tech R&D programmes in order to preserve their share of research budget and other resources. Not only did these powerful research establishments defy reform programmes, local government and industrial enterprises also deviated from original state policies and pursued unit (group) interests once the chance arose. As a consequence, vested interests based on institutional lagacies and the formation of new interest groups made China's S&T policy during the reform period highly complicated, involving *diversified actors* interacting with *changed structures*, often creating conflicts among various policy groups and compromises over final policy outcomes.

Science for Policy: The Improvement of the Planning System

Besides being utilised as a means of achieving political legitimacy, "expertise" was further employed by the Chinese leadership to improve the planning system. In the 1980s, the Chinese leaders came to pay increasing attention to the "scientification of decision-making," which meant adoption of measures to increase the role of professionals—from both the natural and social sciences — in policy-making. Recruitment of educated individuals into leadership positions in both government and Party was advocated; more importantly, organisational innovations in the form of new advisory bodies that would increase and restructure the flow of expert advice available to the leaders were introduced.

Beginning in late 1980, newly appointed Premier Zhao Ziyang—who had successful experience in regional economic reform in the late 1970s—started creating policy research organs to support his search for a new development strategy and concrete economic policies. By 1982-83, several "think-tanks" directly under the State Council and in key state commissions and ministries had sought the advice of well-known social scientists and recruited younger researchers.

These think-tanks undertook a crash course in modern social theory and social indicators research. Simplistic hopes of modernising by merely importing advanced foreign technology began to give way to new views on the relationship between cultural, technological, political, and economic factors in the modernisation process. The role of the cultural component was at this time also being emphasised in the West, e.g. the Japanese example.

The five permanent research centers created under the State Council between fall of 1980 and 1982 were: the Economics Research Center (ERC), headed by Xue Muqiao (who, together with Hu Qiaomu and Sun Yefang, had become influential since the late 1970s by advocating liberal economic theory); the Techno-Economics Research Center (TERC), headed by Ma Hong; the Price Research Center; the Rural Research Center, headed by Du Runsheng, and the Economic Legislation Center, headed by Gu Ming. In May 1985, ERC, TERC and the Price Research Center were combined to form an Economic, Technological, and Social Development Research Center (ETSRC), also run by Ma Hong. The centers brought together experts from both inside the government bureaucracy and outside it, from such organisations as CAS and the Chinese Academy of Social Sciences.

In evaluating and choosing among different capital construction projects and imports of foreign technology, TERC appeared to overlap in function with the State Planning Commission. Undoubtedly, this reflected the leadership's disatisfaction with the Commission's performance. Part of the motivation behind the establishment of TERC was to end fiascos like the Baoshan Steel Mill, on which the leadership had spent millions of dollars in 1978-1979 before realising that the project was poorly planned, badly located, and much too expensive. Such projects were the responsibility of the State Planning Commission (Halpern, 1989:165).

In October 1982 the State Science and Technology Commission established a subordinate National Research Center for Scientific and Technological Development (NRCSTD) to improve planning in the area of science and technology. One aspect of the NRCSTD's work was long-term planning and priority setting in the area of technology. Like the TERC, the NRCSTD provided advice and feasibility studies on specific projects. It was asked to help the State Council resolve the bureaucratic debate over whether and how to proceed with the Three Gorges dam project and commissioned studies from other institutions on different aspects of the project. The stress on professionalism, feasibility and foresight studies provided a strong organisational impetus toward greater consultation and cooperation in the planning stages of major projects. It also created a channel for discourse between experts and political leaders on S&T and development-related policy issues.

The NRCSTD collaborated with foreign research organisations, such as the Science Policy Research Unit at the University of Sussex and UNESCO in the area of S&T planning and indicators research. The publication of a series of white papers on China's science and technology policy in 1986-90 was part of the outcome of this international co-operation.

Premier Zhao's efforts were intended to make researchers' work useful for urgent policy needs. He not only set up think-tanks under his State Council but appointed his aide Ma Hong — an economist — to replace Hu Qiaomu as President of the Chinese Academy of Social Sciences (CASS). Intellectuals were encouraged to "emancipate their thought" and explore new ideas and methodologies that could support the reform programme (Hamrin, 1987: 292 f). Eventually, the Institute of Industrial Economy, the Institute of Law, and the Institute of Political Science of the CASS contributed a considerable number of ideas, theories, and legal codes for the second wave of reform initiated in the mid-1980s (Zhao, 1988:327).

In Western countries, both the concept and the practice of "science for policy" had been implemented for several decades emanating particularly from discussions in the OECD and its S&T policy group. In many cases, the coalitions between social scientists and policy-makers occurred during the "reform mood" of the political systems. How to achieve modernisation generated by technological innovation was often the main focus of their interactions (Wagner, 1987). Even the Soviet Union had committed itself to "scientific decision-making" and "science for administration" to improve its planning system during the Khrushchev and Brezhnev periods.

The complexities of social activities and the ever-changing socio-economic and political situations in the modern era have increased the need for social sciences research and the value of expertise. The establishment of think-tanks during China's reform drive created a channel for discourse between experts and policy-makers which improved the planning system. However, it also led to the emergence of a "technocracy" within the political leadership (Cheng and White, 1990). At times, these young technocrats tended to be over-enthusiastic about Western ideas — such as the "third wave"[1] and "new technological revolution" theories — proposing policy initiatives which were not always appropriate to China's present reality. Their alliance with the research establishments in the pursuit of high-tech R&D programme in 1985-86 was an evident example. The details of the formation of the "high-tech lobby" will be outlined in Chapter 10, Section C.

B. INTERNAL VERSUS EXTERNAL CRITERIA

The Debate on Basic and Applied Research

In the early 1980s, national policy gave the highest priority to the development of science and technology. To facilitate this, the Party accepted the fact that it must withdraw from its over-dominant position, allowing scientists and technicians greater freedom within their areas of professional competence. The Party leaders realised that the S&T sector cannot be over-administered but, at the same time, maintained that it could not be left to its own devices. This resulted in an attempt to find an appropriate balance between central control and delegation of powers.

In December 1980, the first national science conference since Spring 1978 was held. Among the participants, there were representatives from various research sectors and government planning offices. On the base of discussions at the conference, the State Science and Technology Commission drew up an "Outline Report on Policy Concerning the Development of our National Science and Technology" which urged research in production enterprises be stepped up while also guaranteeing the role of basic research, in particular that affecting the development of national economy. This simultaneous emphasis on applied and basic research was an obvious compromise between the scientific community (the CAS) and the SSTC, but when this policy proposal reached the highest level of decision-makers, its content and orientation was altered. After being modified by the CCP Central Committee and the State Council, the report was officially announced as a policy document in April 1981 with an overwhelming stress on applied research and development. The outline summarised the future direction of science and technology policy in five main points:

1. science and technology was to be developed in co-ordination with society and the economy with the primary mission of promoting economic development.
2. applied research on production technology was to be strengthened; the application and dissemination of research results should be promoted, including the transfer of scientific and technological, know-how from the defence sector to the civilian sector.
3. there should be more co-ordination between the SSTC, the State Planing Commission, and the State Economics Commission; long-term planning of science and technology was to take technological, social, and economic factors into considerations.
4. gradual reform of the existing S&T system was to take place. A contract system could be applied between research and production units. In some cases, joint research-production associations (*keyan shengchan lianheti*) could be formed.
5. imports of foreign technology were to be based on national economic requirements and China's absorptive capacities (SSTC, 1986: 305 f).

Although the content of "Outline Report" was rather general, it anticipated most of the reforms that took place in the 1980s and it resulted in the gradual materialisation of the 1985 reform of the S&T system.

Being a privileged establishment in basic research, however, the Chinese Academy of Sciences tended to disregard the external demand for a more application-oriented research policy. It continued to press for internally-regulated research criteria and agenda setting.

The Growing Autonomy of the Scientific Community and Its Pursuit of Basic Research

In May 1981, the Fourth Conference of the CAS Scientific Council was held (the last occasion was 1960). Four hundred members were newly elected and among them both scientists and engineers from the CAS. IHEs, and R&D units of industrial ministries. The CAS Scientific Council began to take responsibility for the evaluation of research projects and research results and, it was now also mandated to undertake planning and feasibility studies.

At the same time, the President of the CAS, Fang Yi, a bureaucratic figure, resigned, and two natural scientists, Lu Jiaxi and Yan Dongsheng were elected by their peers as the President and Senior Vice President respectively (*PD*, 19 May 1981).

At the Conference, scientists again demanded more state investment in basic research. With the consent of part of the political leadership, a research council, or as it is called, the "CAS Science Foundation" was established. It was initially administered by the CAS, then transformed into a national foundation in 1986. From 1982 onwards, the

Science Foundation funded basic research on a project basis through competitive peer review. This was the first time that *the concept of "peer review" was used in China.* Before then, very little research had been evaluated unless it was designed to meet specific needs.

The struggle, over the issue of "academic leadership" starting from the 1950s was finally settled, now, favouring the significance of internal control by the scientific community. On the other hand, the de-emphasis of the Party's role in directing research activities increased the importance of government's role in overall science planning.

The Academy's interest in basic research can be attributed to its institutional legacy and the newly evolved political environment. In Chapter 3, I have argued that the Chinese science system, with its concentrated research center located at the Chinese Academy of Sciences[2] inevitably encouraged the scientists' pursuit of self-interest. The lack of effective mechanisms capable of integrating research and productive activities further encouraged many researchers to neglect the importance of application. In fact, many Chinese scientists, particularly those affiliated with the Academy, often tended to regard applied as inferior to basic research, thereby refusing to surrender their commitment to basic science and "dirty their hands" in the movement to give greater emphasis to applied research (Orleans, 1982: 472-477). There are also fundamental Confucian values that reinforce this tendency. In the Introduction, I have pointed out the historical fact that in traditional China, there was a sharp class division between the intellectuals and manual labour, and that scholars tended to despise craftsmanship and practical matters. This mandarin attitude seems to linger on in the modern era, a typical example being natural scientists who often prefer basic research to applied research and development.

The political conditions accompanying the emergence of Deng Xiaoping's leadership with its economy-based, science-based legitimacy offered the scientific community a unique chance to press for autonomy. As the door to interaction with the outside world reopened in the late 1970s, many senior, often formerly Western-trained scientists were inclined to select research topics following the mainstream of scientific research in the advanced nations. The unrealistic science plan formulated in 1978 reveals some of these tendencies. A major contributor to this state of affairs were the large numbers of ethnic Chinese in the upper echelons of the foreign scientific community who acted as advisers to China's political leaders. Partly under their influence, some leading Chinese scientists apparently believed that the current "pro-science" climate might be their last opportunity to achieve a nationally and internationally recognised scientific accomplishment (Simon, 1987: 358 f). Basic research in advanced fields naturally became their favourite choice.

External Demand on Scientific Research—Renewed Emphasis on Applied Science and the Introduction of Economic Measures

The new found autonomy and prestige enjoyed by the scientific community caused problems of coordination and the direction of research. The Academy's emphasis on basic research was an obvious deviation from the utilitarian-oriented "Outline Report on the Development of Science and Technology" issued in April 1981. It is claimed that

Premier Zhao Ziyang had conflicts with the CAS which he threatened to close down if the Academy continued to pursue self-interest and detachment from social acountability.

On 24 October 1982, Premier Zhao Ziyang addressed the National Science Awards Conference in an attempt to define more precisely the relationship between science, technology and economic development and he took the occasion to stress once again the significance of applied research and economic development. According to Zhao, shortages in energy, raw material, and financial resources were holding back the country's economic growth potential. As a result, the desired expansion could only be achieved through additional S&T inputs. He stated that "it is necessary to activate the economy by relying on scientific and technological progress..." and *"scientific and technological work should be oriented to serving economic construction."* To improve things he suggested a number of practical measures such as setting up "technical development centers," and perfecting the reward and the evaluation systems of research and development. Zhao further proposed that new policies be introduced to deal with pricing, taxation, and the protection of intellectual property.

According to Zhao's speech, four types of "technology transfer" were to be encouraged: (1) from research to production, (2) from coastal regions to interior regions, (3) from defense to civilian sectors, and (4) from overseas to domestic users.

Evidently, there were increasing demands for relevance and accountability imposed on the research sector by the government. Research and development activities which could directly serve production technology and propel economic growth now received the highest priority. At the same time, the "CAS Science Foundation" continued to operate with a limited budget.

While both the "Outline Report" of 1981 and Zhao's policy statement of 1982 emphasised applied research, technology transfer, and a more market-oriented mechanism in the research and industrial sectors, the scientific community's pursuit in basic research became threatened and a split ensued between the scientists and the government bureaucracy over the direction of scientific research.

Although, throughout its history the PRC has always stressed the need for science and technology to serve production, Chinese science and technology has never been application-oriented. In contrast to the achievements of academic scientists, here was a case of gross incompetence in the management of applied science (cf. Simon, 1984: 100; Suttmeier, 1986: 201). According to one study, only 10 per cent of all research could be transferred into production (Xia and Liu, 1981). Due to this low application rate, scientific achievements often remained "samples, display items, or gifts."

The structural defects of China's R&D system have been reviewed in Chapter 8, Section C. The Soviet model of research and industrial designs seriously separated scientific and productive activities. Furthermore, the Chinese planning bureaucracy failed to fulfil its role of coordinating the research and industrial sectors. The root of this problem can be traced back to the late 1950s, when the SSTC was established on the model of its Soviet counterpart. While it planned research in science and technology, it played little role in dovetailing research results with production processes. This was partly because most new technology in the 1950s came from the Soviet Union, with the result that China did not have to rely on its indigenous scientific capabilities for technological advancement. It also stemmed from the fact that the SSTC lacked the funds necessary to set up pilot projects to turn scientific discoveries into economically viable industrial processes (Liberthal and Oksenberg, 1988: 78). In general, the bureaucratic character of China's planning system was in many ways ill-suited to generating technological innovation. It would be impossible for a single centralised bureaucracy to create all the mechanisms efficiently linking research achievement to production needs.

Recognising the defects of an over-centralised planning system, China's science policy of the 1980s tried to initiate new measures that might increase the research/production interface. A rudimentary market mechanism was introduced and encouragement given to both industrial enterprises and research units to organise and have larger control over newly created institutions, i.e. the contract system, research-production associations, consultancy companies, and technology market centers. In other words, R&D activities both inside and outside the production sector were strongly enlarged.

A nationwide consultancy network administered by the China Association for Science and Technology was formed in January 1983. Individuals scientists or groups of scientists could establish formal consulting relationships for the purposes of offering expert advice or assessing the technical feasibility of a proposed project through legal contracts. Growing numbers of research-production companies were established in major industrial cities such as Beijing, Jilin, Nanjing, Shanghai, and Guangzhou. The economic measures introduced in the research and industrial sectors, though not yet practiced on a large scale, laid the foundation of 1985's reform programme of the S&T system.

C. NEW DIRECTIONS IN SCIENCE AND TECHNOLOGY POLICY

The Key Projects: Mission-Oriented Research and Development

In December 1982, Premier Zhao Ziyang introduced the nation's Sixth Five Year Plan (1981-1985) (*PD,* 14 December 1982, pp. 1-4) indicating that, "in the future, as with other sectors of the economy, science and technology would be increasingly governed by economic rather than administrative measures." To stimulate more innovative activities, the plan introduced a "responsibility system" in which managers and directors would gain more latitude and freedom while simultaneously reducing state control over enterprises and research institutes. In this way, industrial enterprises and research institutes were expected to become more "responsible" for their own productivity. The aim here was to reinforce the market measures which Zhao Ziyang's leadership had been advocating since 1981.

Nevertheless, to enhance the practical needs of the State, the Chinese government had to try and create a more efficient balance between market mechanisms and planning. After urging greater use of economic measures and unit responsibility, the government intended to improve the operation of the existing centrally directed S&T structure. It initiated a mission-oriented research policy as part of an attempt to orient scientific research more directly to state demands and social needs. This mission-oriented science policy was called the. "key project" (*gongguan*) with a focus on applied research and development eventually integrated into the Sixth Five-Year Plan for economic development.

In the period 1981-85, the government put priority on 38 major scientific and technological key projects in eight fields, with total investment amounting to 1 billion yuan *(Renminbi)*. As against the eight priority areas of the 1978-85 Science and Technology Plan, high energy physics was now removed from the list. Conversely, the beneficiaries were those areas where the economic benefit would be more quickly felt, i.e., agriculture, textiles and other light industries energy, electronics and machine building, raw materials, the chemical industry the pharmaceutical industry, and transport and communications. According to the plan, three-quarters of the items listed for scientific research were supposed to provide key equipment and solve technological problems the major construction projects due to be built under both the Sixth and the Seventh Five-Year Plans *(PD*, 14 December 1982, p. 2).

To integrate science and technology with economic development, an important new body was created in January 1983 to preside over the system. A supra-ministerial body called the Science and Technology Leading Group was set up directly responsible to the State Council. The group was headed by Premier Zhao Ziyang and drew its membership from key bodies involved in S&T work such as the SSTC, the State Planning and Economic Commissions, the Ministry of Education, the Ministry of Finance, the CAS, and representatives from the defense R&D sector. Its creation signified high level commitment to science and technology, and for the first time since the 1950s, provided an authoritative forum for national policy coordination and inter-ministerial dispute settlement. Thus, China's science policy structure evolved into one authoritative, comprehensive, cross-sectoral policy supposedly to be set at the highest level of government. Key projects from the Sixth Five Year Plan were among the major responsibilities of this new organ, but the right of budget allocation was shared with subordinate agencies such as the SSTC and the State Planning Commission. The S&T Leading Group also started preparing a reform proposal of the S&T system eventually finalised in 1985.

In the West, greater stress on socio-economic relevance since the 1970s has led to government funding for research institutes increasingly being distributed by mission-oriented agencies through whom research priorities cannot always be selected by an ordinary peer review system. This was especially the case in "strategic research" aiming at high technology R&D (Irvine et al., 1990 : 43 105, 121). There has also been an increasing use of the "customer contractor" principle *(also called the Rothschild principle, see Chapter 1, Section B)* in government-financed applied R&D, whereby the government subcontracts a high proportion of its R&D projects to research institutes, then systematically evaluates the research results of the "contractors" (Clark, 1985: 223).

In China, mission-oriented research and development has had a long tradition in the defence sector where it had attained notable successes especially in the atomic weapons and space programme. It was now applied to the civilian sector employing a more comprehensive coordination network. Chinese planners imitated the Western practice of the "customer-contractor" principle and sub-contracted the 38 key projects to R&D units from different sectors.

Among the 38 key projects of the Sixth Five-Year Plan, the Chinese Academy of Science undertook 16 projects involving agriculture, energy, new materials, bio-technology, laser, superconductor, electronics, and environmental protection (Yao, 1987; 158); the others were share by industrial research institutes and IHEs. Not all these projects were made known to the public, partly because a number of developments in the field of military technology were included. These 38 projects were reported to have been completed, yet the transfer of these research achievements to the production units, though free of charge, had disappointing consequences.[3] Though they coordinated research projects more efficiently, government planning agencies were still hampered by their difficulties in narrowing the gap between research and production even in the highly targeted areas.

The commitment to science during the Seventh Five-Year Plan (1986-1990) was substantially greater then the previous period (1981-85) — 5 billion yuan in support of 76 key projects *(Science and Technology Daily*, 8 April 1989).The SSTC was in charge of 36 projects and the rest placed under the auspices of the State Planning and Economic Commission.[4] High-tech R&D, such as microelectronics, information technology, telecommunications, new materials, and bio-technology were among the top priorities of these projects (SSTC, 1986: 111). Not only the CAS, IHEs, and industrial research institutes were involved in these projects; newly emerged high-tech research and development companies and large research-production consortia were also competing for funds. The advantage for research institutes and R&D companies in contracting key projects were multiple — project money, for example, offered extra capital for their ongoing R&D activities, and there was also the question of the prestige of winning contracts.

As a consequence, the "key projects" met no serious resistance from the research establishment. On the contrary, they subtly combined external demand for relevance with the internal interests of the research community. It seemed that the Chinese planners were becoming more aware of the significance of rationalising external regulations over S&T matters not by the means of ideological oppression but through co-ordination and more efficient use of investment funds and evaluation systems.

The decentralisation of project administration and technolgy acquisition which the establishment of contract research promoted was accompanied by highly centralised control over key projects (although there was also a contract mechanism involved). A logic of simultaneous centralisation and decentralisation was thus at work in China's S&T policy. Both methods were designed to speed up domestic technology transfer, with horizontal transfer taking place between production and research units or among enterprises themselves, while vertical transfer occurred within the "key projects" where state organs intended to convey know-how from applied research to development and production (but with limited success at the last stage).

The structural defects of the Chinese S&T system however still frustrated the links between planning, research, and production activities. Intermediary institutions capable of integrating these units, making them more efficient and producing more desirable results were scanty and weak, thereby constituting a serious constraint on the reform programmes of the 1980s.

Technological Transformation in the Industrial Sector

Another major technology development policy of the Sixth Five-Year Plan was the push for the "technical transformation" of the entire Chinese industrial infrastructure. Approximately 130 billion yuan were allocated for this purpose (*PD*, 14 December 1982, p.2)—a much higher figure then the investment sum in key projects since it was designed to bring about a nationwide improvement in industrial technology and equipment. The State Economic Commission were to be in charge of the appropriation of this budget, with the SSTC and the State Planning Commission allocating the budget for key projects.

By the early 1980s, a large proportion of China's industrial plants possessed obsolescent technology and equipment with high energy-consumption and low efficiency. Yet, with the lessons learned in the late 1970s fresh in the minds, Chinese leaders realised that advanced technology could not be simply uprooted form the West and transplanted in China (McDonald, 1990: xx, 16, 51). Therefore, instead of buying new plants and large quantities of equipment from abroad, the Chinese now emphasised rehabilitation of existing plants and facilities.

The specific objective was to improve China's technological levels by the end of the century to those presently existing in industrially-advanced countries, provided they were deemed appropriate to domestic needs and conditions. This was obviously a long-term and complex task, but Chinese planners and policy -makers decided to grapple with the detailed planning and organisation work involved. Between 1983 and 1986, the State Economic Commission convened four national conferences on technological transformation and instructed all industries to work out strategies to improve technology and equipment, based on the targets to be achieved by the turn of the century. The priority sectors for technological transformation during the Sixth and Seventh Five-Year Plans included energy, transport, raw materials, and basic industries (textile, metallurgy, electronics, chemicals, etc.); any new enterprises built had to incorporate the latest technologies (Conroy, 1985: 119; Lu, 1987: 199-120).

A series of trade fairs were held during these years whose aim was either encouraging domestic technology transfer from defense to civilian sectors or promoting technology trade between Chinese enterprises and foreign suppliers.

Historically, Chinese enterprises had been inclined to utilize capital for expanding construction or for purchasing foreign equipment in complete packages, ignoring the significance of depreciating obsolescent equipment and the upgrading of existing technology. These were typical characteristics of Soviet style extensive development strategy.

Brugger (1985: 112-115) and a Chinese study (Guo and Yang, 1982) indicate that 90 per cent of the foreign exchange earmarked for importing technology between 1950 and 1979 was used in purchasing whole sets of equipment instead of advancing the technological level of existing equipment.

Some economists (e.g. Chen, 1990: 103) argue that gains in output achieved during the first three decades of the PRC development experience were more the result of additional inputs of capital and labour force than application of new and more efficient production technologies.[5]

In the 1980s Chinese policy makers were becoming aware of the potential benefits of incremental technical change. They recognised that most of the potential gains in modernising Chinese industry and agriculture would have to derive from increase efficiency and more effective use of inputs rather than from additional capital investment and plant expansion. The key to desired increases in productivity would be factory renovation and technological upgrading.

The reorientation reflected the recognition that the "software" side of technology may be just as vital to increasing productivity as the acquisition of large quantities of advanced foreign equipment. As such, China de-emphasised its previous focus on whole-plant purchases as the major form of technology imports — in the belief that this acquisition vehicle did not provide adequate levels of technology transfer—and stressed the software side of technology imports, i.e., the acquisition of "know-how" and training (Lu, 1987: 201; Simon, 1989: 296-297).

However, despite the new policy orientation, *the "hardware bias"* of the Chinese Industry prevailed throughout the 1980s. Both during the periods of the Sixth Five-Year Plan and the Seventh Five-Year Plan (up to 1988) the purchase of "software technology" only consisted of 5-8% of the total technology imports (Chen and Lu, 1988: 64). Chinese industry again confronted the problem of assimilation which it had already experienced in the 1970s. Due to the high level of sophistication of imported technologies and the lack of specialised personnel, it often took a long time before equipment could run at designed capacity (Qin, 1988: 188-189).

Many of the early technology transfer studies tend to indicate that genuine transfer, in the sense of a permanent capacity to build upon technology imports through enlarging domestic capabilities, often did not take place, mainly because it was not in the interests of the technology supplier to lose an important source of monopolistic control in terms of skills and information. It was often the case that the major suppliers of technologies were multinational enterprises, motivated by business (profit-maximisation) rather than development (social welfare) considerations.

China's experience of technology import for upgrading its industrial infrastructure seemed to confirm this trend. Both the interests of foreign suppliers and Chinese managerial bureaucrats tended to play down the value of "know how" transfer which completely reversed the original intention of technological transformation policy. During the process of technology transfer, Chinese trade officials largely neglected the considerations of development goals, resource endowments, and conditions of application. This problem seems to be common in the less developed countries where many do not appear to have initiated incentives designed to promote adaptation of imported technologies (UNIDO, 1984: (121).

Another widespread phenomenon was the misuse of funds available for the purpose of technological transformation. Following a series of decentralisation measures introduced in the industrial sector in the 1980s, local authorities were encouraged to take their own initiatives in technology purchases. With increasing investment power in their hands, local governments tended to build new factories in the same way that central government had done in the past. Individual enterprises, on the other hand, often utilised their limited investment funds for non-productive projects, especially for housing programmes (Chen and Lu, 1988: 62-63). The problems caused by decentralisation will be further discussed in Chapter 10, Section A and Chapter 11, Section B.

On the whole, the process of technological transformation in the 1980s was sluggish and problem-laden, although some progress was achieved in identifying priorities and formulating development plans for key industrial sectors. A number of large enterprises in the sectors of steel, electronics, and petrochemical, for example, successfully combined the purchase of foreign equipment, in plant technological transformation, and economic efficiency. Internal technology transfer from defense to civilian sectors and the creation of technology market also had a strong impact on the pace and the scale of technological transformation. These issues will be examined in the following sections (the next section and Chapter 10.).

Technology Transfer from Defense to Civilian Sectors

The transfer of scientific and technological know-how from defense to civilian sector was encouraged by the Chinese leadership from the early 1980s. The 1981 "Outline Report on Science and Technology" suggested that "as far as security considerations allow, even the results of military scientific research should be actively transferred to civilian application" (SSTC, 1986:305). Premier Zhao Ziyang's speech of October 1982 further reinforced this policy trend. It was also something that had become a trend in the West where the notion of "dual use" was introduced to refer to technologies that are useful in both the military and the civilian spheres (Elzinga, 1990: 187).

China's defense sector had been favoured in resource allocation during the last thirty years with more and higher-quality manpower, manufacturing and testing equipment, and greater financial and political support. As a result, China was faced with irrational surpluses of manpower and facilities in some fields and severe shortages in others, notably, light industry and agriculture—while defense-related heavy industries possessed the strongest R&D capabilities in the entire industrial sector.

The effort to break down barriers between the civilian and defense sectors was a move to strengthen civilian industry's R&D capabilities and its productivity. The internal technology transfer was also hoped to modernise China's industrial infrastructure and reduce the scale of foreign imports.

Before the early 1980s, the relationship between Chinese military and civilian R&D sectors has been highly compartmentalised. While CAS institutes had frequently been tasked to participate in defense-related projects in the 1960s and 1970s, the same could not be said for military R&D institutes with respect to most large-scale civilian projects. Under the direction of the new science policy, military units were instructed to use their superior resources and more extensive experience in dealing with technology to help solve civilian problems.

Another considerations was based on harsh economic realities. Modernisation is costly, both for Chinese society and the People's Liberation armed forces. Defense spending drained resources needed for economic development. To raise industrial productivity and improve people's living standard, steady reallocation of resources was a necessity.

The CAS, formerly deeply involved in defense-oriented research and development, now came to devote much more of its talents to the civilian sector. There was a general budget cut in the defense sector the 1980s. Military R&D institutes were pressed to shift part of their research activities into civilian oriented R&D, and to link their research projects more with the production needs of civilian enterprises.

The defense establishment was under pressure to improve its economic efficiency. Factory managers in the defense industry began to assume responsibility for profit-and-loss, and therefore had an incentive to manufacture goods above and beyond the levels called for in the State plan. They began to engage in joint ventures, co-production, licensing of technologies, and many other economic arrangements from which they profit by providing equipment or services to the civilian economy. Defense plants began to market motorcycles, refrigerators, and consumer electronics products; ministries of the old military machine-building establishment began to build nuclear power plants and marketing satellite launch services (Simon, 1989: 298, 316). Some of these products and services were intended for the export market (SSTC, 1990: 22).

Nevertheless, as the Western experience indicates, defense technological culture greatly differed from that required by successful business in the civil consumer product market. There are significant differences in institutional arrangements, incentives, and styles of management between defense and civilian industries (Elzinga, 1990: 190). The Chinese defense plants also confronted these problems when they attempted to enter the consumer market and compete with civilian enterprises. The legacy of managerial rigidity and the lack of training in marketing often resulted in low efficiency and competitiveness.

To promote closer co-operation between defense and civilian sectors, 16 provinces set up "Integrated Military-Civilian Leadership Organs" under the leadership of a local government official and drawing members from among the leaders of the local economic, planning, and S&T commissions and the national S&T and industry offices. To promote technology markets and the circulation of commodities, 13 provinces set up National Defense Industrial Technology Development or Consultancy Companies (Saich, 1989: 49). Trade fairs for the transfer of technology had been arranged in collaboration with the SSTC, the State Economic Commission and the reorganised Defense Science, Technology and Industry Commission. Their usual focus was high-tech areas, including electronics, lasers space, energy, oil, medical equipment, etc. As a consequence of such measures, the amount of technology transfer work increased considerably.

Preliminary statistics compiled for 1984 showed that this process resulted in more than 6,800 contracts for technology transfer between military and civilian units, with fees totalling 430 million *yuan*. In 1985, this trade was estimated to an amount close to 1 billion *yuan* (SSTC, 1986: 180).

There was at the same time a trend towards transferring the third-line (western interior) technology to the coastal area. Third-line defense R&D forces began to assist China's entry into new technology-based industry. Enterprises formerly engaged in defense electronics production were transformed into a number of high-tech R&D centers specializing in microelectronics, fibre optics communication, radar and broadcasting products, cathode ray tubes, etc. (*PD*, 21 September, 1987, p. 1).

Despite the promotion of policies, considerable opposition existed within the military to redirecting its work towards the civilian sector (Saich, 1989: 48). The military were also dissatisfied with their share of the national budget, a share that fell from a high of 17.7 per cent in 1977 to about 13.1 per cent by 1984, with a corresponding de-emphasis of industries from which the military derives armaments (Clarke, 1987: 42). According to a 1988 CIA report to the Joint Economic Committee of Congress, Chinese defense expenditures fell from 12 per cent of gross national product in 1978 to 5 per cent in 1987 (Prados, 1989: 33).

In Chapter 8, Section B, I pointed out that China's military-industrial network had established a bureaucratic momentum of its own. To force this establishment into a radically different mould was never going to be an easy task. Western experience in the post-WW II period in attempting to transform the military R&D establishments into civilian-oriented structures had confronted the problems of structural change and bureaucratic resistance. The powerful military-industrial complexes with their enormous interest networks continued to persuade their respective governments with overtly political arguments and so continued to receive large proportions of national R&D expenditures (Clark, 1985: 125, 219). In the 1960s and 1970s the main civilian term of the argument to justify such military spending was "spin off" theory. Later in the 1980s with the Japanese high-tech challenge, there was a shift to the concept of "dual use" (Elzinga, 1990: 187-189).

Under the pressure of shifting priorities in national science policy in the 1980s, the Chinese defense establishment mobilised their most influential figures, such as the rocket expert Qian Xuesen, to negotiate with political leaders and planning bureaucrats using long-established personal ties. In 1982, as part of a larger bureaucratic reform, the two primary offices for overseeing military R&D (National Defense Science and Technology Commission) and production (National Defense Industries Office) were combined into the National Defence Science, Technology and Industry Commission. In some respects, this made the military R&D-production nexus a more powerful force in the bureaucracy. Either through personal influence or bureaucratic links, the defense sector managed to preserve its share of the R&D budget.

According to CIA projections, China's defense research and development spending from 1978 to 1987 increased by roughly 25 per cent, despite a simultaneous reduction in the army's operating expenditures, and a reduction of about one-eighteenth in defense investment. Strategic nuclear forces and related technology were specially exempted from cuts in military spending (Prados, 1989: 33).

Evidently, China's goal of modernising the defense sector was not neglected, only the strategy modified. In the mid-1980s, seeing the increasing market competition as a threat to its vested interests, the defense sector tactically allied with the other powerful research establishment—the Chinese Academy of Sciences—and the think-tanks technocrats to form a high-tech lobby. As a result, the "863 programme" was set up in 1986. This bargaining story will be described in Chapter 10, Section C.

D. STRUCTURAL REFORM OF THE ECONOMIC AND S&T SYSTEMS

The Reform of the Economic Structure

Erik Baark (1990b: 2-3) observes that the 1980s witnessed the emergence of a strong economistic doctrine fuelled by a neo-liberalist interpretation of the economic performance of the Asian newly industrialised countries and the imperatives of global high technology innovation. This doctrine has won support in both developing countries and centrally planned economies as a means of dealing with their deteriorating economic and technological performance. The main tenet of the "economistic" doctrine is a belief in the commercialisation of research and development.

However, it is not enough simply to reform the S&T sector in isolation. There must be sufficient demand, or pull, from the production sector to provide the stimuli and incentives for the S&T sector to undertake the kind of research that is necessary for the nation's economic needs. This means that success is ultimately dependent on effective reform of the economic structure as a whole.

China's policy legacies in economic reform can be traced back to the early 1960s when liberal economists, notably Sun Yefang, proposed the use of market mechanism in socialist economies. Sun's academic circle became active again in the late 1970s and early 1980s, collaborating with Deng Xiaoping's regime in propagating liberal economic theories. During this transitional period, various reforms in the management of state-owned enterprises were introduced, mostly on an experimental and piecemeal basis. These included: enterprises retaining a proportion of profits for workers' bonuses, collective welfare expenditure and small-scale investment; limited freedom for enterprises in selling part of their output; some flexibility in setting prices, and increases in managerial authority over production decisions and personnel matters (World Bank, 1985: 164). These changes, comparable to reforms tried in nearly all socialist countries, produced some good results. They represented only marginal changes, however, the fundamental problem remaining the appropriate relationship between the State and enterprises.

In October 1984, a major reform document modifying the Chinese economic system was adopted — the "Resolution of the Central Committee of the Chinese Communist Party on the Reform of the Economic Structure." This document chronicled the problems of an over-centralised industrial economy noting that "defects in the urban economic sector... seriously hinder the development of the forces of production." The Decision recognised that the "new technological revolution had made vital the need for reform with its provision of new opportunities and challenges to economic growth." According to the Decision "our economic structure must become better able to utilise the latest scientific and technological achievements, promoting scientific and technological advancement and generating new forces of production (*PD*, 21 October 1984, pp. 1-3). The central argument was that science, technology and their proper applications were the keys to socio-economic growth.

The focus of the reform was to introduce a market mechanism into the Chinese industrial sector and to divest the central government of its managerial role. The document called for a "rational price system "in the Chinese economy and suggested a gradual reduction of "mandatory planning" and expansion of "guidance planning[6] meaning more loosely-controlled, less centralised planning. Evidently, the market was not meant to replace planning but as an adjunct to it.

Among the concrete measures proposed was the idea that the State would reinforce and enlarge the "production-responsibility system" introduced during the Sixth Five-Year Plan in such a way that much greater responsibility for profits and losses would be granted to urban, state-owned enterprises (which used to be affiliated directly to their central ministries), with the ultimate possibility of bankruptcy. With increased autonomy for production units and the pressure for competition generated by the responsibility system, enterprises would now be expected to purchase relevant technology when necessary, which would lead in turn to structural change of the enterprises. By revitalising the industrial sector, it was hoped that the typical characteristics of centrally-planned economies plagued by low productivity, inefficiency, and low quality would be altered. Another intended consequence was that the banking system would eventually shoulder a much greater role in making investment decisions jointly with enterprise managers. The task remaining for the central government and ministries would be to formulate development policies and to monitor their implementation. Although a kind of market mechanism was clearly intended by the Chinese reformers, the precise nature and operation of this mechanism was ill-defined. Besides, almost none of the specific policies discussed in the Decision was really new; it simply summed up and deepened a series of economic reform measures practiced in the previous years that reaffirmed the leadership's commitment to continuous evolution of the socialist economy.

With all the above-mentioned reasons, the 1984 document on economic reform can be seen as politically significant rather than as a detailed design for a comprehensive reform in the entire economic system. The idea of linking technological change with economic growth needed further structural reform of the S&T system as a complementary policy package to reinforce this trend of development.

The decentralisation measures and the introduction of market mechanisms enabled both local government and enterprises to gain more autonomy vis-a-vis central government. They emerged as new actors in the economic and S&T systems. While increased economic efficiency and technological progress were expected to result from the reform measures, these actors might also take advantage of the newly evolved structures, and deviate from state policy. Examples have already been given in Section C of this chapter pointing to the phenomenon of misuse of funds by local units. Chapter 10-11 will further elaborate the problems stemming from the interaction between local actors and the new structures during the reform process.

The Reform of the Science and Technology System

From 1978 onwards, the Chinese leadership not only came to regard S&T as a crucial aspect of achieving modernisation but increasingly recognised the significance of economic measures in the management of S&T. Former Minister of the SSTC Fang Yi proposed the use of contracts between industrial and research sectors as early as 1979. The 1981's "Outline Report" and Zhao Ziyang's 1982 policy statement further emphasised the development of the contract system, joint research-production associations, and technical service or consultancy centers. All of these efforts were attempts to improve the links between research and production in order to increase the efficiency of the S&T system.

The establishment of the State Council's S&T Leading Group in January 1983 made it possible for Party leaders, planning bureaucrats, and scientific experts to work together in formulating S&T policy. There was a growing belief among them that managerial deficiencies, bureaucratic rigidity, and organisational bottlenecks were constraining S&T advance. To strengthen R&D capacities within production enterprises and stimulate technological innovation, a wider market mechanism needed to be installed within the S&T system (Simon and Rehn, 1988: 30-32). Acknowledging these circumstances, they drafted a reform programme for the S&T system. It is widely known now that the formulation of this document involved intense political negotiations and compromises. The document was reviewed by top political leaders, such as Premier Zhao Ziyang and Party Secretary Hu Yaobang, and the opinions of a number of Chinese-American scientists were also taken into consideration. After sorting out various controversies, the formal reform document—the "Resolution on the Reform of the Science and Technology System"—was released in March 1985. The new document signalled the beginning of an explicit attempt to link economic reform with that of the S&T system.

Like the Soviet reform programme of 1961-62 and the Hungarian reform after 1968, the main thrust of China's S&T reform programme was to resolve the problem of poor links between scientific research and industrial production. One method was to give science and technology and new ideological label: scientific and technological know-how was to be viewed as commodity which could be exchanged in the market place. The decision to treat technology as a commercial commodity represented an abrupt departure from previous thinking, which treated the product of mental labour as a public good that could not be privatised.

Reform of the funding system was the most important operational change introduced by the new policy. Research budgets for the majority of scientific institutes either belonging to the CAS, the industrial ministries, or local governments were to be reduced gradually, thus forcing research institutes to look for contracts with industrial enterprises or other units to compensate for and supplement their financial needs. This was a form of external contractual funding meant to increase research-production interface. Thereupon, *a knowledge market mechanism was introduced into the research sector.*

The old funding system was based on fixed quotas. The central government controlled the allocation of annual operating budgets to research and development units under its jurisdiction. These allocations depended mostly on the type of institute supported, the size of its staff, etc. The quantity and quality of projects were generally not evaluated. These old funding procedures paid little attention to the academic merits and feasibility of projects. The emphasis on contract-related research was part of an effort to encourage greater cost-consciousness within the research sector, and also to raise the S&T community's enthusiasm through its sharing of the monetary benefits accruing through the fee-paying system.

The "customer-contractor" principle applied in key projects between state and non-state actors was now extended into the technology market with non-state actors (e.g., enterprises, research institutes belonging to the IHEs, CAS, and industrial sector) directly interacting with each other. Now central government only provided general guidance and legal codes to regulate the market indirectly. It was hoped that the contract system would help to direct resources into providing the production sector with the new technology it actually needed, as opposed to the technology which central planners thought it needed.

Accordingly, funding reform shifted the sources of research money into three different areas: government contracts (e.g., the key projects), contracts with industry through technology markets, and funding from research foundations.[7] In this system, state funding still played the major role either through direct allocation or contract, and state planning and management would remained paramount owing to the larger and more diversified channels through which state funds were distributed. In other words, state actors (e.g., government and planning bureaucracies) still played an essential role in China's S&T system. Added to this was a growing number of direct S&T supplier-user linkages covering non-planned projects mainly, most of which were related very closely to immediate production needs (Conroy, 1989a: 522-523).

Technological markets are those sectors of the society where technological commodities (intellectual or physical) can be integrated with production. In the technology market, enterprises purchase both the technology and relevant techniques required to increase production capacity and technological levels. By giving technology commercial value, the Chinese S&T policy-makers tried to stimulate the diffusion of technology through profit-type incentives. They saw technology markets as playing a variety of roles: stimulating production-oriented research and development; speeding up the development time for new products; breaking down administrative barriers; and encouraging S&T labour mobility (Simon and Rehn, 1988: 34).

With the inauguration of the S&T reform programme, China's science policy started to combine the *"science-push" and "technology-push" models with the "market-pull" theory of innovation*. The external role of the State in relation to science was to be shared by the market. Or in Lindblom (1977)'s term, "authority structures" were combined with "exchange mechanisms" to promote technological and economic development. China's S&T policy hence developed greater economic content and her S&T structure further evolved.

The 1985 S&T reform programme also granted research institutes greater autonomy in terms of management power and encouraged enterprises to improve actively and strengthen their technological development capability (SSTC, 1986: 300). The S&T reform document attempted to make explicit the role and responsibilities of the State, research institutes, and production enterprises in science and technology work. By helping to clarify these roles, the Chinese leadership intended to break down the bureaucratic boundaries and related obstacles that had long worked against the effective and efficient use of S&T resources. On the other hand, a Western style of entrepreneurial talent together with market stimuli were encouraged in order to invigorate China's S&T system. Consequently, of new category a actor emerged, i.e., scientist-entepreneurs, the majority of whom came from the CAS and outstanding technical universities. This group of mature professional scientists received support from influential political figures and played a significant role in China's establishment of science parks in the late 1980s.

The S&T reform programme served to complement a number of other initiatives introduced over the preceding years in the area of economic reform and science policy, and also to deepen structural change. Driven by the international trend towards a new technological revolution, China became eager to dovetail science and technology with production in an attempt to achieve the coordinated development of science/technology, economy, and society. By encouraging the commercialisation of research and at the same time promoting the economic responsibility system in industry and facilitating cooperation between civilian and defense units, the leadership introduced several new dimensions to the research-production interface previously absent in the Chinese system.

Here then we can see a series of attempts — either through policy statements, institution-building, or formal policy documents — to improve China's S&T system in the first half of the 1980s. Table 6.1 (see next page) shows that the Chinese Academy of Sciences' only influence was in pushing for the establishment of the CAS Science foundation for supporting basic research: the rest of the new policy initiatives were dominated by state actors i.e., *reformers within the government* (and to a lesser extent the Party), *pressing for higher efficiency and social relevance.* Planning agencies also undertook major tasks in coordinating key projects and speeding up the process of technological transformation and technology transfer from defense to civilian sectors. In 1984-85, the reform of economic and S&T systems integrated most of the S&T-related policies in the previous years, thereby reaffirming the political leadership's commitment to S&T advance and economic growth.

China's S&T policy-makers showed a high-degree of consistency in the period of 1981-85, both in policy statements and attempts at institution-building. The role of the Party in research and industrial units was diluted, the function of government planning agencies was strengthened, and the establishment of "think-tanks" and S&T Leading Group under the State Council helped China's planning and policy-making systems develop in a more efficient and coordinated mode. State actors were diversified into the Party, the government (now a major reformer), and the planning bureaucracies.

Nevertheless, tensions were also created accompanying the introduction of new policy packages. *The government and planning agencies formed the core of bureaucratic culture whose goal of practical developmental needs clashed with the values and interests of the defense and scientific cultures.* The earliest conflicts in research priorities between the government and the CAS were exemplified in the debate on basis and applied research between 1981 and 1982. Later on, the defense sector became dissatisfied with the policy of transferring defense technologies to civilian uses and had difficulties in competing with civilian enterprises in the consumer-goods market. Finally, the cuts in direct state funding implied in the 1985's S&T reform programme were a tangible threat to the majority of research institutes which were ill-trained and ill-prepared for market-type behaviors. However, a small group of entrepreneurs did manage to prosper in the technology market.

TABLE 6.1

Policy Initiatives Relating to the S&T System: 1981-85

Policy (Actors)	*Goals (outcomes)*
Science for Policy, 1981 (State Council and its think-tanks)	improved planning
"Outline Report" 1981 (SSTC, CAS)	— rudimentary market — technology transfer from defense to civilian sectors — coordinated planning
CAS Conference, 1981 (CAS)	— basic research (Science Foundation)
Zhao Ziyang's speech at Science Awards Conference, 1982 (Zhao/government)	market measures — applied research — technology transfer
Sixth Five-Year Plan, 1981-85 (Economic and Planning Commissions)	— key projects — technological transformation
S&T Leading Group, 1983 (mixed actors from state and non-state sectors)	— coordinated S&T planning
Reform of the Economic System, 1984 (government and its think-tanks)	— decentralisation and market measures for revitalising urban industry
Reform of the S&T System, 1985 (mainly Party and government reformers)	— funding reform and technology market for stimulating innovation.

While local government and enterprises benefited form the new economic reform policy, the research sector did not necessarily welcome reform of the S&T system. The achievements and constraints of China's reform programmes and the tensions among various actors/cultures during the implementation process will be examined.

REFERENCES

1. In his book *The Third Wave,* Toffler (1981) argues that the agrarian society which still characterises China is indicative of a "first wave" economy. The industrial economy, which China tried to copy first from the Soviet Union and more recently from the West and Japan, is characterised by "second save" modernisation. Now in the West and Japan, the beginnings of "third wave modernisation" are appearing. This modernisation, based on the information revolution, is capable of minimising waste and transportation costs, since units of production, linked by sophisticated information systems, can be decentralised and dispersed.
2. In the 1980s, the Chinese Academy of Sciences comprised about 10% of China's researchers and consumed 10% of the nation's research funds (Saich, 1989: 66).
3. For example, the results of the application of various key projects coordinated by the SSTC during the Sixth Five-Year Plan were: 20%—high economic efficiency, 70% — poor economic efficiency, and 10% — no results (SSTC, 1988).
4. The State Planning Commission and State Economic Commission were combined into the State Planning and Economic Commission in 1988.
5. One early example of using "technology input" to explain economic growth was Robert Solow (1957) in his article "Technical Change and the Aggregate Production Function." Using

conventional "comparatives static" techniques, Solow attempted to provide a statistical explanation of the causes of US manufacturing growth over the period 1911 -56. He concluded that only 12.5% of the observed growth of labour productivity (output per worker) over this period could be "explained" by increments in the stock of capital, the remaining 87.5% being a "residual" or an unexplained "technological change." In the Chinese case, Chen (1990: 103) estimated that from 1952 to 1982, only 27.8% of the national industrial growth was caused by the input of science and technology, while the rest 72.2% derived from the increase of investment and labour forces.

6. For example, the practice of key projects during the Sixth and Seventh Five-Year Plans is mandatory planning, since those projects are highly targeted and mission-oriented with strong state control. "Technological transformation," on the other hand, is a kind of guidance planning in which no fixed contracts or obligations exist between the central planning agencies and enterprises. Local units are encouraged to take initiatives while following general policy guidance from the Center.
7. By the end of 1988, there were 26 different kinds of research foundations in China (SSTC, 1990: 79).

7

Industrial Reforms and North-South Economic Relations

As the world economy experienced rapid changes in the 1970-1980 period, any industrialised countries faced strong pressures to restructure their manufacturing sector. The responses to these pressures chosen by the industrial countries had important implications for their own societies. Profound restructurings, if successful, could leave enterprises well positioned to survive further pressures, and provide economy dynamism to the home economy—while limited restructuring could leave enterprises, and the economies of which they are part, subject to more severe dislocations in the future. At an international level, the strategies chosen in the industrialised countries could also have major effects on the economic opportunities and position of the developing countries. Extensive domestic restructuring could, under certain circumstances, result in export markets in industrialised countries being opened more widely for developing countries. Or, conversely, domestic restructuring policy could significantly restrict the opportunities facing developing countries.

This article examines industrial restructuring between 1970 and 1980 in Hungary and the Netherlands, with the focus on the implications for developing countries. Two industries are examined, textile and wood products, in which developing countries have demonstrated some export capacity. The first two sections review the experiences of the two European countries at a national level.[1] The third section looks at restructuring changes at the enterprise level.

I. Industrial Restructuring in the Netherlands

Among the countries of the European Community, none were more explicit than the Netherlands between 1973 and 1977 in seeking to protect the interests of the less developed countries in industrial restructuring. A series of institutional initiatives was taken that reflects this: a special restructuring fund (the Pronk Fund) was set up to help Dutch companies shift out of products where the LDCs could fill the resulting gap; a new Centre for the Promotion of Imports from Developing Countries (CBI) assisted LDC enterprises to penetrate the Dutch market; and the existing Finance Company for Developing Countries (FMO) was made a government channel to finance the growth of

LDC enterprises that could export to the Netherlands.

The plywood industry is a good example of the Dutch approach. At the start of the 1970s, this industry produced much standardised plywood using imported LDC logs. In other EC nations such as France, this emphasis on standard qualities continued throughout the 1970s and led to serious problems for French firms — to which the French responded with more protection for their home market against the new standard production coming from the LDCs. In the Netherlands, however, the same pressure led to an energetic government effort to have the country's plywood producers move out of standardised production and into specialised plywood for reinforced concrete work and marine construction.

Interviews with state and company officials stressed that this restructuring initiative was critically important: it persuaded several of the smaller Dutch firms to shift toward such specialities; it led the largest plywood firm (Bruynzeel) to import veneers rather than logs from the LDCs; and it assisted Dutch firms to regain their economic viability without extra import protection. The annual losses of Bruynzeel had reached 7.6 million guilders before the restructuring; as a direct result of the restructuring initiative, the company recovered to an operating surplus of 3.3 million guilders in 1980s.[2] This initiative was financed from the Pronk Fund.

The Pronk Fund also supported the extensive restructuring that took place in the Dutch cotton textile industry. As in the plywood sector, there were early contrasts between the Dutch and the French approach to the industry's problems; while the latter stressed protection for the industry and concentrated on consolidation moves by French multinational firms,[3] the Dutch stressed active restructuring plans for the whole industry. In cotton spinning, the bankruptcy of several large firms in 1974 and the drastic cash flow problems of others led the Dutch government to set up a single publicly controlled spinning firm in which virtually all capacity in the industry was reorganised. Planned by a restructuring commission made up of labour, employer and government representatives, Spinnerij Nederland scrapped 30% of Dutch cotton spinning capacity (all in simpler product lines of interest to LDCs), brought the number of production units down from 14 to 9, regrouped almost all machinery, and initiated a strategy of flexibility and short production runs in response to rapid demand shifts in Europe.[4]

These changes were part of a far-reaching restructuring effort in cotton spinning which, as in plywood, had the effect of opening up much more of the Dutch textile market to the LDCs. A key provision was that the 1,179 workers whose jobs were lost went onto a "transfer list". They received full wages for a year while retraining or searching for new jobs. The success of the approach is shown by two indicators: of the workers on the transfer list, only 232 (19.7%) had to be dismissed into unemployment after the year was up; and the losses of Spinnerij Nederland declined from 65 million guilders in its first full year of operation (1978) to 35 million in 1979, and to only 4 million in the first half of 1980.[5]

This active and interventionist industrial planning approach flagged, however, as the economic crisis deepened into the late 1970s. Therefore the restructuring effort was much less far-reaching in cotton weaving and finishing than in spinning. Although the Dutch trade unions were again able to win transfer list provisions after they mounted national demonstrations, this time the government took no active role in shaping industry plans. Employers in the industry agreed they needed a 25% capacity cut, all in simpler product lines, but they could only agree on seven projects — and these did not come close to reaching this level of reduction. In consequence the movement out of product lines of interest to the LDCs was much slower — and the future vulnerability of the industry remained much greater.

This soon became evident. By 1978 and 1979 the larger textile firms in the Netherlands had restored some profitability to their operations, but in early 1980 there was a serious decline in the textile markets, and within a few months, three of the weaving and finishing restructuring projects failed with 800 jobs being lost: one company shut down completely, eliminating 450 more jobs. The failure to achieve planed capacity reductions had caught up with the industry.

This failure in textile restructuring contributed to more protectionism at the European Community level where protectionist reactions had already become a growing problem for the LDCs. As well as the tougher import quotas under the 1978 Multi-Fibre Agreement, informal quotas were imposed on those LDCs entitled under the Lomé Convention to duty-free exports of manufactured goods to the Community. This significantly hurt some of the textile production which had emerged in Africa.

Thus the deteriorating international economy led in the Netherlands to fewer economic opportunities for poorer nations. But it is perhaps more important to stress how extensive industrial restructuring in plywood and in cotton spinning did contribute to Third World economic gains — in a process that significantly cushioned the impact of change non most Dutch workers, and resulted in more viable enterprises by the start of the 1980s.

II. Hungary and Third World Industry

Like the Netherlands in Western Europe, Hungary has been the most active of the East European countries in restructuring its industry. Hungary has also devoted considerable attention to its ties with the LDCs. In industrial restructuring, the Hungarians, like the Dutch, concentrated on their textile and clothing industries (allocating US$1 billion to reconstruction in that sector between 1970 and 1980)[6] and also on parts of the wood industry (particularly the wooden furniture segment).

These policies led to some increased imports from the Third World. In textiles, planners decided that cotton spinning in Hungary should cease to expand, and the gap in yarn demand as cloth production grew was covered by increased imports, 30% of them in the simpler yarn categories from the LDCs; more recently, the import of low-cost finished goods from South-East Asia (particularly knitted pullovers) was also deliberately expanded as Hungarian enterprises shifted out of such production.[7]

As a part of this change in the international division of labour, Hungary also organised technology transfer to LDCs, often combining the delivery of new factories with buy-back arrangements to supply the Hungarian market. In the wood sector, for instance, at least five such projects were arranged; one in Kenya, for example, was planned to export furniture parts back to Hungary.[8] In textiles and clothing at least five spinning facilities and seven complete garment factories were set up, with buy-back arrangements in a number of these cases.

It might appear, then, that developments in Hungary conform closely to a model of equitable North-South Relations. The reality is more complex. Hungary, even more than the Netherlands, was severely affected in the late 1970s by the changed conditions in the international economy; internal growth rates slowed considerably (per-caput real personal income fell in 1979 after years of increase); and Hungary experienced serious trade deficits and a growing international debt burden.[9] These pressures forced an industrial restructuring aimed at export expansion to the developed market economies and led to a toughening of strategy toward the LDCs.

Rather than a deliberate opening of the whole Hungarian market to manufactured imports from the LDCs, Hungary's industrial strategy in textiles and wood envisaged the retention of most of the home market, a careful release to the LDCs of a few simpler product or input areas, and consequent Hungarian concentration on higher quality product areas, to allow expanded exports to the developed market economies. In effect, Hungary sought to compete more successfully with present LDC exporters to those. That is, the restructuring of textiles and clothing aimed above all at capturing western markets away from the LDCs, and used increased LDC imports to Hungary in a few selected areas as part of this aggressive strategy.

The evidence for this is clear. The Hungarian domestic market has remained highly protected. Because it takes much more time and bureaucratic effort to purchase imports than domestic goods (owing to the need for foreign exchange licences), Hungarian commercial enterprises will opt for imports only if the domestic producers have their order books so full they cannot provide the needed items.[10] Thus Hungarian textile manufacturers interviewed reported no competition from LDC imports. And, in the case of wood, the Hungarian foreign trade company responsible for imports indicated that simple wood products (such as ladders) were *not* imported from the LDCs — because these would damage the small Hungarian cooperatives and craft enterprises which produced such items domestically.[11] Thus, while the Hungarian textile and wood industries restructured, the changes at the national level differed radically from those in the Netherlands. Cotton fabric production grew by 15% between 1970 and 1979 in Hungary and declined by 42% between 1965 and 1976 in the Netherlands; Hungarian plywood production rose 64% between 1970 and 1979, while Dutch production fell significantly.[12] Hungarian enterprises have been improving their quality, reorganising their production systems with foreign help, upgrading their designs and product selection, forming cooperative arrangements with firms in the West to obtain know-how, and investing in machinery.[13] This reconstruction has been aimed at winning new export markets in Western Europe and North America.

Enterprise interviews in Hungary suggest the success of this drive. In textiles and clothing, exports reached one-third of all production by 1980, with 60% of exports going to the capitalist economies; in wooden furniture, 12 to 20% of 1980 output was exported, two-thirds of it to the developed market economies.

In its competition with LDCs in Western Europe, Hungary enjoyed the considerable advantages of proximity, better infrastructure, and more industrial experience, so that the Hungarian drive inevitably damaged LDC prospects and opportunities in those markets — because of direct Hungarian sales competition or because the cut-make-trim option has given West European enterprises another means of meeting LDC competition and defending their home markets.

World economic pressures have pushed Hungary toward tougher strategies also in its direct dealings with the LDCs. At the enterprise level, where much of the decision-making now takes place, Hungary has become distinctly sceptical and calculating regarding technology transfer to the LDCs. Textile and clothing enterprises interviewed reported unhappy experiences with buy-back arrangements from the LDCs (delivery delays and problems of quality). It had therefore been decided to pull out of such arrangements for the future. The enterprise selling garment factories in the LDCs was promoting its services even more vigorously as of 1981, but it no longer was prepared to arrange buy-back provisions for the Hungarian market.[15]

Nor does there seem to be much prospect of major future LDC export gains in predictable areas in the textile and clothing sector. Dutch textile enterprises, for example, have greatly increased their imports of low-cost grey cloth from the LDCs. But both enterprise management and Ministry of Industry officials in Hungry reported that they did not expect to arrange any such import increases in coming years.

Despite considerable industrial restructuring in Hungary, then, the country's response to the international economic crisis has been to intensify its export competition to the detriment of LDC trade and to adopt a tougher attitude in its direct relations with the LDCs. In both textiles and clothing and wood products, Hungarian enterprises have preserved their home market for themselves; the few selective LDC import gains that have occurred have contributed, in textiles and clothing, to an aggressive export strategy to compete with the LDCs in the West European market. The extensive restructuring of Dutch plywood making and cotton spinning, with its major gains for LDC producers, has not been paralleled in Hungary.

III. Restructuring at the Enterprise Level

Industrial restructuring has a significant impact on future enterprise viability and on national economic potential as well as on international income distribution. This section now returns to those considerations at the enterprise level, focusing on the textile sector. In examining this change, the following indicators within the enterprise are considered: shifts in production patterns; changing vertical integration; mergers or divestments; the degree of modernisation of production technology; the extent of exports; and the extent of R&D (since this is expected to contribute to ongoing change).

In the Dutch case, five large and medium-sized textile firms were examined that restructured successfully in the 1970s (regaining profitably through sweeping changes in strategy and production in the face of the severe pressures in the industry); the five accounted for almost 100% of synthetic textile production and the great bulk of cotton and cloth production in the country.[16] Table 7.1 summarises the restructuring thrust of these enterprises, and indicates how far-reaching the shifts were that took place in the 1970-1980 period.

In all firms there was widespread closure of facilities, and the rationalisation of production into higher-quality, more skill-intensive items; most lines of interest to LDC exporters were phased out. But column 1 reveals that more was involved than rationalisation; all five enterprises moved into new product lines as part of their strategy. In three cases this involved extensive moves into non-textile production; one enterprise began producing sailing boats; another diversified into industrial laundry; and a third innovated several entirely new products (which increased its turnover from one million guilders in 1969 to 170 million in 1978). The two other firms shifted into different textile sector activities. Meanwhile all three of the enterprises with important cotton spinning facilities in 1970 had ceased such activity by 1979 — a sign of the major change spurred by the planned creation of Spinnerij Nederland.

This points to two major elements which were not part of Dutch restructuring. There was no emphasis on vertical integration; indeed, several of the enterprises deliberately moved in the opposite direction, in order to be able to purchase imports like grey cloth independently on world markets. Nor was there any emphasis on mergers as a means of creating larger firms, in order to capture larger market shares. Both takeovers and divestments took place in the Dutch industry between 1970 and 1981, but they were means to achieve production pattern shifts rather than ends in themselves.

On the other hand, modernisation of technology was a major effort. This was true for all four cotton sector enterprises, and was also evident in Spinnerij Nederland, in which, the bringing together of machinery from fourteen separate facilities meant 90% of production equipment was new since 1970. The state support to the industry, aside from facilitating employment reduction via transfer-list payments, went mainly for the introduction of new machinery. The result has been factory facilities highly mechanised in all procedures, from the core production process to handling functions. Enterprises have also tended to stress R&D (although, this was less true for the two smaller firms). Particularly in synthetics, R&D spending was seen as central to restructuring — via innovation of new products — and had in fact *increased* as a share of enterprise turnover.

From these changes developed a set of highly flexible, economically viable textile enterprises in the Netherlands, so that, despite the highest textile wage levels in the European Community, these firms survived. Their strategies stressed change and responsiveness, recognising that the niche left for European textile enterprises in the world economy was a precarious one in which the premium was on adaptability, specialised services and a highly skilled workforce that could rapidly adjust to new production requirements. One sign of Dutch success in this process was the high export levels that four of the firms had achieved.

Table 7.2 of comparative data from Hungarian textile enterprises suggests some contrasts with the Dutch situation. Perhaps most striking is the limited change in enterprise activity compared to the Dutch cases; only one example of divestment was evident in the Hungarian case, and the shifts in production patterns noted in Column 1 were much more limited than in the Netherlands. No movements into non-textile production took place (although enterprise regulations in Hungary do permit this); and only in two enterprises (Nos. 2 and 5 in Table 7.2) did significant shifts in textile product output occur.

During the 1970s, Hungarian economic planners put the emphasis on what is termed "light industry" in the country, and this led to a modernisation of machinery in the textile sector. However, there are contrasts with the Netherlands. First, the general emphasis on this in Hungary as less — this is particularly clear in Enterprise 1, the largest cotton cloth manufacturer, in which only 57% of machinery was new since 1970. Second, even in enterprises where more modernisation took place, such as Nos. 2 and 3, the breadth of modernisation was limited; in Enterprise 3, only 65% of weaving looms were automatic by 1981; and in Enterprise 2, though the core production process was comprehensively modernised during the 1970s, little mechanisation of handling processes took place. Capital constraints in the Hungarian economy were a key factor in these limitations.

Another contrast with the Dutch firms was evident in R&D. Hungarian enterprises depended much more on foreign technology and licensing agreements, with all five firms having such external ties. In some cases, this involved obtaining rights to a specific brand-name product that could be sold at home and abroad. In other cases, new production technology was transferred through the agreement. But perhaps most important in recent years has been the transfer of new means of setting up the production system in factories so as to achieve higher labour productivity. Enterprise 5, for instance, stressed that this was the major benefit from its blue jeans venture with a U.S. multinational—organisational techniques and machines were introduced in the new factory that permitted production of a pair of trousers in 13.8 minutes, compared to 50 minutes in other facilities — and some of these techniques were then successfully transferred to these other facilities. Most of these Hungarian enterprises demonstrated considerable indigenous technological capacity, being able to choose their own machinery from a wide variety of sources, and organising transfers effectively with technology suppliers. But the stress on innovation as a restructuring strategy, evident in some Dutch cases, was not present in Hungary.

As noted earlier, exports were also stressed in the sector, and four of the five enterprises in Table 7.2 had achieved healthy export increases. The export reductions in Enterprise 1, however, cannot be overlooked — especially since this enterprise was the largest in the textile sector.

A comparison between Enterprises 1 and 2, is fact, in instructive. Enterprise 2 is a model of rapid and extensive change in production patterns, in machinery, in organisational technology and (consequently) in exports. Its emphasis on flexibility and responsiveness in output, on maximum training of workers and on specialisation in high-quality lines is very similar to that in the highly adaptable Dutch textile cases. This successful and comprehensive restructuring strategy was reflected in excellent enterprise financial results, with profits rising 22% from 46,645,000 forints in 1975 to 57,037,000 in 1980. Enterprise 1, on the other hand, had not found it possible to restructure in that way, and had been forced back onto the home market; its profit increases were less and it faced increasingly serious problems for the future. This is because the enterprise system in Hungary now rewards export increases with increased access to domestic credit facilities and to foreign exchange for purchasing new technology from abroad — which in turn generate further export earnings in the future.

Overall, then, there seems to have been more limited enterprise restructuring in Hungarian textiles than in the Netherlands. Less modernisation of machinery was undertaken, less product diversification developed, less rationalisation was organised and no real innovative capacity was built. This limitation on change has shown up in problems in the largest textile enterprise in Hungary, which was losing its export markets. This, in turn, raises questions about Hungary's broader efforts to develop an adaptive, efficient and internationally competitive industrial economy in the European context; this evidence suggests that the extensive enterprise restructuring necessary to achieve such goals is not taking place across the whole Hungarian economy — in part because the pressures of developing country competition are being kept out of the Hungarian domestic market.

IV. Conclusions

This analysis has examined industrial restructuring efforts in Hungary and the Netherlands, focusing on economic relations with developing countries. It has demonstrated that, relative to the patterns of change evident in the Netherlands, Hungary has been quite restrictive in its strategy toward developing countries, and more limited in its industrial restructuring. Section 3 suggested that certain large enterprises in the Hungarian economy may face problems as a consequence of this.

In the Dutch case, the failure to restructure extensively in weaving and finishing caught up with those firms that had followed a limited strategy. It is likely that consequences of limited change will also damage the Hungarian economy: not via enterprise shutdown in the Hungarian case, given the way the domestic market is being preserved, but via growing inefficiency (relative to other European textile enterprises) and declining exports in such large textile enterprises as Enterprise 1 in Table 7.2 above. These inefficiencies in turn damage the Hungarian economy's overall efforts to become internationally competitive.

The LDCs have also been affected adversely by the Hungarian approach. Potential LDC export gains in wood products and textiles have been prevented. Dutch industrial restructuring aimed to assist developing countries, and has done so in various specific ways in the two sectors analysed. Hungarian strategy, at last in recent years, has not done likewise. For the sake of Hungary's own economic development, there seems good reason to change that strategy.

NOTES

The research on which this paper is based was supported by the Social Sciences and Humanities Research Council of Canada, Cariebn University and the Hungarian Institute for Cultural Relations.

1. For a more detailed treatment of these experiences, see S.W. Langdon, "North-South, West and East: Industrial Restructuring in the World Economy". *International Journal*, Vol. 36, No. 4, 1981, pp. 768-782.
2. Interviews, Bruynzeel, Zaandam, 1978 and 1980.
3. L.K. Mytelka, "Crisis and Adjustment in the French Textile Industry", in H. Jacobson and D. Sidjanski (eds.), *The Emerging Economic Order: Dynamics, Constraints and Possibilities*, Beverly Hills, 1981.
4. Interviews, Spinnerij Nederland, Twenthe, 1979 and 1980.
5. Interviews, KRL Association, Arnhem, and Spinnerij Nederland, 1979 and 1980.
6. Interviews, Hungarotex, Budapest, 1981.
7. Interviews, Hungary, Ministry of Industry, Textile Section, Budapest, 1981.
8. Interview, Hungarian National Chamber of Commerce, Budapest, 1981.
9. See J. Fekete, "The Crisis of the International Monetary System and Its Effects on the Hungarian Economy". *New Hungarian Quarterly*, Vol. 21, 1980, pp. 33-36.
10. Interviews, Ministry of Industry, Textile Section, and Ministry of Foreign Trade, Developing Country Section, Budapest, 1981.
11. Interview, Lignimpex, Budapest, 1981.
12. *Statistical Pocket Book of Hungary 1980*, Budapest, 1981, pp. 17 and 92; OECD, *The Textile Industry*, Paris, 1979.
13. Interviews, Hungary National Bank, Budapest, and textile, clothing and wood enterprises, 1981.
14. Interviews, Hungarotex, and Ministry of Industry, Wood Section, Budapest, 1981.
15. Interviews, Ministry of Industry, Textile Section, Budapest, and enterprises, 1981.
16. The five firms were Enka (synthetic fibres), Nijverdal-Ten-Cate (cotton and other cloth), Gamma-Vlisco (textile printing and finishing), Twenthe (cotton and other cloth), and Blydenstein-Willink (cotton and other cloth).

TABLE 7.1

Industrial Restructuring in Dutch Textile Enterprises

Enterprise	*Key changes in production patterns*	*Changes in vertical integration*	*Mergers or divestments*	*Acquisition of new machinery*	*Exports as per cent of sales*	*Research and development*
1.	1970 - 100% spinning and weaving 1980 - no spinning; 35-40% non-textile products	Reduced - cut out spinning	Divested spinning; takeover of several non-textile firms	All new last 10-15 years	50% (1979)	1-1.5 of sales (1979)
2.	1970 - 100% spinning and weaving 1980 - no spinning; no cotton cloth production; laundry 20% of turnover; verosol blinds 10%	Reduced - cut out spinning	Merger-takeover of laundry firm (1979)	Details not provided (but high priority)	45% (1979)	2 researchers (1979) under 1% of sales
3.	1969 - 67% textile and carpet fibres 1979 - 43% textile and carpet fibres, two important new products innovated	No change	Three major divestments	Little new since 1974	80-85% (1979)	3.6% of sales (1978)
4.	1969 - 20% of turnover spinning, 63% weaving, 9% knitting, no printing 1979 - no spinning, 55% weaving, 22% knitting, 15% printing	Added printing in 1971; cut out spinning	Knitting takeover 1973 divested spinning	75-80% new in 1970-1979 period	15% (1979)	Under 1% of sales
5.	1972 - printed fabrics, 60% of turnover, interior products 32% 1977 - printed fabrics 48%; interior products 48%	No change	Takeovers in carpets and wall coverings (1976, 1977)	Virtually all new in 1970-1978 period	70% (1977)	3% of sales

Source: Enterprise Interviews, December 1978, September 1979, August 1980, in Almelo, Arnhem, Helmond and Twenthe, The Netherlands

TABLE 7.2

Industrial Change in Hungarian Textile Enterprises

Enterprise	*Key changes in production patterns*	*Changes in vertical integration*	*Mergers or divestments*	*Acquisition of new machinery*	*Exports as per cent of sales*	*Research and development*
1.	1970 - 79% cotton cloth, 20% blended cloth, no knitting, little clothing 1980 - 75% cotton cloth, 15% blended cloth; 10% knitting, more clothing production	Increased - more stress on clothing	One segment, divested	50% new since 1970	1970 - 56% 1980 - 40%	1.2% of sales; technology agreements with foreign dye companies
2.	1970 - 60% simple cotton, no blends, no fancy weaves 1980 - 35% simple cotton, 12% blends; 11% fancy weaves	No change	None	90% new since 1970	1970 - 31% 1980 - 50%	Technology agreement with Austrian company
3.	Increased texturising of output; basic production pattern maintained	No change	None	Most modern texturing machinery; only 65% of weaving looms automatic	1970 - 15.5% 1980 - 23.8%	Foreign technology licences
4.	Move to style specialities and higher quality items - all men's clothing	Increases via spcialisation among units	Shift production units to countryside	100% new since 1970	1970 - 52% 1980 - 66%	Foreign technology licences
5.	Cut out 5-10% of products over 1970-1980; Major new production of jeans	No change - have own retail shop	None	Much new since 1975	Increased to 1980 - 50%	Technology agreement with U.S. company

Source: Enterprise interviews, Budapest and Györ, Hungary, April 1981.

8

Business Environment and Trade Potential in Europe

Introduction

The 1990s create the possibilities for a new system of co-operation in Europe in both the political and the economic sense. One of the important determinants of this new European co-operation is how the integration programme formulated in the "White Book" of the European Community in 1985 will be realised by the set deadline, i.e. the end of 1992.

By analysing the formulated objectives and the realisation process that can be observed so far, the present volume of studies seeks an answer to the question how consistent and realizable the objectives themselves are.

We have examined the questions in three large blocks, i.e. macroeconomy, microeconomy, and geopolitics. We have been of the opinion that surveying these three areas of examination is suitable for forming a judgement concerning the genuine interests and chances of the Twelve for integration.

It can be assumed that the regional integration process of the decade of the 1990s will be shaped in Europe on the basis of numerous new political and economic factors. Among these the fate of the EC '92 programme will be just a single one. But one of the most substantial ones.

This compilation undertakes primarily to evaluate the chances of the integration of the Twelve out of the integration concept itself.

VISIONS AND REFLECTIONS CONCERNING THE "EC 92" PROGRAMME: A SUMMARY

1. Europe 92: On the Integration Model Based on the "White Book" and the Single European Act

In the "White Book" adopted in 1985 and in the single European Act adopted in

1987 the EC set the goal of qualitative development for the decade of the 1990s. Relying on these documents, by the beginning of the 1990s the EC will become a single market where the supranational institutions of market regulation guarantee the assertion of the four freedoms (persons, goods, services, and capital).

In accordance with this integration objective, the concept deals with the "internal affairs" of the Community. Its philosophy is based on the assumption that while in the preceding period the Community only expanded but did not become developed in depth, now this will be exactly the other way round. In other words, the Community will not expand, but the co-operation will become deeper. The expansion from six to twelve members involved the experience that in practice the expansion and the deepening of integration cannot be realised successfully simultaneously.

The single market planned for the 1990s is in fact an objective which is derived from the Treaty of Rome (1957) itself. The name of the Common Market itself indicates that the founders wanted to establish an integrated market. In the mirror of the four freedoms, the EC is not a "common market" as yet. Consequently, the integration planned for the 1990s is in fact but the creation of the conditions of an integrated market, of movement without borders and restrictions. The goal itself raises for the external world the problem that to the extent that the unification of the internal market of the EC is realised, a new power centre is established in the world economy which sets also new institutional barriers to the external world.

Consequently, the first question for the external world is to what extent the EC will function in the coming decade as a fortress. The Integration model of the EC does not deal with this question directly. Economic co-operation with the external world is determined for the EC considerable by numerous international institutions and agreements regulating international trade. Nevertheless, the fortress character is involved in the integration process in at least two respects.

First, this is indicated by the practice itself which has been exercised so far. By the manifold instruments of anti-dumping procedures and the national regulation of competition the community has already restricted considerably the entry into the market of external competitors in areas which were considered sensitive by the member countries.

Second, the new the integrationist fervour has been brought about exactly by the circumstance that in the 1980s the international competitiveness of the EC diminished noticeably in some key areas (for instance, electronics).[1] This is shown convincingly in the changes in proportions which occurred in world trade in this decade (at the beginning of the decade the share of the EC was approximately 38% in world trade, and by the end of the decade this fell to a level of around 30%. To the world economic challenge the Community wants to give an integrationist response which sets as a goal a considerable improvement also in the size-specific aspects of its competitiveness. For this reason, it intends to raise the intensification of business relations to a qualitatively higher level primarily within the EC.

In this approach the concept itself can be considered rather consistent: through market integration the achievement of the increase of external competitiveness. The trouble with the concept begins when it wants to make everybody a winner in this process. It should count with at least three losers. (The external world—this, of course, in a differentriated way —, the underdeveloped regions of the EC, and the sectors which are falling behind or are condemned to regression.) The reason is that the rise in the competitiveness of the EC involves inevitable that the strong become stronger. The integration concept would be much more convincing if it paid special attention to the disadvantages caused by the intensification of the integration process. But instead, at the moment, it can only be seen that the very strong publicity wants to mobilise, intends to convince every single citizen of the Community that he will feel much better, and that the integration is even the only chance for him. However, with the advance of time it is primarily the consequences of the reactions by the companies that become the main shapers of the population's mood. The increase of competitiveness usually is accompanied by a more rational management of labour, which frequently leads to the increase of unemployment. In the countries of the Twelve this danger is already being felt, although 1989 brought the biggest boom of the decade for the Twelve.

This publicity is needed, because the entire philosophy of the single market relies on the requirement that the barriers which at the moment belong to the national competencies and are consequently dependent on the national will must be wound down for the sake of the unification of the market. The rules adopted in the various common institutions of the Community can exert an influence only if the member countries can introduce them into their own domestic economy.

The Brussels Commission of the EC is the institutional engine of the unification of the market. Looking at it from the side of the Commission, the realisation of the Europe 1992 concept means the solution and introduction of approximately 300 new fundamental tasks. And that by the end of 1992. If we look at the process of the unification of the internal market in this way, the progress becomes transparent and easily measurable.

However, it is not certain that the integration can be examined exclusively in the process of the realisation of these rules. Since the expansion of the membership of the EC from six to twelve, i.e. the meeting of the developed North and the underdeveloped South within the framework of integration, the manageability of the differences in the grade of development has become most decisive from the aspect of the degree of integration. Let us have a look at some data about the size of the differences in the grade of development.

From the aspect of the differences mentioned in the level of development between the North and the South, the data show two things unequivocally. First, the fact of the stubborn difference over three decades, and second, the just as stubborn trend of the continuous reduction of this difference. However, all this does not mean that the differences in the level of development had shrunk to be so small that they would make a truly single market possible. These comprehensive indicators show clearly that there are considerable regional differences, and consequently regional regulation within the EC is necessary. And that in questions affecting the essence of "freedom" (e.g. restriction of the free movement of labour).

TABLE 8.1

Per Capita GDP (E.C. = 100)

	1960	*1973*	*1986*	*1989**	*1990**
Belgium	95.4	100.6	101.1	102.4	103.0
Denmark	118.6	113.1	118.0	108.0	107.1
F.R.G.	117.2	110.1	114.4	113.3	113.4
Greece	38.4	56.3	56.0	54.0	53.6
Spain	59.2	77.4	72.2	75.7	76.3
France	104.3	109.3	110.0	108.5	108.6
Ireland	61.4	59.9	63.4	66.0	67.3
Italy	91.2	98.8	104.0	105.1	105.2
Luxemburg	134.5	123.9	126.3	128.0	128.7
Holland	117.8	112.1	106.4	103.5	103.1
Portugal	37.3	54.2	52.8	54.5	55.4
United Kingdom	127.6	107.2	104.2	104.6	103.7
E.C.	100.0	100.0	100.0	100.0	100.0

* September/October 1989. Forecast.
Source: Jahreswirtschaftsbericht 1989-1990.
Kommission der Europäischen Gemeinschaften.

The change in the level of development involves sacrifices, and among these unemployment is perhaps the biggest from the social aspect. The integration must handle this question. It is consequently worthwhile to survey the situation of the twelve member countries in this respect.

Th data indicate primarily that compared to the great competitors the rate of employment was significantly higher in this five-year period in the whole of the EC. And this draws attention to the fact that the Community is in a more acute situation than its competitors. If we think of this, it is not so surprising that in 1989 the weight of the Left and of the extremists rose in the European Parliament.

In this context that it has to be formulated as an open and rather serious question from the aspects of the future of Europe what the role of leftist ideas and movements will be in the process of building the single market? Because it can be declared unequivocally that the strengthening of the Left does not favour the market-based integration.

For the sake of increasing international competitiveness — exactly on account of the size-specific disadvantages — it is necessary to integrate. The principles laid down in the White Book are supported effectively by the survey led by Paolo *Cecchini* and conducted by experts appointed by the EC Commission, about the costs caused by the fragmentation of the EC market. According to this study, the abolition of border controls would lead to a gain of approximately 13-25 billion ECU. The realisation of "Europe '92" could establish 2-5 million new workplaces. The increase of the size of production series could lead to a saving of 2% of the GDP. These are the sources and new possibilities which are referred to when one wants to emphasise the beneficial effect of the unification of the market for everybody. These are indeed real and very imposing benefits. However, the matter has a blemish. The millions of new workplaces must be accompanied by an end to millions of old workplaces. And, for structural reasons, one cannot make up for the other. The abolition of borders within the EC can increase the already considerable great migration of the Modern Age.

TABLE 8.2

Number of Unemployed in the Percentage of the Civilian Working Population

	1986	*1987*	*1988*	*1989**	*1990**
Belgium	11.9	11.5	10.4	9¼	8¾
Denmark	5.8	5.8	6.4	7½	7¼
F.R.G.	6.5	6.4	6.4	5½	5¼
Greece	8.2	8.0	8.5	8½	8½
Spain	21.2	20.5	19.6	17½	16½
France	10.4	10.5	10.2	9½	9
Ireland	18.3	18.0	17.8	16¾	16¼
Italy	10.6	10.1	10.6	10½	10½
Luxemburg	2.7	2.7	2.2	1¾	1⅓
Holland	10.3	10.2	10.3	10	9½
Portugal	8.3	6.8	5.6	5¼	5¼
United Kingdom	11.5	10.6	8.7	6¾	6½
E.C.	10.8	10.4	10.0	9	8¾
U.S.A.	6.9	6.1	5.4	5	5¼
Japan	2.8	2.8	2.5	2½	2½

* September/October 1989. Forecast.
Source: Jahreswirtschaftsbericht 1989-1990.
Kommission der Europäischen Gemeinschaften.

The concept of EC '92 would be better founded if it presented the market-conform treatment of the disadvantages. This would be especially important because the advantages do not preceed the disadvantages in time.

The idea of the single market is tied closely to the building up of the supranational institutional system. In other words, to the macro-monetary integration, and through it to the future political union of the twelve member countries. This logic is followed also by the integration concept of the EC from the White Book through the Single European

Act to the Delors report. Thus the gradual evolution builds three steps onto each other; single internal market—economic and monetary union—political union. In other words, the vision of the concept is a road from the Common Market to the European Union. Logically it can be also assumed that the EC will be a genuine common market if it becomes also an economic and possibly a political union. Merely on the level of logic, this is true in the reverse too. If it will not be a union at least in the economic sense, it will not be a common market either.

This is the reason why concerning the planned extent of unification the Europe '92 concept harbours even also the possibility of failure. It should, of course, be made clear what could be considered a failure from the aspect of the concept. For the EC Commission it would certainly be already a big failure if by December 3, 1992 it were not able to tick off the full implementation of all the three hundred new regulations. It is most likely that in numerous respects a single system of standards will be achieved in the EC member countries by the end of 1992. It is also likely that these will not serve exclusively as weapons of trade policy against the external competitors, but will represent a serious step in the process of the evolution of the single market, the completion in time of which cannot yet be foreseen.

In this process it is far from being certain that 1992 will be a milestone. If we set out in the consideration of the time factor from what the concept itself sets out from too, viz. we reckon with factors within the EC only, then some aspects can be formulated which can have a considerable influence on the pace and direction of the integration. In fact, all solutions are built around a single question. And the decisive question is to what extent the integration manifested from above, through the supranational institutions, will be underpinned or followed by the integration of the market from below.

If we assume that one of the indicators of market integration can be trade among each other, then it is worthwhile to survey these data.

The data show clearly that trade within the Community played a decisive role in the international trade of all member countries, and it exceeded significantly the weight of trade with any other region. With a small exaggeration (with the exception of Denmark and the United Kingdom) it can also be established that 50-70% of the trade of the member countries was transacted among each other. This represented a huge stabilising factor from the aspect of maintaining the Community. In respect of the proportions of trade, the difference between the developed Northern and the underdeveloped Southern member countries is far from being as big as in respect of the per capita GDP. This shows clearly how much closer in respect of the directions of trade the relationship between the developed Western Europe and Southern Europe is than between Eastern and Western Europe. The trade structures built on each other, if they also carry a dynamic in the longer-term, can represent the most stable foundations of the intensification of integration. It is exactly this dynamism that the concept of Europe '92 wants to promote through the unification of the market. The question is how successful this reversed logic will be.

TABLE 8.3

The Share of the E.C. in the Total Imports and Exports of the Member Countries in 1987

	EC		*Japan*		*U.S.A.*		*Others*	
	imp.	*exp.*	*imp.*	*exp.*	*imp.*	*exp.*	*imp.*	*exp.*
Belgium	72.4	74.0	2.6	1.0	5.1	5.0	19.7	20.0
Denmark	53.6	48.5	3.6	3.7	4.9	7.2	37.9	40.6
France	66.7	60.6	2.9	1.5	5.7	7.2	25.7	30.7
F.R.G.	54.6	52.9	5.7	1.9	5.8	9.4	33.9	35.8
Greece	61.2	67.1	4.1	0.9	2.6	6.7	32.1	25.3
Ireland	71.3	73.5	3.3	1.7	14.5	7.8	10.9	17.0
Italy	56.7	56.1	2.1	1.6	5.3	9.6	35.9	32.7
Holland	61.5	75.7	3.7	0.7	7.4	4.1	27.4	19.5
G. Britain	51.3	49.2	6.0	1.9	10.6	14.0	32.1	34.9
Spain	54.9	59.1	4.1	0.7	8.2	7.5	32.6	32.7
Portugal	63.5	71.3	3.9	0.6	4.9	6.5	27.7	21.6

Source: Die Gemeinschaft 1992: Ein Markt mit neuen Dimensionen. Europäische Dokumentation Zeitschrift 2/1989.

The triad of the White Book, the Single European Act and the Delors report covers the period which has passed since 1985. These three documents represent a vision of integration in which the "what" is more exactly outlined than the "how". And if the "how" is open from many aspects, then the question of "why" is also open.

About the details of the concept outlined by the three documents, I shall enumerate some out of the ideas of a German and a British researcher, in order to provide examples for the lack of solution of large-scale and essential problems of the plan and for the "visioning" which is unfolding throughout the Community.

Horst Werner[2], who works at the Institut für Wirtschaftspolitik of the University of Cologne, focuses on the question of "how", concerning the economic and monetary union.

He considers the harmonisation of taxes to be achievable through the instruments of competition. In this respect he points out that the harmonisation of the value added taxes and of the sales taxes arose in respect of the stipulations of the Community primarily with the abolition of the controls of the member countries at their border with each other. In the single internal market expanded to a size of approximately 430 billion DEM the gain from the abolition of internal border control would amount to 22 billion DEM. At present there is border control, because the tax rates of the country of destination apply if the rates differ in the selling and the buying country. Thus the exporting country of origin is exempt from the tax, which burdens the country of destination. This procedure demands border control. The obvious solution would be a changeover to taxation according to the country of origin. This, however, is unrealizable for political reasons. The different rates threaten the countries of regions where tax is relatively higher with a competitive disadvantage. However, in respect of the principle of country of destination and of origin it should be revised whether the Community law would be the best for the harmonisation of taxes. The equalisation of the tax systems can also be achieved through the competition of the taxation systems, which pays attention to the differences existing in local conditions of the various member countries. In this context frequently no unequivocal reference is made to the circumstance that the tax revenues do not represent a burden only but can also considerably improve the living conditions on the given scene.

It is also worth quoting the arguments of Horst Werner concerning the common regulation of competition. In the Common Market the competition can be achieved primarily through open markets, because the competition coming about here can restrict the elbowroom of the companies which dispose of market power. Towards third countries the market of the Community can become open if company concentration becomes activated through a Europe-wide industrial policy for the purpose to promote, for instance, the competitiveness of the European electronic industry or the aerospace industry. A European cartel office would be needed against the tendencies of monopolisation and dividing the market, which would have to investigate whether company mergers are worth prohibiting on account of the danger of market domination. The closing of the domestic market against competition from third countries is becoming a growing trend supporting protectionism with such arguments as "environmental dumping" or "social dumping". Chances for an open market competition would be enhanced if anti-dumping accusations were referred to the competency of the European Court. This, however, meets with resistance from the EC Commission, which — with the increasing stream of anti-dumping procedures — has until now counteracted the entire openness of the EC market.

The ideas quoted from Horst Werner throw light, behind the investigation of the integration model, on an interconnection which is frequently mentioned in the German press, viz. the interconnection between the Brussels Commission and a given integration model, the path of economic unification guided from above through instructions.

The solution concerning the regulation of competition and mergers deserves special mention. According to this, there is no international competitiveness in high-tech industries without a strong internal concentration of capital, and without this there is no real chance for opening the EC market to third countries. Ideas kindred to these can frequently be read from the industrial circles of the F.R.G. Namely that in high-tech industries the international competitiveness is size-specific, and in this area the Community suffers a serious disadvantage compared to the USA or Japan.

Brian *Hindley*[3] leads a project in the Trade Policy Research Centre in London. Seeing the ambitious integration plans, his basic question is what happens to the EC after 1993? In connection with this question Hindley stresses three subjects: the establishment of the European Central Bank, the extension of the EC with social dimensions, and the possibility of retreating to the idea of the fortress Europe.

About one of the most important objectives of the Delors plan, the Common Central Bank, Hindley has a devastating opinion. The supporters of the Delors plan argue that the European Central Bank is indispensable in order to ensure the convergence of economic policies and social policies in the EC. According to him, although this argument is plausible, it raises numerous problems. For example, this logic, in fact, assumes that the individual national central banks — overestimating their actual freedom — commit many errors, which would not be committed by the common bank. Such typical errors are the deficit of the balance of performance, or the strong devaluation of the national currency, when the governments come under pressure to introduce foreign exchange control. In other words, the central banks commit errors which involve serious consequences. Seeing this, Hindley's question is the following: is it better if, instead of the central bank of a member country, the European Central Bank commits the errors, which would affect the whole EC?

In connection with the common central bank, the British researcher also discusses what would happen to the function of the regulation of money supply, which is so important from the aspect of the functioning of the economy. There are member countries which want to achieve the increase of employment by a higher rate of inflation. There are others which have already learned that the long-term effect of inflation is the rise of unemployment. If the common central bank had to be established, it would also have to be invested with the responsibility for the stability of prices. The connection between the prices and the quantity of money is judged differently by the individual banks. Most of these diverging views would be represented in the European Central Bank. In the end all this would lead to an incalculable economic policy. and thus certainly also to no member country being satisfied with the activity of the common bank.

In connection with European enterpreneurial law and the social charter, the author takes a stand for the free open market but is far from being certain about its feasibility. Therefore, he closes his train of thoughts by formulating the following question: "Will the internal market of 1992 indeed bring about a more open market of high intensity competition?" this indeed is at stake.

The British researcher presents the problem of fortress Europe rather vividly on the example of the motor industry. In this connection he points at the different reactions of the member countries to the intrusion of the Japanese motor industry. Britain maximised the share of Japanese cars on its market to eleven percent, France to three percent, while Italy admits an infinitesimal quantity. Other Northern member countries of the EC have not applied any quantitative restriction at all. This practice is contrary to the Treaty of Rome, which referred the external EC trade policy to the competency of the Commission and of the Council of Ministers. The Commission has for years tried to make itself independent of national restrictions. The basic problem is that those member countries where it would be higher, are unwilling to accept the Community quota.

The Commission recommends a part solution for the single market in order to regain its influence on trade policy. If a uniform EC standard applies to cars and internal border controls have been abolished, the governments of the member countries will no longer be in the situation to maintain the national restrictions. In this case, a Frenchman, for instance, would be able to buy his car in Belgium, be it Japanese or not. The European motor industry is not interested in the bringing about of such a situation and, in order to avoid it, it is able to influence also the governments. It thus becomes questionable whether the governments influenced in this way will at all permit that the unification of the market should occur in this area.

The cited considerations of the German and the British researcher point out emphatically that by leaving the question of "how" open, the Europe '92 concept has given rise to serious doubts about its feasibility, but at least whether it can be realised by the time limit set. It seems on the basis of these considerations that the EC becoming integrated from above, i.e. the introduction of framework regulations will not really be able to manage the problems, and conflicts of interests which surface in the wake of harmonisation.

This is why building from the bottom up appears to be more successful. This path of evolution cannot be excluded in the EC, not even if the three documents mentioned do not take a stand in these questions, or in some cases expressly prefer the other way. One thing can certainly be established: EC '92 cannot be considered a thoroughly thought through and properly elaborated integration concept. (This is perhaps why is so stimulating).

2. The E.C. Commission on the Fulfilment of "Europe '92" at Half-time[4]

The adopted programmes have made the unification of norms and technical prescriptions one of the most important areas of the unification of the EC market. This is a huge, time consuming task in the course of the realisation of which the legislation and the application of law by the member countries will become much better known and "experienced" by the EC Commission and the member countries as well. The EC Commission is responsible for the realisation of the objectives adopted in the common documents. Consequently, so far it has been able to gather knowledge mostly about the introduction of Community decisions by the member countries. The basic philosophic questions of the integration model can — by nature of things — not arise in the course of this work. Thus the fulfilment of the program can be measured, and concrete causes can always be found for delays, which are usually linked to the particularities of the practice of transplantation into the national frameworks.

In this logical section, the appraisal of the Commission concerning the fulfilment o the programme reads as follows: "The Council has already made final decisions about 130 measures figuring in the Internal Market Programme. Together with the common stands and part-decisions this accounts for more than 50% of the programme."

The adoption of the Single European Act has cut short the time necessary for passing the final decisions. (From the earlier 70 months to 30-15 months). In this regard both the EC Commission and the Council decided that the acceleration of the decision-making process has strengthened the credibility of the objectives, and thereby has made the realisation of the internal market of the EC irreversible.

According to the evaluation of the Commission — based on an opinion poll in economic circles — everybody has understood the importance of the deadline of 1992, even if this has in part given rise to concern. This has contributed to the companies developing their strategies paying attention to the European dimension. Investment into Europe has become one of the most attractive goals for foreign firms, as a result of which the number of unemployed fell to the 1983 level.

The Commission mentions as a critique that in respect of the "Europe of citizens" the progress is unsatisfactory. There are difficulties in respect of the introduction of the general right of residence as well as in taxation matters.

The success achieved in the fulfilment of the programme on the level of the Community has not always been accompanied by a similarly accelerated pace in the introduction within the national framework. It is thus not coincidence that in Brussels the EC Commission pays emphatic attention to the implementation or non-implementation to the tasks to be fulfilled within the national framework. It points out emphatically that, as the Commission stressed in its latest comments concerning the implementation of the White Book, it is insufficient for fulfilment to pass the necessary measures. In addition, it is also necessary to create the conditions for application and that the guidelines should be transplanted by the time set.

Adequate control is first of all necessary because the players in the economy are mostly not confronted directly with Community law, but only with the measures and administrative steps transplanted by the individual states. If the principle of support must be maintained, this must not lead to the reintroduction of distortions which must cease with the introduction of Community law.

Even if not directly, this finding refers rather unequivocally to the national counter-interests to some basic principles decided on the level of the Community. And the critique of the Commission is voiced in connection with the systems of support which rather fundamentally determine and spin a fine web right across the functioning of the national economy. And this means that the national economies of the member countries dispose of distinctive basic characteristics which may even put a question mark to the harmonisation of regulations, to the unification of the internal market of the EC.

Examining the causes for delay, the Commission begins its material with a threat worthy of attention. It declares that the problem of national introduction is already to a certain extent the consequence of an irreversible evolution in connection with the target of 1992; this is due mainly to the acceleration of the decision-making process. At the same time this problem questions the credibility of the political will of the Community and thereby threatens the irreversibility of the evolution.

Although the internal mechanisms of national introduction are not yet adjusted in he member countries to the new rhythms of the decision-making process, several member countries are aware of this problem.

It is difficult to tell whether the sentences quoted above reflect the fear of the Commission concerning the sustainability of the set time limits, or whether it bows its head to the time-honoured stability of the national economic frameworks and limitations, linked to the attempt at passing on responsibility. In any case, the irreversible evolution concerning the targets set for 1992 and the danger of reversibility are described in two sentences following on each other. They certainly point out that the reasons for the delay must be explored, the method of solution must be found, and not only procedures against the violations must be looked for.

The Commission publishes its opinion in detail about the reasons for the delays. It mentions four reasons. The most important one is the internal organisation established in the member countries for the control of the transplantation of the main guidelines. The second reason is that in some cases the authorities have difficulties concerning the interpretation of these main guidelines. The third reason mentioned is the legislative procedure existing in some member countries. The fourth reason is that an adequate transparency is missing in transplantation to the member countries.

In view of "December 31, 1992, which is an important political date", the Commission will now issue information every six months about the situation of the national introduction.

Concerning the problems of interpretation, the Commission sees the solution in calling expert meetings in questions which are especially intricate, where the introductory measures applied in the individual member countries must be harmonised to the fullest possible extent. These meetings can also be used for reminding the national authorities of their obligations. This procedure will be applied systematically in all working groups and committees. The question is whether — co-ordinated by the EC Commission — the authorities of the member countries will show greater inclination to present their different national economic arrangements, and even for their harmonisation. These methods proposed by the EC Commission must be viewed with some scepticism, although it cannot be excluded that all this can contribute to the national bureaucracies becoming European, i.e. eurocrats. Whether this will then be useful from the aspect of a competitive open European market integration, is difficult to tell.

The cause for delay is frequently seen by the Commission in the circumstance that in some member countries the legislative procedure makes the transplantation of the basic principles the task of parliament. In the future — as the Commission points out — one has to reckon with guidelines frequently which will demand participation of the legislature (including e.g. the recognition of diplomas, the new concept of financial services and taxation matters, etc.).

It follows from all this that the Commission has adopted the guidelines, i.e. the from time to time lengthy practice of national introduction, and counts on unification in this way. At the same time it warned very cautiously of the undeniable usefulness of the application of dispositions from the aspect of the time plan (1992!).

It appears that the date of 1992 and the way in which the new regulations are introduced cannot get into a relationship where the date gets the primacy. The Commission takes no stand in respect of why the matter of national legislation adjusts with such difficulty to the integration objectives of the EC. Presumably the question is left open, because the fact of delays in the practice of legislation is considered by the Commission a phenomenon which is linked to the lack of information and consequently can also be eliminated.

On the basis of all this, the supremacy over the states, which is embodied in the existence of the Commission, does not appear to be free of problems in the EC. In vain does the "Europe '92" programme progress according to the plans adopted by every member country, if the approved national introduction the procedure, as could be seen above, cannot be supranational. With some exaggeration, it is possible to see in this fact that in respect of the integration model the from building from the bottom up has come to the fore, because the other is being scuttled by the existing order of national legal practice. It depends on this practice, on the one one hand, to what extent the market is finally unified, and on the other, to what extent the institutions of supranationality will be removed in the EC from the specialised executive bureaucracies, or to what extent they will be left in the hands of the legislative organs consisting of the national legislature and the leaders of state power.

The sovereignty of the national parliaments lives on in the course of the implementation of the "Europe '92" programme, and this means that in practice the national conflicts of interests will be clearly expressed, and not the Commission but exclusively the affected nations will be called upon to resolve them.

The assertion of this procedural method may at the same time have the effect that the time plan of integration is condemned to failure. The question consequently is whose interest it is to keep the time plan? Is this in the interest of the national legislators? The question is open, and the answer will be provided by the practice of the next couple of years.

The transparency of the process in the codification of the Community statutes is especially underlined by the Commission. This is linked to the large and increasing number of statutes. For the sake of textual exactness and correspondence, an adequately transparent practice is indispensable.

The demand for smoother national introduction and its method, the achievement of a higher degree of integration demand the construction of a very fine and manifold network, and this can be realised through a series of practical attempts. It can perhaps be assumed that the over-emphasis on the year 1992 as a milestone will serve the purpose of developing and stabilising the most adequate and practised method of interconnections between the member countries and the integration institutions in the development of the regulations. Certainly a link in the chain is involved which is important from the aspect of integration.

The Commission has dealt repeatedly with the question of the national transplantation of the guidelines. The time needed for this is usually 18 months. Investigations by the Commission have led to the conclusion that keeping to the deadlines represents an organisational problem in some member countries. This is not considered a very fundamental problem. It is certainly not considered a problem which would demand changes in the deadlines.

In essence it has been possible to learn from what has been said how the Commission—which is most interested in keeping to the time plan—judges the problem of implementability. In sum it can be established that the appraisal of 1989 did not leave any doubt that the deadlines could and must be maintained. This approach will again and again raise the demand of the Commission to see its power extended.

3. On the Chances of 1992 in 1980-1989—EC Appraisals

1989 was in the EC countries a year of economic boom compared to the preceding period. This can be linked primarily to the rise in investments. It was already mentioned in the preceding chapter that—conscious of the increasing competition of the single market—foreign investors started vigourous investments. The same reaction could be observed with the companies of the EC without the internal market programme, private investments would have increased in the European Community by 7% only instead of 8.5%. According to the appraisal of the Brussels authorities, 17% of the increase of private investments was due to the internal market effect. After an 8.4% rise in the past year, and 7% in the current one, the Commission counts on an increase of 5%. In contrast, between 1985 and 1987 the increase was only 3.6%, and between 1982 and 1987 there had been no increase at all. According to an all-round inquiry addressed to the EC companies in mid-year, numerous companies increase their investments as the preparation for the internal market without border, but after 1992 this trend might become weaker. According to the survey, the companies of the less wealthy member-countries are rather inclined to invest in their own country, while the German, the French, and to a smaller extent the British companies like to invest also in other countries of the Community. In the opinion of the Commission, the growing investment activity can contribute in the poorer regions to the reduction of regional disequilibria, which the annual report mentions as the central problem of the Community. By realising the single market by the time set, the EC would be able to moderate inflation and simultaneously improve other economic indicators, e.g. the balance of trade. The precondition for this is certainly the closest reconciliation of the economic policies of the member-countries,—the Commission emphasises.[5]

What was described in the preceding chapter might even lead to the conclusion that the realisation of "Europe '92" is in the universal interest of the companies and citizens of the member-countries, and only the state bureaucracies of the member-countries delay the process, primarily on account of the lack of knowledge and difficulties of interpretation. It is likely that the coming about of the single market is unstoppable and irreversible, if the micro-level intertwining continues, and mainly if the North indeed integrates the South. However, this is a slow process, certainly slower than would be required by "Europe '92". Perhaps this is one of the reasons why the question of human approach has been raised to one of the primary problems from the aspect of realising the Commission's programme.

This can be indicated by a short quotation from the speech by Jacques *Delors*, president of the EC Commission, delivered as an opening address to the College d'Europe in Brugge in October 1989: "We live through an unmatched experience. We build a Community.... in unusual circumstances,... this model will be unique, without any example in history." This is why the endeavours of the Twelve are considered a "first performance" in history, because it unites countries which were earlier frequently hostile to each other, and

— has nine official languages,
— covers regions of very different economic power,
— evolves along a peaceful path,
— sticks to the principles of democracy.
— passes resolutions in the Community institutions."[6]

Delors stressed that the logic of European history taught that integration needed will. According to Delors, the existence of this will is confirmed by the resolutions of the European Parliament passed by large majorities, as well as numerous opinion polls and initiatives which bear witness of the positive approach of companies, trade unions, representatives of workplaces and local institutions. According to Delors, every citizen of the Community must feel that the Community is its second homeland.

These ideas show clearly that the EC Commission sketches down a large-scale perspective concerning the future of the Western half of Europe. Their image of the future is shaped taking into consideration the failures of the European past.

It is in fact possible to interpret Delors's quoted ideas in such a way that for the sake of belonging together politically some correction of co-construction on a market basis can also occur. Although the linking together of the strong North and the weak South in an integration is a lofty European idea, if we think of the four freedoms and the 1992 time-plan, doubts arise. As may be seen, the Delors plan strives for a European integration of a historic horizon, embedded in its approach into the European past, because "without remembering there is no progress."

For the sake of implementing the Delors plan, the EC Commission submitted to the Council for approval, inter alia, the following: "In order to achieve lasting growth without inflation in the Community, linked to a high degree of employment, and to be able to achieve the extent of economic convergance which is necessary for the first grade of the successful monetary union, the Council — with regard to the unification of the internal market and its economic and social coherence — undertakes multilateral control... Multilateral control covers all aspects of economic policy, including the short and long-term perspectives."[7]

As may be seen, one of the focal elements of the Delors plan is the supranational co-ordination and control of the member countries. It is food for thought that when taking into consideration the regional differences, the mitigation of the differences becomes the centre of integration according to these propositions. Although the content of multilateral control is not sufficiently clear, it can be established that the EC would put tremendous power into the hands of its supranational institutions if the treatment of regional differences became their tasks.

4. On the Questions of Macro-Economic Integration (Finances, Technical Development, Trade Policy) in the EC

Macro-economic integration affects on the one hand those questions of national economic control which influence the market processes of financial management, and on the other, those which represent the objectives (technical catching up) and instruments (unified trade policy) of the answer to be given to the challenge of the external world.

The Delors plan formulates it clearly that in the last resort the macro-economic integration amounts to an economic and financial union. Consequently, in connection with the financial integration processes of the EC the question is what the consequences of the integration of the real sphere are in financial co-operation, and whether these lead in the direction of monetary union.

The progress of integration in the real economy assumes the free movement of capital in the territory of the EC. The period between 1986 and 1989 brought considerable progress in the EC in the freeing of capital movements in the general sense. It was exactly the developments in this direction that called attention to the circumstance that the fixed exchange rates and the capital taxis different from country to country represented a serious problem and that the capital movements rendered free hand undesirable effects. Thus this freedom provided to the profit-oriented microsphere made necessary a much closer co-ordination of the governmental financial functions. However, contrary to what would be deduced from its name, this co-ordination assumes that the stronger should support the weaker.

The functioning of the EMS is a good example of this problem of integration and of its handling. There were many who did not attach hope to the functioning of the EMS. It has been in operation for ten years. But the positions of the stronger and the weaker currencies compared to each other would have supported those who had a sceptical approach if the Deutsche Bundesbank had not undertaken the co-ordinated support of the weak currencies. In consequence, financial stability became in the EC "dependent on the West Germans". It is questionable to what extent this can represent a firm foundation in the long-term for the integration of the macro finances. By a little simplification it may even be claimed that the financial stability is the privilege of the strong, while the fate of the weak in the process of following the lead is instability. The task of integration should be the mitigation of this situation.

The question is interesting from the aspect whether evolution will proceed on the basis of the stability logic of the EMS and the present role of the ECU, according to the Delors plan. Although 1990 represented the first year in the implementation of the plan, we have to say that the question is completely open.

The free movement of capital is a universal market interest for all the Twelve member-countries. It can consequently be assumed that the sacrifice mentioned will be undertaken in the future. The open question is whether this represents a sufficient foundation for the supranational competency of the central bank functions or does not.

In the Community of "uneven stability" the free movement of capital is closely linked also to the questions of taxation. If the Community united economies the strength of which was similar, the differences of the tax systems, which had come about as the result of different national historic evolution, could even be enforced by market competition. But in this case this cannot really be undertaken. Thus, what is left is the road of harmonisation developed by the integration organs of the EC by instructions from above. However, as witnessed in 1989, this road is full of pitfalls to the extent that it may even block the realisation of the plan. In 1990 the opinion became more and more universally held that in the issue of the harmonisation of taxes it was not possible to reach a final solution by the end of 1992. Formulated more pointedly, the objective economic compulsion exists concerning the harmonisation of taxes in the market, but the protection of the less developed regions does not exist, and if the harmonisation exists through instructions, the situation is exactly reversed, and in this case nothing can restrain the national lobbies which have a strong bargaining position.

The integration concept of the EC considers financial stability (rate of inflation, exchange rates) a real and indispensable goal. It is far from being certain that the intensification of financial integration and the desired stability are possible at the present level of differences in the stage of development.

Let me quote an opinion which is close to this summary philosophy, in order to strengthen the certainly more pessimistic vision concerning the time horizon. According to the ideas of a famous European financial authority, André *Kostolany*[8], today the government of every EC member-country conducts a sovereign interest rate, credit and taxation policy, which subordinate to different domestic and foreign political, social and psychological developments. On the other hand, they are influenced by such factors as the national character, style of life, or the attitude of the trade unions—phenomena which change from time to time. In one country full employment is the supreme command (at the expense of stability), in the other stability (at the expense of the labour market). One country conducts a monetary policy, the other a fiscal one. "To lump the Scots and the Sicilians, the Danes and the Greeks together reminds me of the story of La Fontaine "The marriage of the carp and the hare".

One of the basic areas of the macro-economic integration of the EC is the acceleration of technical development in the countries of the Community. It was exactly the losing of ground in the world economy in the area of the high-tech industries in the 1980s which gave rise to the "Europe '92" programme. The objective is clear, but the question is how. The integration institutions of the Community want to contribute to the achievement of the goal through several programmes of various types.

It is characteristic of all programmes that the financial resources that can be devoted to them on the level of the Community are rather small. This is linked to the strongly tied expenditure structure of the EC budget. To prove this, let us see some proportions of the budget.

It can be pointed out with assurance that while the budget of the Community increased more than 3.5 fold in the ten years and within it the share of expenditure of an R+D nature was quadrupled, the absolute sum remained insignificantly small. (At the same time, it can be stated with unequivocal certainty that throughout the ten years the dominant item was agricultural subsidies. It is worth mentioning that the question of agricultural policy is not at all raised by the White Book).

TABLE 8.4

Percentage of Some Summary Items in the EC Budget

	1979	*1981*	*1984*	*1987*	*1989*
Share of expenditure of an agricultural nature in the total expenditure	81.1	72.7	72.9	64.8	64.5
Share of expenditure of an R+D nature in the total expenditure	1.3	2.2	6.1	6.2	5.2

Source: European Trends 1981, 1988, 1989.

In a somewhat paradoxical way, these tied proportions led the Community to a more efficient stimulation of R+D. The stimulation of R+D activity provides the Brussels Commission primarily with tasks of co-ordination, the participation in the programme being voluntary, and the programmes operating with decentralised means in respect of financial sources.

Co-ordination by the integration (supranational) institutions helps the establishment of contacts between partners, which results in the reduction of the numbers of parallel research, may exercise an influence in the direction of the desirable concentration of capital, can strengthen the increase and higher efficiency of applications. In sum, it can reduce the negative effects (e.g. the secret enclosure of innovations into companies) of the increasing acceptance of roles by the companies, which is overwhelmingly very positive from the aspect of the economy.

The R+D activity represents the most important element of company strategies, and if the programmes do not reckon with this, then they necessarily "sabotage" them in practice. Consequently, the supranational institutions must restrict themselves to a role which does not want to cancel out the success of the R+D activity which is linked to the competitive position of the company. Companies have remained key players in the R+D activity, and international co-operation is possible to the extent which the company judges to be in its interest.

However, all this means also that in questions of technical development the importance of the supranational integration institutions remains limited. The integrating role is fulfilled mostly by the market. It is shown convincingly by the behaviour of companies in 1989 that — counting on the unified EC market — the optimum magnitude, the competitive size, i.e. the mergers have come to the fore. It must however be noted that the capital concentration and the built-up institutional system of the money market are interconnected. It can perhaps be expected that in the movement of money on the market the weight of the companies will grow. All this can mean in the EC the foundation and princial engine of a market type integration.

In high-tech production and application the positions of the member-countries of the Community have continuously been deteriorating in the world-wide competition. It is a question whether Europe is able at all to change this trend. It is very likely that the essence of this problem is provided by the competitiveness of companies. And company attitude will be change towards improvement of the world market positions, if the protection of the internal market of the Community against the external competitors ceases. The statement can perhaps be risked that successful R+D activity within the Community will depend not only on the programmes but at least to the same extent on trade policy. And to this may perhaps be added the unification of the market, including the uniform technical standards and norms.

It is worth mentioning here that — exactly on account of the steep life curve of products in high-tech industries — the development of standards has taken shape in the course of the competition and co-operation between the companies. Even in the question of technical norms, what is involved is that under market constraint a readiness for co-operation among companies arises, which assists standardisation on the international scale. Thus out of an authority function this activity becomes a category of company competition. Consequently, the readiness of the company for international co-operation depends on its market motivation.

Of course, this "market philosophy" strongly exposes the EC countries to international competition also in those areas where Europe is less competitive. And here it has to be supposed that the market-conform regulation would lead to the gaining ground of foreign companies exactly in these high-tech sensitive sectors. In the 1980s, the Japanese market successes in electronics, the irrepressible hard "samurai" business proved with an almost shocking power that the companies of the EC were not competitive against imports. And it was perhaps exactly this recognition which drove import policies to a considerable extent to the Community level. And this import policy is unequivocally protectionist.

The viability of companies is determined primarily by the dynamic of their sales potential. It is perhaps due to this that export policies have remained within the national framework. All this raises the question whether the competitive disadvantage which arose in the area of high technologies in the 1980s does not move the Community towards an "effective" protectionism, and in order to enhance the bargaining position, toward a strengthening protectionism. If in the area of macro-finances integration is possible only in the rather long-term, and if the invigoration of technical development is linked expressly to the comfortable, protected position of the companies of the EC an exactly contrary trend can be claimed concerning trade policy intentions and constraints. Namely, the co-ordinated and strengthening protectionism, partly directed from above (from Brussels).

If the possibility of integration approached from the macro-economic aspect was concentrated primarily on protection against the external world, this would mean undoubtedly that "Europe '92", as the programme of the construction of a single internal market has become scuttled. And consequently those areas of integration were left which had become crystallised in the course of the practice of the preceding three decades. It is unlikely that the short-term future of EC integration must be considered so darkly. This is so, inter alia, because the strengthening of protectionism would conflict even in case of the most refined tactics with the interests of important trading partners. It is unlikely that the majority of the EC member-countries should not have an elementary interest in increasing trade outside the Community.

It is today still rather difficult to size up the influence of the external market, as an important factor concerning the internal integration of the EC, beyond asserting that it exerts an influence against the fortress Europe. It cannot yet even be seen what will be realised by 1993 on the basis of the internal interest relations of the EC. The unification of the market in itself makes the EC rather more attractive for foreign investments (as was shown in 1989). If it were not necessary to reckon with a strengthening protectionism as an alternative, it is unlikely that in 1989 the interest of the external business world would have been so strong towards the EC.

5. Micro-level Interests and Reactions Assuming the Realisation of the Single Market

The business world of the EC member-countries has got into a peculiar situation concerning the integration programme. To wit, the most powerful influence, the inevitable constraint of reaction is exercised by the unification of the internal market of the EC exactly on business life, on the companies. The companies must prepare themselves for the radical change in the conditions of competition, and must provide a strategic answer. But this is only one side of the peculiar situation. The other is that the future which is being assumed in general by the business world is realised exactly through preparing themselves to this future, through this self-fulfilling mechanism. And as long as there is no unequivocal image of the process of unification being realised by 1993, the companies get ready for a unified and new competitive market of 320 million inhabitants.

The possible variants of partial market unification are placed on a broad scale between "no" and "yes". This keeps the companies in the EC member-countries in a state of uncertainty. And it is perhaps this that the company uncertainty and fear registered by the Brussels Commission an be deduced from. Perhaps 1989 did not bring in respect of the market unification the actual progress which the companies had expected.

Let us see here a very competent opinion. The German Industrial Association (Bundesverband der Deutschen Industrie, BDI) called on the EC summit held in Strassbourg at the end of 1989 that the implementation of the single internal market should be given priority. "The BDI calls on the heads of state and government of the EC member-countries to take an emphatic stand for the internal market action, so that it should not be deadlocked. Of primary importance are the continuous transplantation into the national legal systems of the Community measures, as well as the soonest possible resolutions of he Council of Ministers on public tenders, communication, the liberalisation of telecommunication, and the abolition of border control. These are the resolutions which would made it possible that not only a large but a free market should be brought about, and would reduce the administrative burdens of the companies. By such halfway solutions as additional administrative burdens inflicting the companies and the removal of border control to the background, the qualitative goals of 1992 cannot be achieved. Only the bringing about of a unified internal market creates the economic basis for the economic monetary union. Its realisation depends on whether the single steps are taken in the right sequence. At present the decisive thing is that the resolved liberalisation of the movement of capital should be realised, as far as possible, in an irreversible way, and every member-country should joint the EMS exchange rate mechanism with the same rights and obligations. After the realisation of the first grade of the monetary union every national central bank should be given full autonomy. Only an independent European Central Bank can represent the sole warranty for the stability of the Community."[9]

The ideas cited above show unequivocally that the BDI would indeed like to achieve a single market and that it has doubts concerning its realisation. It seems that the goals of the Brussels Commission coincide with the goals of the BDI. However, the matter is much more complicated than this. The free EC market without administrative restrictions is probably a desired goal for every competitive company. But the contrary probably applies to the potentially weaker. After this the question is who will delay in the interest of whom?

The essential information transmitted by the lines quoted is the dissatisfaction of the companies. Still another German opinion is worth mentioning concerning the effects of the functioning of the single market. "In the 1990s there will be more co-operation, more intertwining of capital, acquisition of companies on the European and the international scene, which subordinates the weak to the strong in the market, the slow to the quick, the company of low capital strength to the company of higher capital strength and to which is more innovative. The trend towards larger units is unmistakable in almost all sectors."[10]

Preparations by companies for the single market in the EC after 1992 certainly speed up mergers. An attractive effect of the not yet existing but for the near future assumed single market is the demand for increasing the scale. While the unification of the EC market occurs primarily on paper, the mergers take place in practice. New market positions, new power centres are established. It is probably this market force which can and possibly will integrate on the fragmented EC market. On the logic and power of the mergers let us see again an example taken from the German economy.

The large merger affair of 1989 (which may even be termed scandalous) was the merger of Daimler-Benz AG and Messerschmitt Bölkow-Blohm GmbH. In its application for approval of the merger Daimler made use of the following arguments: after the merger the sales share of the Daimler-Benz Group in the area of aerospace is still much smaller than that of its foreign competitors. In sales American companies occupy the first nine places. The largest European aerospace company, British Aerospace, is tenth on the world list. The expanded Daimler-Benz Group will be in twelfth position. The more foreign companies will figure as the leaders of international co-operation, the smaller will be the opportunities for orders for the German manufacturers and suppliers.[11]

These company endeavours and attempts are characteristic of the large companies which have power, autonomy and influence. The "small is beautiful" and rather useful too, represent a principle which is reflected much rather in the direct and indirect support plans of the Commission than in the company strategies. It can be assumed that—although to a different extent from country to country — the attachment of the small enterprises to a given location is big, and thus the unification of the internal market of the EC will certainly leave the largest part of the microsphere unaffected.

Where exporting and dynamic small enterprises are concerned, or firms which are strongly exposed to competition in some other way; the reaction and preparations for 1993 rely on similar principles as in case of the large companies. They try to increase their bargaining position on the basis of the identity of interests. These ambitions necessarily include alliances directed at the mitigation of the positional advantages of the large companies. The Brussels Commission has also elaborated numerous projects which assist co-operated and thus increase the bargaining power.

It is very probable that in the course of preparations for 1993 a large demand for money aimed at modernisation will arise on the EC market. Thus the attitude of the banking sphere will have a decisive importance. The banks too want to protect themselves from the unpleasant effects of the 1993 competition by mergers. This interest and process will be harmonised with the growth and modernisation interests of the small enterprises as well as with the endeavours of the large companies towards merger.

From the aspect of the single market, the reaction by large companies can be considered the perhaps decisive change which occurred in 1989. It seems that another kind of group and level of the integration forces is involved. This force of integration acts within the region in the direction of differentiated development. It cannot be seen clearly whether anti-monopoly regulations or the establishment of companies of a European status will succeed in preventing or restrict the coming about and functioning of this force, or whether it would be useful to restrict it at all.

6. On Some Geopolitical Interconnections Concerning the Integration Endeavours of the EC, in Brief

The "Europe '92" programme has expressly taken aim at the internal integration of the Twelve, wanting to intensify it. Where the external world enters the picture is to what extent it must or wants to tolerate this process from the outside.

It can be assumed that the USA and Japan will prevent their being shut out, i.e. one-sided protectionism of the EC, by market and power instruments. The system of reciprocal concessions will become stronger, especially as far as Japan is concerned. The European outsiders are in a different position. Their bargaining power is much smaller. But the chances of the EFTA are better, since — even if in a differentiated way — a closely knit network ties the individual countries to the EC. It can be assumed that these connections are not at risk. Presumably, the bargaining power of the EFTA will be sufficient for the EFTA countries to achieve equitable contractual procedures, to the extent of the integration of the EC, on this traditional market.

The situation of the COMECON countries is entirely different. In fact, they have almost no bargaining power in the economic sense, including the Soviet Union. The EC can "treat" all of them in an almost sovereign way.

Irrespective of all these external forces and intentions, or in spite of them, the internal integration of the EC is unstoppable from the outside. However, the German unification can give a new direction to the European process of unification and integration both in the economic and the political sense. Today we are still at the beginning of the process, so that only the fact of the effect can be stated unequivocally, but not yet its characteristics and the path of its realisation. It is very likely that German unification will act counter to the fortress-like integration within the EC and will bring about new and livelier relations with Europe outside the Twelve. Thus, presumably, the 1990s will be in Europe not only the decade of the fullness of integration in the EC, but also the period of intensification of a variegated regional integration process in the whole of Europe.

NOTES

1. DIW 32/1989.
2. *Werner*, Horst: Perspektive und Probleme des Gemeinsamen Marktes 1993 (Perspectives and Problems of the Common Market 1993). In: Supplement to the Weekly "Das Parlament", June 9, 1989.
3. *Hindley*, Brian: Die Europäische Gemeinschaft 1993 (The European Community 1933). In Supplement to the Weekly: "Das Parlament". June 9, 1989.

4. Mitteilung der Kommission uber die Instrumente zur Verwirklichung des Binnenmarktes, (Communiqué of the Commission about the Instruments for the Realisation of the Single Market). Brussels, September 7, 1989.
5. Monatlicher Brief zum Europa ohne Binnengrenzen (Monthly letter for Europe without internal borders) No. 10, December 1989.
6. Vorschlag für eine Entscheidung des Rates (Proposal for a resolution by the Council). Brussels, October 13, 1989.
7. Ibid.
8. Kostolany, André: Europa-Rat (Council of Europe). In: Capital, No. 8/1989.
9. BDI Pressemitteilung (BDI Press Communique). Köln, December 6, 1989, No. 121/89.
10. *Sombers*, Gerd: Forum Binnenmarkt 1992 (Single market 1992 Forum). In: Auf dem Weg nach Europa (On the road to Europe). July 25, 1989. No. 30.
11. Von Bonn wenig begeisterte Daimler und MBB. (From Bonn little enthusiasm for Daimler and NBB). In: Neue Zürcher Zeitung, August 5, 1989.

9

Case Study in Global Business Environment: The EEC

EXPECTED TRENDS OF THE TRADE POLICY OF THE EUROPEAN COMMUNITY

The programme of the renewal and intensification of West European integration, which is symbolised by the magic figure of the year 1992, has called forth great interest all over the world. This is far from having happened by chance. The "Europe '92" programme formulates, extraordinarily ambitious targets, it nevertheless being a big question what will become realised of all this.

It can be stated with certainty that one of the central problems of the long-term evolution of West European integration, one of the main points contested is how the division of work between the European Community and the world economy will develop.[1]

In my opinion we can seek the answer to this question in the external relations aspects of he unified internal market of the European Community, as well as in the intentions of the Common Market, in the likely outcome of the internal conflicts of interests concerning the external policy of the Community. It is consequently the purpose of this study to provide an answer to these issues.

1. External Relations Aspects of the Unified Internal Market of the European Community

In connection with the external economic aspects of the unified internal market of the West European integration it has to be stressed that the company circles and governments which are outside the European Community but are interested in economic co-operation with it are fully aware that they have to face a qualitatively new stage of the West European integration centre, the birth of a European economic formation which has heretofore been unknown.[2]

Among the outsider countries it has called forth uncertainty—and in this connection no little dissatisfaction—that the programme of the unified internal market of the European Community does not contain a separate chapter about external relations and that the White Book does not even refer to these external relations, although the abolition of the internal border controls will necessarily have consequences for the regulations to be applied to imported goods on the common external border.

For the countries which are outside the West European integration, the questions concerning the future principles of the foreign trade policy of the European Community have the greatest importance, since it is decisively dependent on these to what extent they will be able to share in the benefits of this expanding and dynamic economic region.

From a theoretical approach, the full liberalisation of the internal market can be accompanied by two kinds of external trade policies. It can be imagined that the internal opening will be accompanied by an external opening. According to this liberal view, the competition which is expected to become considerably stronger will offer a favourable opportunity for the Community to become even more open towards the outside world. According to the other approach, the internal opening, the unrestricted competition of the member countries among each other, will represent such a huge shock to the countries of which the competitiveness is weaker that this cannot be added to by the unrestricted admission of external competition. According to the advocates of this second view, it is inevitable that internal opening should be accompanied by external protection. In this context it is absolutely necessary to comment that the interest of the European Community is obviously that the benefits of the livelier internal market should be enjoyed first of all by its own companies. Consequently, the perspective of "fortress Europe" can certainly not be considered lacking a foundation in principle.[3]

For the companies and governments which are outside the West European integration but are interested in economic co-operation with it, the question must certainly be clarified on what principle the Community wants to treat the outsiders on the occasion of their admission to the unified internal market. In Brussels's view, the unified internal market provides extraordinary advantages also for the companies of the external countries, and consequently the opportunity to enter the wide internal market cannot be made available "free of charge". Consequently, in the Community proclamations describing the plan of the unified internal market the requirement of "reciprocity" appears, which has been received by the outsider countries with suspicions and reservations, since the interpretation and range of application of this concept is rather obscure.[4] What is involved is that this beautifully sounding principle is extremely suitable for justifying a procedure of "an eye for an eye" in international economic relations.

The European Community's requirement of "reciprocity" gives rise to a number of problems of interpretation. [E.g. the practice of which EC member-country (countries) is decisive in the establishment of reciprocity; does the Community demand identical ("mirror") regulation; is it necessary to establish mutuality within a sector, or is a certain global reciprocity sufficient, etc.]. The question of the area of application is not clarified either, although under the pressure of the dissatisfied outsider countries claiming most favoured nation treatment according to the GATT (first of all the United States) the European Community has tried to find an internationally presentable form for its demand of "reciprocity". According to the interpretation of the Commission, the demand of reciprocity voiced at an early stage of the description of the unified internal market programme applies only to those special areas of services and investments which are not yet covered by GATT regulations.[5] (Such areas include, for instance, banking services, investment services, or the order of public tenders). Seeing that the regulation of world trade in services forms an important point on the agenda of the Uruguay Round of the GATT, the demand for reciprocity lasts, according to the intentions of the European Community, until a universally adopted regulation is achieved.[6] As may be seen, the problem of reciprocity tied to conditions has not yet been removed from the agenda for discussion.

In the instrumentarium of the common internal market affecting the outsiders, the classical instruments of trade policy occupy a relatively modest place. The "Europe '92" programme does not touch on the tariff duties at all, since the Community as a customs union forms a single customs area. The countries outside the European Community are worried mainly about the future of quantitative restrictions to be applied to their imports by the Common Market.

Two problems arise concerning the quantitative restrictions applied by the West European integration. First, it has to be pointed out that the European Community—by a conscious contravention of the valid rules of the GATT—applies special discriminative quantitative restrictions to the "socialist" countries, as well as to the outstandingly competitive Far Eastern Exporters. The second—much more important—problem is that in the West European integration the quantitative restrictions of imports—in a way which is in principle impermissible in the case of a customs union—have been left in the hands of the member-countries, and in addition these show rather big differences from country to country. In 1988, Italy applies restrictions to 487, France to 156, while the F.R.G. only to 15, the United Kingdom to 18 groups of goods. In the same year, 121 different quantitative restrictions were in force against Japanese exporters to the European Community. But the breakdown of these by countries has shown extremely big inequalities, because while in Italy and in France separately more than 20 quantitative restrictions were in force in respect of Japanese goods, in Ireland the last quantitative restriction affecting imports from Japan were abolished on December 19, 1988.[7] The differing import regulation practice of the member-countries of the West European integration is indicated by the fact that Italy authorised in 1987 the importing of 4000, in 1988 of 3300 Japanese cars, while in France the market share of Japanese cars was set at three percent of annual sales. In contrast, in Great Britain a market share of eleven percent was permitted to the Japanese manufacturers. And the Dutch and the West German regulation was even more liberal than the British.[8]

All this undermined to a considerable extent the unity of the common trade policy, which should have been applied in principle, and made in practice impossible the realisation of the objectives of trade policy. After 1992 these differences will be completely unacceptable from the aspect of the Community, since the differing national trade policy measures do not only make difficult the united stand of the Community towards third countries, but divert the competitive external exports towards the less protectionist member-countries, which results in a large-scale distortion of the conditions of competition, and this is impermissible from the aspect of the single internal market. For the sake of balanced competitive conditions and a truly effective trade policy, the unification of the different quantitative restrictions has become a commanding necessity. However, in connection with the unification of quantitative restrictions attention must be called to the circumstance that although each member-country of the European Community has recognised the necessity and unpostponability of the unification, practical implementation has nevertheless made very slow progress, on account of the considerable differences existing in the internal competitiveness and the trade policy practice of the member-countries.[9]

It is worth mentioning that in questions concerning the counteracting of harmful effects caused by the sudden growth of imports, the member-countries of the European Community have renounced initiatives on the national level. By virtue of a resolution by the member-countries of the integration, the possibility to initiate protective measures on the legal basis of various bilateral and multilateral agreements, has come to be handled by the Community. Although classical instruments of import regulations are concerned, which by the principle of the common trade policy would be due to the Commission of the European Community, the member-countries—if they had to renounce initiatives on the national level—have transferred this right to the Council, which can pass its resolutions by a qualified majority.[10] (It should be noted that—with reference to the principles of integration—the Brussels Commission launched a sharp protest against this solution which has infringed on its competency to a considerable extent).

Despite the undoubted progress of integration, the raising of an increasing proportion of trade policy decisions from the national framework to the Community level will result in the protraction of the process of decision-making, its considerable slowdown, since in the given circumstances approximately 50 ministries have to be consulted in the process of decision-making. (This figure arises, because in the twelve member-countries of the European Community the ministries of trade, of industry, of agriculture, and of finance are in all cases affected by the various questions of trade policy, but it is not possible to count mechanically with four ministries in each country, because in Italy, for instance, there are three ministries the activities of which cover the competency of a Ministry of Finance).

To the outsider it follows from all this that after 1992 they will have to face a much more complicated, slower, and not least much less transparent system of regulation than earlier. This is indicated, inter alia, by the circumstance that earlier the outsider country already won its case if it succeeded to obtain the support of two larger member countries of the integration. However, with the new system of majority voting the possibility of this has ceased for once and for all.

Concerning the external relations aspects of the single internal market of the European Community it can be stated in sum that it can be expected that after 1992 a system of regulation will come about within the Community which the outsiders will be able to acquaint themselves with and to follow to a certain extent, but the formulation and primary benefit of which will be exclusively the internal affair of the Community. It is unlikely that in the sectors critical to it the Community will by one stroke renounce all kinds of protection, but this is far from meaning that the outsiders should count on a crude and traditional import protectionism on the part of the Common Market. Measured by the classical yard-stick, the European Community is one of the most liberal trading powers in the world: its tariff level is low (average 4.2%) and it applies quantitative restrictions within a relatively narrow range.[11] In all probability, the walls of the assumed "fortress Europe" will be built primarily of non-tariff barriers, and will provide, through the internal legislation, standards and various prescriptions competitive advantages to companies within the Community versus the outsiders. And how high the walls of the "fortress Europe" will be, will depend basically on the internal conflicts of interests concerning the Community's external economic policy, or to be more exact, on their outcome. It seems nevertheless useful to survey briefly the internal interest relations of the European Community, with special regard to the likely outcome of the internal conflicts of interest.

2. Interest Relations in the European Community, and the Likely Outcome of the Internal Conflicts of Interests

The European Community unites countries which have rather different economic potential as well as very different internal economic structures and external economic relations. However, the articulation of particular interests occurs not only according to the national framework, but rather frequently also on a sectoral basis. The reason for this is that the trends of the various sectors and their competitiveness in world markets differ extraordinarily from case to case, and consequently in such cases the dividing line is not the national interest but it is drawn along the line of the structural characteristics of the manufacturing industries operating in various countries. However, all this does not exclude at all the possibility that the companies active in the individual manufacturing sectors should formulate stands completely opposed to each other in questions concerning the functioning of the given sector. (One of the best example for this is the difference in attitude which characterises that West European car manufacturing companies versus Japanese car imports or the West European siting of the Japanese car factories.[12]

It has already been mentioned that despite the extension of the scope of common trade policy the trade policy autonomy of the member-countries of the integration has basically survived unimpaired, because the really important fundamental decisions continue to be taken on the national level. The Brussels Commission must continue to stick closely to the expectations of the member-countries. Consequently, it is useful to concentrate the examination of the internal conflicts of interests affecting the trade policy of the Community on the interest relations and conflicts manifesting themselves in national frameworks.

The differences among the member-countries of the West European integration are most conspicuous exactly in regard to joining in the international division of labour, international trade and structural adjustment. The competitiveness and ability to adjust in world markets are highly different in the individual member-countries of the Community, and thus it is not surprising that one of the most contested questions of the long-term evolution of the West European integration is whether the internal opening should be accompanied by an external opening, or on the contrary, the internal opening should involve the increase of external protection. In connection with this question, the economies which are more open to the world economy are more competitive, or which can imagine the strengthening of the national economy only parallel to liberal world trade, including the F.R.G., Great Britain, Denmark and Holland, emphasise the necessity of the openness of the European Community towards the world market. This is not contradicted by the circumstance that in recent years the so-called "liberal economy" countries have also more and more frequently taken recourse to measures restricting external trade, because their world economic interests, traditions and mentality inherited from earlier periods continue to make them supporters of freer world trade. In contrast, France as well as the new South European member-countries, but also Italy—which is at present expanding on the West European market—give preference to relations within the integration over relations between the Community and third countries.

The protectionist wing within the European Community, which in addition to the Latin member-countries of the integration enjoys in some areas—on the level of the industrial interest groups—the support of almost every member-country, brings up two arguments against an external opening simultaneously with the internal opening. First, market competition will grow substantially already in consequence of the removal of the internal borders, and this would be added to, as a sort of second wave, by the external competition swamping the extended market. Second,—and this argument is far from being theoretical—it is highly probable that in an unrestricted competition ensuring equal chances, the most important external competitors—first of all the countries of the Pacific region—would easily outrival the weaker member-countries of the European Community, for whom the benefits of belonging to the integration would become whittled down in this way.[13]

Beyond the intra-relations, different member-country interests manifest themselves in the differences of regional emphasis linked to the external economic orientation of the Community. France pays, special attention to its earlier colonial empire, the Mediterranean region and Black Africa. French policy wants to strengthen its traditional African orientation, inter alia, by Community instruments, and consequently lays great emphasis on assisting the Black Continent, which—on the other hand—is considered mainly by Great Britain—at least in the form imagined by the French—"money thrown down the drain". The interests of the West German economy are attached primarily to the expansion of relations with the European market economies, the East European countries and the United States, as well as some Latin American countries. In the case of the F.R.G., political, historic and psychological reasons also play a role in the relative strength of

West German interests attached to "Eastern trade". The Eastern trade of the F.R.G. surpasses by far not only in its absolute figure but also in respect of the share in the total trade of the member-countries that of all other E.C. countries.[14]

The above statement already leads to the analysis of the French-German relationship, which has until now been decisive in the internal equilibrium of the Community. In respect of the French-German relations it has to be stressed first of all that its future depends on a whole number of world political developments. It follows from this that within the framework of the present study only a few approximative comments can be made. For the time being all indications show that the firm and mutual interests characterising the relations between he two countries will continue unchanged. However, disturbing factors can arise, such as, on the one hand, the pressing West German trade surplus, and on the other, the French policy towards Europe which has become spectacularly more active in the eighties, and which tries to carry the F.R.G. to the "French course". It is beyond doubt that recently almost all integration initiatives in merit have been initiated by the economically strengthening France (trade policy, common industrial and research activity, unified internal market, social domain).[15] The main reason for this is that the increase of France's weight in the world economy and world politics can only be achieved through the dynamisation of the European Community and the leading role adopted in it. It is undeniable that this French endeavour—accompanied by a suitable economic policy—has recently given an impetus to the further development of integration. However, meanwhile some of the traditional French interests have also been put at risk. It is still early to decide how far this has been conscious, and if yes, in the interest of what has this step been undertaken.

It can happen that a transition leading to a global economic opening is involved, when a certain—true, not national but West European—protectionism is still needed. (It is nevertheless questionable whether such transitions are possible in a world economy which is fast becoming internationalised. The theory of the "regional training ground" undoubtedly sounds attractive, but it is very doubtful whether West European industry, on a protected market, can be strengthened to the extent that it should soon be able to enter the world market without any fear). It is however much more likely that strategic considerations play a role here, which look much farther but have never been pronounced aloud. What is involved is that seeing the improving East-West relations and the rapidly changing East-European social-political processes which harbour a mass of uncertainties, the binding of German power and interests to Western Europe has again become a goal of first order for French policy. Despite their public declarations, it can be almost excluded that the few decades which have passed since the Second World War with their contrary experience should have rendered nil the reminiscences of the centuries old French-German controversy. True, the F.R.G. would hardly be able or would hardly want to leave the European Community, but this does not yet tell anything about what kind of Europe it wants and what West-European policy it wants to conduct. Every West-German step which strengthens the all-European framework, obviously increases the European importance of the F.R.G. and diminishes that of France. Beyond this, the

German-French relationship has also a world economic component: every West-European protectionism or any unification which would involve a separation from the worldwide processes, may reduce the world economic weight of the F.R.G. and its international competitiveness, which would be unacceptable to the Germans. The F.R.G. does not consider the European Community a "fortress Europe", but an instrument increasing competitiveness. In this question the F.R.G. can count on the support of the United Kingdom. The special importance of British support is due to the fact that through its strengthening economy and leading role in the West-European liberalisation process, Great Britain can in the near future influence decisively the future of the integration processes of the Community.

Concerning the likely outcome of the internal conflicts of interests affecting the trade policy of the European Community, it can be stated in sum that Great Britain and the F.R.G.—enjoying the support of Holland, Denmark and partly Ireland, as well as the outsiders, the United States and Japan, will in all probability be able to thwart the efforts of the French-led Souther (or Latin) wing of the integration directed at the establishment of a "fortress Europe". Nevertheless, on account of the losing of ground by the West-European integration in the world economy the fall in its international competitiveness, and the structural problems of the member-countries appearing to be lasting, the survival of protectionism can be forecast with great certainty. Although the "spokesman" of a Community-type industry, the UNICE warns not to commit on the external borders the same mistakes which were committed on the internal borders,[16] it can be considered likely that from the aspect of the safeguarding of internal interests and integration benefits of the Community, the external protection—indispensable according to some member-countries and accepted or tolerated by others—accompanied by the internal opening will form the common platform. At this point it is absolutely necessary to stress that the intensity of the protectionism of West-European integration depends to a large extent on the likely evolution of the world economic cycle. It can result in the moderation of protectionist trends in the European Community if, as a result of the considerable economic liberalisation carried out in the second half of the 1980s, the earlier trend of deterioration in the position of French industry is brought to a halt, and the international competitiveness of France is improved considerably.

In connection with the differences in regional emphasis in the external economic orientation of the European Community it can be stated that the importance of the Central-East-European region, of "Eastern trade", will grow considerably in the system of external relations of the West-European integration. The main beneficiary of this will undoubtedly be the F.R.G. The potential opening up in Central-Eastern-Europe strengthens further the German position within the Community.

France will at most be able to slow down the unfolding processes, but not to stop them. There are all indications that the French endeavour has failed which was directed at chaining West German power and interests to Western Europe. The German question has received an impetus and this can change power relations fundamentally within the West-European integration.

THE EUROPEAN MONETARY SYSTEM AND THE ECU IN THE LIGHT OF 1992

1. The Road of Political Decision to the Plan of the Monetary Union

The European Monetary System (EMS) established by the European Communities in 1979 has in the past more than ten years—despite all kinds of technical doubts and national particularities—been able to prove its favourable effects, and has brought about a stable exchange rate zone where the extremes of monetary policy and significant fluctuations of exchange rates have ceased to exist.

The stability of exchange rates has contributed considerably to the expansion of trade and to the further integration of markets. The EMS has had a favourable effect on the formulation of economic policies by the high inflation countries making use of the exchange rate limits in their anti-inflationary programme, while the low inflation countries benefited through its effects of increasing their exports and as a result stimulating their economy.. Within this framework co-operation has been expanded in various forms, especially in the area of monetary policy. In time the results have created the conditions for winding down the remaining barriers to the movement of capital, and made possible the objective of creating the "single European market".[17]

The monetary union[18] is an important complement to the single market and the process of economic integration. For this, a central monetary institution and a common currency become necessary. The establishment of a common central monetary institution—e.g. a European Central Bank (ECB)—is in fact not a primary task, although there are numerous monetary and currency questions which can depend to a considerable extent on the existence of the ECB, and consequently some decisions can have important long-term effects. This is why the number is high of those who consider it essential that the EC should decide already at this stage about the forms and structure of the monetary system.

1.1. Comments on Monetary Co-operation

The Single European Act adopted in 1986 in the spirit of the Treaty of Rome of 1957, indicated as the principal objective the bringing about of the unified internal market of the EC by 1992.

Following this, in September 1987 a decision was made within the Framework of the Basle-Nyborg agreement on closer co-operation concerning the monetary policies. The two main points of this agreement are the granting of short-term credits to support the interventions serving the enhancement of the flexibility of the system, and at the time of pressure on the exchange rater—the ensuring of a higher symmetry in the movement of interest rates.

In the debate concerning the questions of the exchange rate system and the EMS, this change in emphasis stressing the wider monetary union has mainly become the consequence of two factors:

(a) The "single European market" programme[19] in connection with which primarily the question may arise whether a single market leads to an optimum result and whether it can function satisfactorily if the national currencies—and with them the possibility of changes in the exchange rates among them—remain. The reason is that in case of the continued functioning of the national currencies one has to reckon with

(1) the transaction costs arising on account of the differing currencies,
(2) the continued possibility of the adjustment of exchange rates, and
(3) the fluctuation of daily exchange rates, which in their totality cause considerable difficulties to the free flow of the factors of production (capital, goods, services, people). And all this can already impede the coming about of a single internal market.

(b) the liberalisation of the movement of capital proclaimed as part of the "single European market" programme[20] represents the other factor. The step to be taken towards the bringing about of the unified internal market and the aim of the satisfactory functioning of the EMS have raised the dilemma that unified internal market is not possible without a fully integrated European money market. It was due to this that the decision was made that the EMS—which is increasingly characterised by the harmony of economic growth and common procedures in numerous areas of monetary and exchange rate policy—must be complemented with the full liberalisation of the movement of capital, and that by June 1990.[21]

Agreement in the contested questions went so far that in June 1988, at the Hannover summit meeting of the EC, the idea of the elaboration of the European Monetary Union was adopted. The "Delors-committee" formed for this task has been entrusted with studying and making propositions for concrete steps which lead to the economic and monetary union.

The Delors-committee published its report in April 1989 and then delivered it at the Madrid session of the European Council in June. This summit meeting again confirmed its resolution to gradually establish the Economic and Monetary Union in Western Europe.

Six months later, at the beginning of December, 1989, at the Strassbourg meeting of the heads of state and government of the EC member-countries agreement was reached on the acceleration of the realisation of the European Monetary Union. By virtue of this, negotiations about the Monetary Union would begin before the end of 1990, i.e. even before the creation of the unified West European capital market and the full liberalisation of the movement of capital. It was also decided to co-ordinate the economic and monetary policies more closely after July 1, 1990 and that the pound sterling would join the monetary system.

1.2. The Delors-report

The Delors-report has numerous similarities to and differences from the Werner-plan proclaimed in 1971. The Delors-report has taken over a number of targets and points from the Werner-plan, but it has certainly developed further its ideas concerning the monetary union. It is a similarity that both plans recommend implementation in three degrees, but while the Werner-plan also set time limits, the Delors-report has not set a time frame. One of the decisive reasons for this is that the member-countries imagine the implementation at various paces. While France, Italy and Spain want more rapid progress, the F.R.G., Great Britain and Luxemburg argue for a more considered policy.

Mainly for political reasons, the objectives do not include the plan of establishing a European Central Bank at an early phase. It is first of all the view of Great Britain according to which a monetary union can be realised without the immediate establishment of the European Central Bank and of a single European currency. On the other hand, theory and in part practice show—as is generally asserted by the other EC member-countries—that a monetary union demands a common monetary policy, a common currency, or at the minimum a fixed exchange rate system.

The balance of the advantages and disadvantages caused by a full monetary union disposing of a common currency, foreseen also by the Delors-report, demonstrates its success. It is relatively easy to define the advantages. If an identical currency is applied, the risk of uncertainties caused by exchange rate fluctuations cease, and the settlement of accounts becomes simpler. All this makes possible the ore efficient utilisation of economic resources.

It is difficult to estimate the disadvantages of the monetary union on account of their complexity. The two main losses derive from the loss of the autonomy of national monetary policy and the end to the changing of exchange rates as an instrument of economic policy serving adjustment. The possibility for exchange rate adjustment is interesting especially where the price of capital and labour calculated in the domestic currency is relatively inflexible and labour is relatively immobile. In such a case the exchange rate certainly can have in the short-term an important influence on changes in competitiveness and can provide protection against certain shock effects.

For the implementation of the monetary union sketched down in the Delors-report the Committee proposes three stages:

In the first stage in aim is a further increased convergence in economic development through the strengthening of the co-ordination of economic policies within the existing institutional framework. For this sake, if economic indicators develop unfavourable, an agreement must be reached through consultations. It is during this period that the unified domestic market must be realised (where the free flow of capital, labour, goods and services will be ensured), the complete freeing of the money and capital markets, and the bringing about of a unified money market. The member-countries have already agreed on the deadlines of these, i.e. 1992, and in some cases 1990. In this stage the existing exchange rate mechanism of the EMS will continue to be applied. In essence, the adjustment of exchange rates will still be possible, but should be avoided as much as possible. Rendering the adjustment of exchange rates more difficult points in the direction of the formation of the monetary union, where the exchange rates will then be fixed for good. However, it seems doubtful to numerous experts already whether this degree of exchange rate co-ordination can be achieved in the first stage already.

In the second stage new organisations will be established, or respectively, the earlier institutions will be given new functions. The main task will be the transition from the co-ordination of the autonomous national monetary policies to the elaboration and implementation of monetary policy on the Community level. From the institutional aspect, the task is primarily the establishment of a new common monetary institution: the European system of Central Banks. The decision-making power will still be left within national competency. Changes in exchange rates need not yet be eliminated from the instruments serving adjustment, although at this stage it will be possible to make use of them for the sake of adjustment in exceptional cases only, and other kinds of mechanisms will primarily be involved. Thus the margin of exchange rate fluctuations can be narrowed further. This, of course, necessitates the approximation of the rates of inflation. Thus the asymmetry of the EMS[22] which rests at present in essence on the stability of the DEM, can be terminated *de facto* as well.

In the third stage the exchange rates will already be fixed irretractably, and in the last resort a common European currency will replace national currencies. This assumes that the transitory stage to the common monetary policy should become complete.

2. Theoretical and Economic Policy Questions of the Monetary Union

2.1. *Theoretical Foundations of the Monetary Union*

The foundations for the European monetary union are provided by the theory of the optimum currency zone, which unfolded primarily in the wake of the works of *T. Scitovsky, R. Mundell* and *R. McKinnon.* Attention turned towards this theory, because—as opposed to a freely floating exchange rate system—belonging to a monetary union can, to a certain extent, protect an economy presumably from external shock effects. Looking at it from the aspect of economic theory, joining a monetary union involves the reduction of national economic policy sovereignty, since the possibilities for monetary policy are narrowed down or come under common control. Simultaneously, the building up of a flexible and selective regional fiscal system must include the unification of the budgets of the member-countries to a considerable extent, as well as the control of their functioning by a special common institution. Even participation in an exchange rate system with adjustments demands a strong commitment in order that the operational reliability of the exchange rate system should remain. Thus joining a monetary union already surpasses considerably the scope of economic decision-making and becomes a substantial political question as well.

2.2. *Alternative Strategies of the Development of the Monetary Union*

The process of the establishment of the economic and monetary union necessitates inevitably the taking of further steps. From this aspect, a wide range of various approaches has developed. On one side of this we find the "activist strategy", which urges the rapid realisation of the monetary union, as an important instrument serving the achievement of economic integration, and in this context also some important regional political questions emerge. The other side, the "minimalist strategy" considers progress towards the monetary union, a step which is entirely dependent on the building up of general integration. Between these two extreme views numerous other views exist, which foresee the pace of the realisation of the monetary union dependent on general integration to different degrees.

The efficiency of the "activist strategy" cannot be established with certainty, because it can speed up in principle the pace of economic integration by e.g. the trade increasing effect of a smaller exchange rate fluctuation. At the same time, it can also have the result that it increases the pressure on the divergence of regional development, i.e. some regions will be affected unfavourably by the monetary union. Long-lasting structural problems can only become graver, because the risk exists that the trend of real wages will be much more towards the higher levels than would be justified by the levels of productivity. The risk of this is the greater, since—within the framework of the required centralisation of macro-economic policies—some income and welfare allowances will also be unified. In such circumstances the monetary union can have such unfavourable effects as increasing unemployment in the low productivity regions.

The implementation of the "evolutionist strategy" would have other results. The steps towards the creation of the monetary union would not precede the process of general economic integration and the coming about of the optimum conditions necessary for the establishment of the common currency. The constitutional and organisational changes would only be undertaken when these were necessitated by the expanding relations among the EC member-countries. This strategy would not represent a passive behaviour from every aspect, since it accepts the tasks of the first phase of the Delors-report, especially the creation of the common European market.

According to the ideas of an intermediate "parallel strategy", the simultaneous development of the dual target of economic integration and monetary union is the most suitable solution. It is not easy to determine at what pace it is necessary to proceed along the road leading to the achievement of the monetary union, and how at the different points in time the institutional changes necessary for this can be ascertained. Similar to the evolutionist strategy, the decision-making structure on the EC level would to a decisive extent be the function of the economic and social conditions.

Concerning the establishment of the monetary union, the opinions of the EC member-countries, or of their central banks and economic ministries respectively, are also divided to a certain extent. The bringing about of the monetary union as soon as possible, including the single European currency and the European Central Bank is supported vigorously by the EC Commission in Brussels and by the central banks of numerous member-countries, primarily by that of France. Opposed to this, a relatively strong counter-block has also come about with the participation of the Bundesbank and the Bank of England, and the treasuries respectively.[23] which support rather a more moderate approach and make the establishment of the monetary union dependent on the pace of the progress of the economic union.

The following questions represent important open problems:

1. taking the institutional aspects into consideration is the establishment of an ECB or of a central monetary agency more useful;
2. a number of questions of regulation, including banking regulation and supervision, the questions of the application of foreign exchange control and of tax harmonisation;
3. monetary measures, which are linked in essence to this future of the EMS and of the ECU.

The institutional and regulatory questions need not become factors impeding the monetary union. Although it is likely that the question of the ECB has become the problem giving rise to the biggest controversies.

The liberalisation of the movement of capital within the framework of the single European market may involve the risk that this process occurs in institutional and organisational circumstances where the harmonisation of economic performances and policies is not yet adequate and consequently the drop in the differences of the rates of inflation can stop and begin to grow, the imbalances in the balance of trade may increase, the fiscal policies continue to remain outside the main streams of co-ordination, and substantial budgetary deficits occur in some countries.

Taking the above problems into consideration, the views relatively differ as to whether the full liberalisation of the movement of capital is reconciliable with the present situation and institutional system of monetary co-ordination. A faulty monetary co-ordination may undermine the holding together of the exchange rates. Thus the paradoxical situation may arise that the smaller the constraint of the stability of the exchange rates is, the bigger is the probability that destabilising portfolio flows will begin and the domestic money demand will suddenly increase.

The creation of the single internal market—including also the money markets and their regulation—through the removal of the internal barriers is an indispensable precondition for the development of common monetary policy and the introduction of a single European currency. There are endeavours to further strengthen the EMS, which has demonstrated considerable stability since the last exchange rate adjustment in 1987. The reason is that a thorougher co-ordination of fiscal policies is necessary.

The question of the monetary union is essential, because in the territory of the EC the mobility of the factors of production will increase after 1992, and a common currency and unified monetary policy are instruments necessary for this.

The success of the "optimum currency zone" depends decisively on the political cohesive force of the monetary union. The diminishing difference in the rate of inflation and the rate of economic growth reduces especially the probability that significant shortages should arise in the external balance of payments. Fiscal integration cannot be considered a precondition of the monetary union, but it is very important for efficient co-operation.

2.3. The Monetary Co-operation

The abolition of the barriers affecting the flow of capital, which figures among the objectives of the unification, will certainly exert a pressure on the present framework and forms of monetary policy and the EMS exchange rate mechanism. The alternative answers to this are: (a) the EMS continues to rely on a relatively loose exchange rate agreement, which would represent a considerable step back from the aspect of the creation of a single European market; (b) the bringing about of a fixed exchange rate and single currency within a well-organised framework.

In connection with the functioning of the EMS, the argument has arisen whether it will be able to function smoothly and to exist at all after the complete liberalisation of the movement of capital. According to numerous opinions, the EMS is being held together only by the broad capital restricting measures, which represent a sort of compensation versus the different economic and financial power of the countries, and prevents large scale speculative movement of capital of various origin, which would otherwise make possible exchange rate adjustments. On the other hand, the fixed exchange rates, the free movement of capital and autonomous monetary policies are mutually irreconciliable.

According to other opinions, the adjustment of the exchange rate would continue to be possible without the coming about of a speculative pressure of a significant magnitude as long as these adjustments are relatively small and are sufficiently frequent in accordance with the differences. It is essential that the harmonisation of economic policies should become stronger, and the free movement of capital has certainly a disciplinary influence on this.

According to the evolutionist principles, considerable progress can be made in the area of co-operation without this involving already a monetary union or assuming the existence of a common monetary authority. Monetary co-operation on a larger scale would first of all require:

(a) The strengthening of the EMS by

- the reduction of the margins of exchange rate fluctuations,
- the pound sterling joining the exchange rate system,
- improvement of the interventionary co-operation in respect of times when the system is under strong pressure.
- more general utilisation of the ECU as a European means of payment.

(b) An enhanced harmonisation of fiscal policies, which affect primarily the taxation of savings.

(c) Economic indicators as the reduction of differences from country to country in the rates of inflation and the rate of interest, co-ordination of fiscal policies in order that the imbalances of trade of the EC countries and of their budget deficits should cease to exist.

3. Instruments of the Monetary Union

3.1. The ECU

Since its establishment the ECU has achieved a relative dual result, which means that the "official" ECU has played a relatively moderate role until now, while the "private" ECU has become a relatively successful participant in the international financial market operations. Although according to the original agreement of the EC member-countries the ECU should be in the centre of the EMS, it has mainly been trade in the private ECU that has grown gradually. This considerable success would probably not have been possible without the institutions of the EC and the EMS. The question now is how the role of the official ECU can be increased in a system which pays attention to the changing circumstances and to the interests of the EMS members.

There are in essence two ways open towards the creation of a common European currency. One is the development of the ECU as a parallel currency besides the national currencies, the exchange rate of which is fixed and the currencies can be substituted for each other. The other road is that the conditions have first to be developed on this basis, and thus the exchange rates are stabilised in relation to each other through the reduction of the exchange rate fluctuations and the co-ordination of economic policies. As soon as the exchange rate fluctuation ceases, the currencies can become substitutable for each other, and a common currency can be introduced in the place of the national currencies.

The ECU must be strengthened for it to become a common European currency, and its utilisation must be increased both in the state and in the private sector.[24] At present the private turnover in ECU is being influenced spontaneously by the market forces. In the beginning the growth was very rapid, mainly in the financial sector. It can be assumed that the private trade in ECU has achieved a level the exceeding of which would already necessitate institutional changes.

According to the Delors-report, the ECU is potentially suitable for fulfilling the functions of a common European currency. But for this it is necessary that the currency basket nature of the ECU should cease and that it should become an independent currency, i.e. in future its value should not be determined on the basis of the currencies in the basket. For becoming an independent currency it is necessary that in order to influence its value the emission should be controlled by an autonomous monetary institution.

3.2. The European Central Bank—European System of Central Banks

According to some plans, through the strengthening of the European Monetary Co-operation Fund (EMCF) a monetary institution can be developed which should be able to accept the role of the European Central Bank. After this, the national central banks would implement the monetary policy of the European Central Bank. Fundamentally this system would be similar to the activity of the Fed, which fulfils the role of the Central Bank of the USA.

In the view of the Bundesbank, the EMCF would not be a suitable institution in its present form, since its activity depends on the decisions of the EC Council of Ministers, and thus it is politically not autonomous. According to this view, only the monetary committee and the extension of the competency of the committee of the central banks could provide a framework for the European monetary body.

The establishment of the ECB need not be considered a goal which must be realised in one go, at a point in time which appears propitious, but an evolutionary process in the framework of which the monetary functions would become centralised gradually in circumstances where the interest rates are stable and the currencies are substitutable. Thus the existence of the ECB will only be justified when there is already a common European currency which must be controlled.

NOTES

1. *McDonald,* F.E.: Completing the Internal Market: Or Making the European Community a Common Market! In: Economics, No. 1/1988.
2. *Bressand,* A.: Beyond Interdependence: 1992 as a global challenge. In: International Affairs, No. 1/1990.
3. *Inotai,* A.: Eröviszonyok és tagállami érdekek a nyugat-európai integrációkban, különös tekintettel 1992-re. (Power relations and member-country interests in the West European Integrations, with special regard to 1992): In: Külpolitika (Foreign Policy) No. 4/1989.
4. *Garten,* J.E.: Significance issues wide open in Japan-EC ties. In: The Japan Economic Journal, Vol. 27, No. 1364/1989.
5. *Weinstein,* M.E.: Washington and Europe 1992. In: Europa-Archiv, No. 5/1990.
6. *Nicolaides,* P.: The problem of regulation in trade services: The implications for reciprocal liberalisation. In: Europa-Archiv, No. 5/1990.
7. *Kunihiro,* M.: The external implications of 1992. A Japanese view. In: The World Today, Vol. 45, No. 2/1989.
8. Far Eastern Economic Review, No. 41/1989.
9. Financial Times, March 19, 1990.
10. European File, No. 4/1988.
11. Arnold, M.—Bronckers, C.: The EEC new trade policy instrument: Some comments on its application. In: Journal of World Trade, Vol. 22, No. 6/1988.
12. The Japan Economic Journal, November 22, 1989.
13. *Jens,* V.: Offenes Europa?—Über den Protektionismus der Gemeinschaft (Open Europe?—About the Protectionism of the Community) In: Wirtschaftswoche, No. 11/1990.
14. *Hoffmann,* S.: The European Community and 1992. In: Foreign Affairs, Vol. 68, No. 4/1989.
15. *Adam-Schwatzer,* J.: Germany and France and European Integration. In: Studia Diplomatica, Vol. 41, No. 1/1988.

16. The Economist. Vol. 308, No. 7558/1988.
17. This was done through the Single European Act adopted in 1986.
18. The monetary union means in practice that (1) the convertibility of the currency is full and irreversible, (2) the margin restricting the exchange rate fluctuations becomes unnecessary, (3) the exchange rate parities are fixed for good, (4) the movement of capital becomes full liberalised.
19. Within the framework of this, the EC member-countries abolish by 1992 all restrictions that still exist in the movement of goods, persons and services among each other. The main objective of the single internal market programme is the "Resolution on the Single Europe" which was adopted by the member-countries in 1987 and has brought a number of changes in the basic Treaty of the EC.
20. The basic Treaty of the EC contains the acceptance of obligations for the gradual liberalisation of the movement of capital to the extent that this should ensure the adequate functioning of the Common Market (Article 67). In reality not much progress has occurred since the beginning of the 1960s. As late as a couple of years ago numerous member-countries took steps backwards from the earlier level of liberalisation, with reference to the protective clause.
21. In the case of some countries which still apply regulations restricting the extensive movement of capital (Greece, Ireland, Portugal, Spain) this transitory period lasts until 1992, and in the case of Greece and Portugal this may even be extended by further three years. Belgium and Luxemburg have accepted formally too that they will abolish the dual money market by the end of 1992.
22. The asymmetry of the EMS means that the uneven burden of adaptation bears down, in the course of the exchange rate adjustments, on those countries which respectively have a deficit and a sufficit, or a strong and a weak currency.
23. See the declaration by J. *Major* (1989) in the British House of Commons.
24. Settlements are accounted in ECU in respect of approximately one percent of the EC's trade turnover.